THE CATHOL
QUAR
MONOGRAPH SERIES

D1191487

15

RICH AND POOR IN THE *SHEPHERD OF HERMAS*
AN EXEGETICAL-SOCIAL INVESTIGATION

by

Carolyn Osiek

RICH AND POOR IN THE *SHEPHERD OF HERMAS*
AN EXEGETICAL-SOCIAL INVESTIGATION

by

Carolyn Osiek

The Catholic Biblical Association of America
Washington, DC 20064
1983

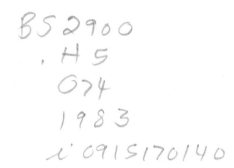

RICH AND POOR IN THE *SHEPHERD OF HERMAS*
AN EXEGETICAL-SOCIAL INVESTIGATION
by Carolyn Osiek

©1983 The Catholic Biblical Association of America
Washington, DC 20064

PRODUCED IN THE UNITED STATES

Library of Congress Cataloging in Publication Data

Osiek, Carolyn A.
  Rich and poor in the Shepherd of Hermas.

  (Catholic Biblical quarterly. Monograph series; 15)
  Originally presented as the author's thesis (doctoral)—Harvard Divinity
School
  Bibliography: p.
  Includes index.
  1. Hermas, 2nd cent. Shepherd. 2. Wealth—Biblical teaching. 3. Poor—
Biblical teaching. 4. Wealth—History. 5. Poor—History. I. Title. II. Series.
BS2900.H5O74 1983   234'.5   83-7385
ISBN 0-915170-14-0

You servants of God know that you reside in a foreign land, for your city is far from this one.

Hermas, Similitudes 1.1.

TO THE SOCIETY OF THE SACRED HEART,
A HOME IN MISSION

CONTENTS

ACKNOWLEDGMENTS

This study was originally a doctoral dissertation for the Harvard Divinity School under the direction of Professor Helmut Koester. To him and to the other members of the dissertation committee, Professor John Strugnell and Professor George Williams, and to Professor Glen Bowersock, who was then in the Department of Classics, Harvard University go my sincere thanks for their encouragement and helpful critique of the first version.

ABBREVIATIONS

The abbreviations used in this study are those given in the common style sheet of the *Journal of Biblical Literature* 95 (1976) 331–46 and the *Catholic Biblical Quarterly* 38 (1976) 437–54; those in *A Greek-English Lexicon*, ed. H. E. Liddell, R. Scott, and H. S. Jones (rev. ed.; Oxford: Clarendon, 1953); those of well-known primary sources in the fields of classics and church history; and the following:

Bull. di Arch. Crist.	*Bullettino di Archeologia Cristiana*, 1863–94
Diehl, *ILCV*	Ernest Diehl, *Inscriptiones Latinae Christianae Veteres*, 3 vols., 1925–31; 2d ed., 1961–
ICUR	Giovanni Battista de Rossi, Angelo Silvagni, Antonio Ferrua, *Inscriptiones Christianae Urbis Romae Septimo Saeculo Antiquores*, New Series, Rome 1922–
OCD	*Oxford Classical Dictionary*, ed. F. L. Cross (London, New York, Toronto: Oxford University, 1963)
PIR	E. Klebs and H. Dessau, *Prosopographia Imperii Romani Saeculi I, II, III*, 3 vols., 1897–98 (2d ed., E. Groag and A. Stein, 1933)
Rend. Pont.	*Rendiconti della Pontificia Accademia Romana di Archeologia*, 1921–
Riv. di Arch. Crist.	*Rivista di Archeologia Cristiana*, 1924–

NUMBERING SYSTEMS FOR THE *SHEPHERD OF HERMAS*

In M. Whittaker's critical edition (1956) a new numbering system was introduced for the sections of *Hermas*, a simpler consecutive numbering rather than the more complicated traditional system of independent numbering of chapters and sections within each of the three major divisions.

Whittaker's system is undoubtedly easier to follow than the traditional system; however, it is unfamiliar to most readers of the Apostolic Fathers. Consequently, not only Whittaker herself but also most translators and commentators since have felt it necessary to use both systems, which is somewhat cumbersome. (There are exceptions. J. Reiling, *Hermas and Christian Prophecy*, ignores the new system; A. Hilhorst, *Sémitismes et latinismes dans le Pasteur d'Hermas*, and D. Hellholm, *Das Visionenbuch des Hermas als Apokalypse*, use it exclusively.) Moreover, there is the added difficulty that works written before 1956 do not use it at all.

For these reasons, it has seemed easier in this study to retain the traditional system of numbering. A conversion table is given below (adapted from Whittaker, p. xxiv).

Concordance of old and new numbering systems

Vis.	1.1–4	= 1–4		*Mand.*	10.1–3	= 40–42
Vis.	2.1–4	= 5–8		*Mand.*	11	= 43
Vis.	3.1–13	= 9–21		*Mand.*	12.1–6	= 44–49
Vis.	4.1–3	= 22–24				
Vis.	5	= 25		*Sim.*	1	= 50
Mand.	1	= 26		*Sim.*	2	= 51
Mand.	2	= 27		*Sim.*	3	= 52
Mand.	3	= 28		*Sim.*	4	= 53
Mand.	4.1–4	= 29–32		*Sim.*	5.1–7	= 54–60
Mand.	5.1–2	= 33–34		*Sim.*	6.1–5	= 61–65
Mand.	6.1–2	= 35–36		*Sim.*	7	= 66
Mand.	7	= 37		*Sim.*	8.1–11	= 67–77
Mand.	8	= 38		*Sim.*	9.1–33	= 78–110
Mand.	9	= 39		*Sim.*	10.1–4	= 111–114

I

INTRODUCTION

The Context in Current Scholarship

In the last decade the field of social history has become a major direction in the study of the New Testament and early Christianity. Those who have attempted to document the progress of this movement have been careful to distinguish between social description and analysis on the one hand and the application of sociological theory on the other.[1] Few biblicists and church historians have either the training or the willingness to learn a new discipline that is required for the rigorous use of sociological models. Those who do have produced pioneering works, which, by the admission of the authors themselves are burdened with the difficulties of applying a science meant to be used with live subjects in a contemporary culture to communities from nearly two millennia ago that produced literature and inscriptions which were never intended to communicate the kind of information we now attempt to wrest from them.[2] Nevertheless, this type of work is a valuable aid to understanding the formative factors of early Christianity.

Those who pursue the less exacting but no less important task of social description and analysis encounter the same difficulties but have greater

---

[1] See J. Z. Smith, "The Social Description of Early Christianity," *RelSRev* 1 (1975) 19–25. Smith distinguishes four levels of social investigation: description of social facts (*realia*); social history; social organization and institutions; social world. It is particularly in the latter two categories that sociological theory can be applied. See also D. J. Harrington, "Social Concepts in the Early Church: A Decade of Research," *TS* 41 (1980) 181–90; and R. Scroggs, "The Sociological Interpretation of the New Testament: The Present State of Research," *NTS* 26 (1980) 164–79.

[2] Especially J. G. Gager, *Kingdom and Community: The Social World of Early Christianity* (Englewood Cliffs, NJ: Prentice-Hall, 1975); B. J. Malina, "The Social World Implied in the Letters of the Christian Bishop-Martyr (Named Ignatius of Antioch)," SBLASP (1978) 2.71–119; idem, *The New Testament World: Insights from Cultural Anthropology* (Atlanta: John Knox, 1981); H. C. Kee, *Christian Origins in Sociological Perspective: Methods and Resources* (Philadelphia: Westminster, 1980); G. Theissen, *Sociology of Early Palestinian Christianity* (Philadelphia: Fortress, 1978).

1

methodological freedom to discover new perspectives on old texts.[3] The recent work of John Elliott on 1 Peter deserves special notice with reference to the method and scope of the present study.[4] His "sociological exegesis" undertakes to combine literary, theological, and social dimensions of the text through historical-critical analysis with the intended or actual social impact on the text—or, to put it simply (this is my interpretation), not only where the text has come from but also where it is going, or at least where the author hopes it will go.[5] While I have some hesitation in calling this a "sociological" method rather than a social analysis, I subscribe fully to its assumptions and find that we proceed along very similar lines.

One of the most important subjects of social analysis is economic status, and several studies in recent years have sharpened the understanding of this crucial factor in the life of early Christians.[6] There has been no thorough examination of *Hermas* from this perspective in spite of the abundance of material.[7] The present study is intended to be a contribution to the social

---

[3] To name only a few, D. E. Aune, "The Social Matrix of the Apocalypse of John," *BR* 26 (1981) 16–32; R. M. Grant, *Early Christianity and Society: Seven Studies* (San Francisco: Harper and Row, 1977); R. F. Hock, *The Social Context of Paul's Ministry* (Philadelphia: Fortress, 1980); A. J. Malherbe, *Social Aspects of Early Christianity* (Baton Rouge: Louisiana State University, 1977); W. A. Meeks, "The Man from Heaven in Johannine Sectarianism," *JBL* 91 (1972) 44–72; idem, "The Image of the Androgyne: Some Uses of a Symbol in Earliest Christianity," *HR* 13 (1974) 165–208; idem, "'Since Then You Would Need to Go Out of the World': Group Boundaries in Pauline Christianity," in *Critical History and Biblical Faith*, ed. T. J. Ryan (Villanova, PA: College Theology Society/Horizons, 1979) 4–29.

[4] J. H. Elliott, *A Home for the Homeless: A Sociological Exegesis of 1 Peter, Its Situation and Strategy* (Philadelphia: Fortress, 1981).

[5] See the full discussion in Elliott, *A Home for the Homeless*, 7–14.

[6] L. W. Countryman, *The Rich Christian in the Church of the Early Empire: Contradictions and Accomodations* (Texts and Studies in Religion; New York/Toronto: Edwin Mellen, 1980); L. T. Johnson, *The Literary Function of Possessions in Luke-Acts* (SBLDS 39; Missoula, MT: Scholars Press, 1977); R. J. Karris, "Poor and Rich: The Lukan Sitz im Leben," in *Perspectives on Luke-Acts*, ed. C. Talbert (Special Studies Series 5; Danville, VA: Association of Baptist Professors of Religion, 1978); G. Theissen, *The Social Setting of Pauline Christianity: Essays on Corinth* (ed. and trans. J. Schütz; Philadelphia: Fortress, 1982). Three other works written for a less scholarly audience are important and should not be overlooked: M. D. Guinan, ed., *Gospel Poverty: Essays in Biblical Theology* (Chicago: Franciscan Herald, 1977); M. Hengel, *Property and Riches in the Early Church: Aspects of a Social History of Early Christianity*, trans. John Bowden (Philadelphia: Fortress, 1974); W. E. Pilgrim, *Good News to the Poor: Wealth and Poverty in Luke-Acts* (Minneapolis: Augsburg, 1981).

[7] This is not to say that no one has been aware of its significance; already Dibelius saw the principal patterns of the material in *Hermas* and its implications both for the author's community (*Der Hirt des Hermas* [HNT Ergänzungsband; Die Apostolischen Väter 4; Tübingen: J. C. B. Mohr (Paul Siebeck), 1923] 552, 555–56) and for the development of a Christian theology of wealth and poverty (*A Commentary on the Epistle of James*, rev. H. Greeven [Hermeneia; Philadelphia: Fortress, 1976] 45).

history of early Christianity by means of a historical-critical analysis of the text and an interpretation of its function within its historical and social context. By "function" I mean here what Elliott would call response to and intended effect of the text upon its situation. It will be left to others, building on these foundations if they choose, to apply sociological models and theories.

Why the *Shepherd of Hermas*?

Assessments of the value of the *Shepherd* for our understanding of early Christianity have varied considerably in this century.[8] On the one hand, "if such men as Hermas had become the real leaders of Christianity, if such books as his had made up the New Testament, the Church could hardly have survived."[9] On the other, ". . . more recent study has re-enthroned *Hermas* as an important witness to second-century Christianity in Rome."[10] It is my conviction that the *Shepherd*, far from being merely a dreary treatise on penitential discipline, as some would see it, has much to yield toward an understanding of the life and problems of second-century Christianity as it

---

[8] Editions, commentaries, and translations include F. X. Funk, *Patres Apostolici* 1 (Tübingen: H. Laupp, 1901), edition of the text; K. Lake, *The Apostolic Fathers*, 2 (LCL; London: W. Heinemann, 1913), text and translation; M. Dibelius, *Der Hirt*, in 1923 (German translation and commentary, still the most complete and still not translated into English); for earlier editions, see the bibliography and Dibelius, *Der Hirt*, 416. Since Dibelius have appeared H. Weinel, translation and introduction in *Neutestamentliche Apokryphen* (ed. E. Hennecke; 2d ed.; Tübingen: J. C. B. Mohr, 1924); R. Joly, *Hermas le Pasteur* (SC 53; Paris: Editions du Cerf, 1958 and 1968), edition, translation, and commentary; G. Snyder, *The Shepherd of Hermas* (Apostolic Fathers 6; ed. R. Grant; Camden, NJ: T. Nelson and Sons, 1968), translation and commentary. None of these has superseded the work of Dibelius in thoroughness. His volume did not include a critical text, however, and new manuscript discoveries since the last one by O. Gebhardt and A. von Harnack in 1877 made the lack more noticeable; see H. Musurillo, "The Need of a New Edition of Hermas," *TS* 12 (1951) 382-87. That need was partially satisfied by Joly's edition, but better with the appearance of M. Whittaker's critical text two years earlier (*Der Hirt des Hermas* [GCS 48; Die Apostolischen Väter 1; Berlin: Akademie, 1956 and 1967]). All Greek citations from *Hermas* are taken from this text unless otherwise indicated. The best summary of manuscript evidence, uses by ancient writers, and editions is found on pp. ix–xxiv. Reaction to Whittaker's edition has been overwhelmingly favorable, e.g., H. Chadwick, "The New Edition of Hermas," *JTS* 8 (1957) 274–80. Both Whittaker and Joly were able to utilize the newly discovered Michigan papyrus fragment that includes a large central section of the *Similitudes* (C. Bonner, "A Papyrus Codex of the Shepherd of Hermas," *HTR* 18 [1925] 115–27; idem, *A Papyrus Codex of the Shepherd of Hermas (Sim. 2-9) with a Fragment of the Mandates* [University of Michigan Studies; Humanistic Series 22; Ann Arbor: University of Michigan, 1934]).

[9] W. J. Wilson, "The Career of the Prophet Hermas," *HTR* 20 (1927) 35.

[10] L. W. Barnard, "The Shepherd of Hermas in Recent Study," *HeyJ* 9 (1968) 29.

struggled to maintain its integrity in an environment that it found hostile in more subtle ways than political persecution. In a community increasingly threatened by material preoccupations and indifference to the hard sayings of the Gospel, the author works with the biblical traditions about wealth and poverty and produces a new interpretation adapted to the exigencies of his own social situation. Thus he stands in continuity with the New Testament and carries its legacy into his own age.

Within the last twenty years a number of major studies on specialized aspects of *Hermas* have appeared.[11] In 1959, Erik Peterson published three form critical studies on the *Visions*, showing both their strong Hellenistic literary background and the influence of Jewish literary forms and ascetic traditions.[12] An important study of the ecclesiology of *Hermas* was done by L. Pernveden, who held that the eschatological realization of the Church is the key to understanding the whole of the book.[13] In *Hermas and Christian Prophecy: A Study of the Eleventh Mandate*,[14] J. Reiling has given us a carefully executed study of the function of prophecy in *Hermas*, showing that in spite of the intrusion of Hellenistic forms of divination into early Christianity as shown by the eleventh *Mandate*, the form of prophecy used there stands solidly within a Jewish Christian tradition.

Three recent studies of the language of *Hermas* have proceeded with different methods toward different goals. J. C. White's *The Interaction of Language and World in the "Shepherd of Hermas"* undertakes an analysis of language patterns in categories suggested by the text itself and attempts to relate them to the literary tradition and conceptual world of the author.[15] A. Hilhorst's *Sémitismes et latinismes dans le Pasteur d'Hermas*, after an

---

[11] Earlier studies include a number on the subject of repentance in *Hermas* (see Snyder, *Shepherd*, pp. 69–72 for bibliography) and the works of O. Seitz on *dipsychia*: "Relationship of the Shepherd of Hermas to the Epistle of James," *JBL* 63 (1944) 131–40; "Selected Subjects in the Thought and Terminology of Hermas" (Th.D. thesis, Harvard University, 1945); "Antecedents and Signification of the Term *DIPSYCHOS*," *JBL* 66 (1947) 211–19; "Afterthoughts on the Term 'Dipsychos,'" *NTS* 4 (1957–58) 327–34; "Two Spirits in Man: An Essay on Biblical Exegesis," *NTS* 6 (1959–60) 82–95.

[12] "Beiträge zur Interpretation der Visionen im 'Pastor Hermae,'" "Kritische Analyse der fünften Vision des Hermas", and "Die Begegnung mit dem Ungeheuer," in *Frühkirche, Judentum, und Gnosis* (Freiburg: Herder, 1959) 254–309. Peterson's method and conclusions will be discussed further below on p. 9.

[13] *The Concept of the Church in the Shepherd of Hermas* (Studia Theologica Lundensia 27; Lund: Gleerup, 1966). See the critique of Pernveden by Barnard in "Hermas and Recent Study," 33–34.

[14] (NovTSup 37; Leiden: Brill, 1973).

[15] (Ph. D. dissertation, Temple University; Ann Arbor, MI: University Microfilms, 1973).

exhaustive examination of the evidence that the author(s) of *Hermas* may have spoken Hebrew, Aramaic, or Latin as well as Greek, concludes that there is no evidence of either semitisms or latinisms in the language of *Hermas* that would not have already been established in Christian Greek through the influence of the LXX and a Latin environment.[16] The most ambitious undertaking of the three is that of D. Hellholm, *Das Visionenbuch des Hermas als Apokalypse: Formgeschichtliche und texttheoretische Studien zu einer literarischen Gattung*, of which only the first volume has so far appeared.[17] Through the application of semiotics Hellholm is attempting to establish the relationship between modern text theory and form critical method, by means of an assessment of the language of *Vis.* 1–4 as characteristic of apocalyptic genre. In a detailed analysis of the text according to a method based on the linguistic theory of scholars like K. Hempfer, E. Gülich, W. Raible, and F. de Saussure, Hellholm seeks to set the interrelationship between form, content, and Sitz im Leben in the text on firmer ground than has thus far been possible.

It is within the context of the more historical and theological of these recent studies of specialized areas of *Hermas* that the present work lies. Previously the interest has been in the development of doctrine and ascetic practice, and hence such subjects as ecclesiology, christology, and repentance have been of central concern in *Hermas*. Investigation of the theme of rich and poor does not cease to be theological. What *Hermas* has to say about it comes from a long biblical tradition of wrestling with the mystery of the unequal distribution of wealth vis-à-vis the justice and mercy of God. The author is just as much a creative theologian when he joins this stream as when he formulates his understanding of the Church or of Christ.

There is, moreover, another perspective added to the theological task in this case, with the assumption that if the integration of rich and poor into the community presents a theological challenge for the author, it also presents a challenge in the concrete social reality from which he writes. Once established, this assumption gives rise to the questions that express the broader framework and scope of the present study: First, what can the theological and literary development of the theme of rich and poor in *Hermas* tell us about the social composition of Christian society in his time and place, in

---

[16] (Graecitas Christianorum Primaeva 5; Nijmegen: Dekker and Van de Vegt, 1976). This conclusion regarding Latin runs counter to the earlier theory of Christine Mohrmann ("Les origines de la latinité chrétienne," *VC* 3 [1949] 67–106 [74–78]; "Statio," *VC* 7 [1953] 223–45), who proposed that the author's language was Latin.

[17] (ConBNT 13:1; Lund: C. W. K. Gleerup, 1980). The bibliographies of Hellholm and Hilhorst (*Sémitismes*) are the most recent and up-to-date listings of studies on *Hermas* and should be consulted for other less significant works that are not mentioned here.

this case, mid-second-century Rome? Second, what is Hermas' message to that situation and how does he intend to influence its direction by means of that message? Before turning to these questions, some clarifications about authorship, sources, setting, and reliability of historical data are in order.

Introductory Questions

The Problem of Composite Authorship and Sources

Nearly all serious students of *Hermas* in the last century have arrived at the conclusion of multiple authorship.[18] The manuscript evidence alone suggests an original separation between *Vis.* 4 and 5, making *Vis.* 1–4 a unit with a strong apocalyptic orientation toward a coming tribulation.[19] *Vis.* 1–4 is also the only section that features the female figure of the Church as revelatory agent. Both this figure and the particular apocalyptic language of the section are absent from the rest of the book. *Vis.* 5–*Sim.* 10 presupposes a past persecution that produced apostates, and it features the Shepherd as revelatory agent. Yet *Sim.* 9 recapitulates and reinterprets the theme of the tower from the *Visions* and is three times longer than its nearest competitor in length, *Sim.* 8. It may be an interpolation into the *Similitudes.*[20]

Many scholars have tried their hand at unraveling the tangle.[21] One of the most complex attempts is that of W. Coleborne, who, on the basis of a linguistic analysis of *Hermas*, would divide the book into the following sections: *Vis.* 1–4; *Vis.* 5; *Man.* 1–12.3.3; *Man.* 12.3.4–*Man.* 12.6.5; *Sim.* 1–7; *Sim.* 8; *Sim.* 9.1–30 (by the nature of the method, *Sim.* 9.31–10.4, which are not preserved in Greek, cannot be considered). Coleborne's theory posits six different authors and seems unnecessarily complicated.[22]

---

[18] Exceptions are Joly (*Pasteur*, 2d ed., 11–16), who accepts the theory of several stages of formation but summarily dismisses Harnack's (and everyone else's) proposal of multiple authorship as "une de ces acrobaties gratuites dont est si friande l'érudition allemande" (p. 15), and Hilhorst (*Sémitismes*, 19–31), but Hilhorst's conclusion is based only on the linguistic evidence yielded by his study, which was guided by a different set of questions.

[19] For a discussion of the manuscript evidence, see Whittaker, *Der Hirt*, xiii; Snyder, *Shepherd*, 3–4.

[20] For a summary of the other reasons for this possibility, see Snyder, *Shepherd*, 4–6.

[21] E.g., Dibelius, *Der Hirt*, 420–21; Wilson, "Career," 20–21, 50–54; Snyder, *Shepherd*, 3–7; Barnard, "Hermas in Recent Study," 32.

[22] "A Linguistic Approach to the Problem of Structure and Composition of the Shepherd of Hermas," *Colloquium* 3 (1969) 133–42; "The *Shepherd* of Hermas: A Case for Multiple Authorship and Some Implications," *Studia Patristica 10* (TU 107; Berlin: Akademie-Verlag, 1970) 65-70. These works summarize a dissertation of the same title as the first article (Newcastle, 1965).

A simpler approach, one more integrated with the historical data while still giving careful attention to linguistic and stylistic differences, had been tried several years earlier by Stanislas Giet. His study, *Hermas et les pasteurs: les trois auteurs du Pasteur d'Hermas*, proposes that *Vis.* 1–4 constitutes the oldest part of the book and was written in the late first or the early second century by the original Hermas, a contemporary of the author of *1 Clement*, to whom he refers in *Vis.* 2.4.3.[23] The second section written was *Sim.* 9, composed by the brother of Bishop Pius in the middle of the second century, in keeping with the data of the Muratorian Canon.[24] The third and final section comprising *Vis.* 5–*Sim.* 8 and *Sim.* 10 was written a few years later by an unknown "Pseudo-Hermas", who utilized more Jewish Christian material and a christology of adoptionist persuasion.[25]

Certainly Giet's theory is one of the most lucid thus far proposed, yet one suspects him of having assumed the authenticity of the reference to Clement and of the reference to the brother of Pius in the Muratorian Canon, a position which of necessity expands the time of writing over half a century. In addition, the adoptionist christology of parts of the *Similitudes* corresponds more smoothly with what we know from outside sources about the theological climate in Rome later in the second century. Thus Giet's theory is a creative and to a large extent a credible attempt to have the best of three worlds. His attempt to harmonize the outside data on both ends may be a bit strained, but his proposal is the one most consistent with the internal evidence. It will serve in general in this study as the underlying assumption regarding authorship, though no consistent patterns in the material about rich and poor can be correlated with any theory of composite authorship. Taking an absolute stand on this complicated question would serve no purpose.

On the question of sources and influences on the author(s) of *Hermas*, the studies of Peterson on the *Visions* and of Reiling on *Man.* 11[26] demonstrate in two sections as in a microcosm the phenomenon present in the whole book: both Hellenistic and Jewish backgrounds are strongly represented, and neither can be proved dominant at the expense of the other. If anything, it can perhaps be proposed that Hellenistic images are more frequent in the *Visions*[27] and *Sim.* 9 (e.g., the Sybil in *Vis.* 2.4.1, the twelve

---

[23] (Paris: Presses Universitaires de France, 1963).

[24] For more discussion of the witness of the Muratorian Canon, see below, n. 41.

[25] See the summaries and critiques of Giet in Barnard, "Hermas in Recent Study," 30–32; Hilhorst, *Sémitismes*, 20–21.

[26] See above, nn. 12, 14.

[27] See esp. Peterson, "Beiträge."

mountains of Arcadia in *Sim.* 9.1.4[28]), while Jewish literary influence seems stronger elsewhere[29] (particularly in the form of biblically based paraenetic material), but this distinction is not to be pushed. Rather, any thorough investigation of the sources and background of *Hermas* must conclude that it is not a question of Hellenistic material inserted into a Jewish book, nor the opposite, the whole thing being subsequently Christianized; nor is it a question of a Jewish Christian book into which Hellenistic images and patterns have been worked, nor the opposite, but instead, "the blending of genuine Jewish-Christian elements with these unmistakable hellenistic elements which constitutes the milieu of Hermas."[30] As in so many other cases in early Christian literature, the world of language and thought patterns from which *Hermas* arises is already a cultural mix that defies reseparation into distinct categories.

The Reliability of Historical and Social Data

Authors like W. J. Wilson have attempted to construct a biographical and psychological portrait of the author based on data given in the book.[31] Dibelius was sharply critical of any attempt to view the intriguing references to Hermas' family and personal life as historical. Rather, he considered the family as the personification of the whole community, so that their way to salvation in the form of repentance was also that to which Hermas was calling his community. Similarly, he considered the Rhode episode in *Vis.* 1.1 not a reflection of experience but a type of romance in Christian form.[32] He held that literary constructs such as *Vis.* 3 (the tower) or *Sim.* 8 (the willow sticks) deal with an original kernel of actual experience, now completely clothed in traditional language.[33] At the same time, though, Dibelius was

---

[28] Though even Arcadia and the twelve mountains have Jewish Christian echoes (see *Sim.* 9.17.1) and may be Jewish in origin (see the summary of theories in Snyder, *Shepherd*, 128–30, esp. that of G. H. Box based on 4 Ezra 9:26).

[29] Parallels have been suggested between themes in *Hermas* and the Jewish liturgical cycle (e.g., J. M. Ford, "A Possible Liturgical Background to the Shepherd of Hermas," *RevQ* 6 [1969] 531–51) and the Qumran literature (J.-P. Audet, "Affinités Littéraires et Doctrinales du Manuel de Discipline," *RB* 60 [1953] 41–82; A. T. Hanson, "Hodayoth vi and viii and Hermas *Sim.* VIII," *Studia Patristica 10* (TU 107; Berlin: Akademie-Verlag, 1970] 105–8).

[30] Reiling, *Hermas and Christian Prophecy*, 26.

[31] "Career"; more recently also to some extent, J. C. White, *Interaction of Language and World.* See *Vis.* 1.1–3; 2.2–3; 3.6.7; *Sim.* 7.

[32] Dibelius, *Der Hirt*, 419–20, 427–30. He posited as the basis for the Tiber encounter "ein Romanstoff—natürlich in christianisierender Abwandlung"; he considered Hermas' family "als Typen für Sünde, Busse, und erneute Begnadigung der Christen," and he concluded that it was doubtful that the *Visions* contained anything of biographical value (p. 419).

[33] Ibid., 420.

aware that the accumulated force of the paraenetic content carried implications for the actual situation of the readers, e.g., that Hermas' concern with possessions indicated a community in which there was a growing problem in that regard, at least in Hermas' opinion, and that the author is not simply developing a favorite theme as a literary exercise devoid of any function his work might play in the community.[34]

E. Peterson, however, in his short studies on the *Visions*, takes an even narrower interpretation on the question of the historical reliability of details in *Hermas*. For him the use of the Jewish apocalyptic genre as well as the commandment and parable forms to convey the theme of repentance is so dominant that any specific information given in the text is there only to serve this end. Hence, nearly all geographical references are "phantastisch": *Hermas* is chiefly valuable as a witness to the development of Jewish Christian ascesis and therefore belongs more to Palestine than to Rome. In fact, "Es ist ein methodologischer Irrtum, wenn man aus dem Hirtenbuch etwas für die Geschichte des Christentums in Rom herausholen will."[35] Even if it is true that Peterson has done thorough studies of inestimable value on the *Visions*, even if "methodologically . . . they are one by one models of the way in which Hermas is to be studied,"[36] this conclusion is unwarranted. The ultimate implication of such a statement is that all apocalyptic literature is "Buchprophetie" produced in a Jewish apocalyptic "school" with little or no relationship to historical situations. This position would be untenable, for it would mean the negation of much carefully constructed work on the Sitz im Leben of apocalyptic books and would suggest that the writers produced their work out of sheer literary fascination rather than for the benefit of their communities.

While Wilson was certainly not correct in taking every personal reference in the *Visions* as literally true and psychologically revealing, neither is Peterson correct in discounting completely any biographical, geographical, or situational reference. Dibelius's position lies somewhere in between, and most other students of *Hermas* have more or less followed him.[37] It may be that Hermas' "family" is the literary convention for his community.[38] That does not, however, provide any compelling reason to deny the reliability of

---

[34] See, for example, ibid., 555–56.

[35] "Kritische Analyse," 275-77, 282-84.

[36] Reiling, *Hermas and Christian Prophecy*, 21.

[37] E.g., Reiling, *Hermas and Christian Prophecy*, 24–26; Joly, *Pasteur*, 17–21; see their documentation for others.

[38] Even though in *Sim.* 7.3 Hermas is called the head of his household (*hē kephalē tou oikou*) and there is no indication elsewhere that he occupies a position of authority in the community.

the geographical references nor those to situations of stress or prosperity. To do so is to uproot *Hermas* from any connection with historical reality.

Date and Place of Writing

Though Origen in his *Commentary on Romans* 10.31 identifies Hermas with the Roman Christian of the same name greeted by Paul in Rom 16:14, this identification is usually discounted. Instead, there are two later chronological poles between which most daters of *Hermas* take a position: *1 Clement* and the Muratorian Canon.

In *Vis.* 2.4.3 the Church personified instructs Hermas to send one copy of his heavenly message to Clement, who will then send it out to the other cities, for he is charged with this activity. Most scholars are inclined to accept this text as an authentic contemporary reference to the author of *1 Clement*, a prominent figure in the Roman Church at the end of the first century. This position necessitates assuming that at least the *Visions* date from that time or shortly after, while Clement was still active.[39] A few scholars reject the authenticity of the reference to Clement and consider it a literary conceit to give the impression of antiquity.[40] There is also the possibility that the Clement referred to in *Vis.* 2.4.3 is a different and otherwise unknown person. However, his job description makes it unlikely that the reference is, authentically or not, to anyone other than the author of *1 Clement*.

The Muratorian Canon, generally thought to be a Roman document of the late second century,[41] ascribes authorship of the *Shepherd* to the brother of Bishop Pius, thus placing Hermas in the middle of the second century.[42] Opinions on the authenticity of this anchor hold are much more divided.

---

[39] E.g., J. B. Lightfoot, *The Apostolic Fathers* (2 vols.; 2d ed.; London and New York: Macmillan, 1890) 1.1, 359–60. J. A. T. Robinson (*Redating the New Testament* [London: SCM, 1976] 319–23) accepts the reference to Clement as authentic and, according to his total schema, dates the writing of the entire *Shepherd* in the eighties or early nineties of the first century, *before* the "episcopate" and literary activity of Clement.

[40] E.g., Mohrmann, "Origines," 77.

[41] Though A. C. Sundberg ("Canon Muratori: A Fourth-Century List," *HTR* 66 [1973] 1–41) gives a convincing argument that it is really a third- or fourth-century Eastern document. In any event, Irenaeus accepted and quoted *Hermas* (*Adv. haer.* 4.20.2 = *Man.* 1.1), and Tertullian both quoted it (*De orat.* 16 = *Vis.* 5.1) and later rejected it as scripture (*De pud.* 10 regarding *Man.* 4.4), so that the terminus ad quem is still the late second century. Sundberg easily solves the difficulty for late authorship, that the reference to *Hermas* says *nuperrime temporibus nostris*, by showing that the expression need not mean "in our lifetime" but could mean rather "in our epoch," on the basis of comparison with Iren. *Adv. haer.* 5.30.3 (pp. 8–11).

[42] Text in Dibelius, *Der Hirt*, 421, and Snyder, *Shepherd*, 22; lines 73–80 of the full text in KIT 1.9.

Mohrmann, Reiling, and Dibelius accepted it, though Dibelius rightly questioned why it would situate the writing in the time of the monarchical episcopate in Rome, against the internal evidence of the book itself.[43] Among rejectors of the Muratorian witness are H. Chadwick and E. Peterson. Among the undecided are Snyder and Hilhorst.[44] Giet, as has been discussed above, tries to accept both the reference to Clement and the Muratorian Canon as authentic.

Joly and others erroneously claim the incompatibility of the theory that the author is the brother of Pius with the internal data of *Vis.* 1.1, where Hermas claims to have once been a slave sold in Rome to a woman named Rhoda, whom he later sees in the Tiber. Joly's supposition is that Hermas, who had several masters and came from elsewhere, could not possibly have maintained ties with a brother whom he finds again in Rome.[45] The case is romantically overstated. Only two owners are required by the narrative—the one who raised Hermas, and Rhoda. Hermas need not have come from outside Rome: *eis Rhōmēn* according to usage elsewhere in the *Shepherd*, may mean "in" as well as "to."[46] Family ties in the city could have been remembered even though members belonged to different masters, and there is besides the possibility of adoption, a common Roman custom.

In view of the conflicting interpretations and the lack of conclusive evidence, certainty about the dating of Hermas is impossible. The reference to Clement in *Vis.* 2.4.3 does not seem authentic because it is so obvious. Though other names are used in the *Visions* (Grapte in the same passage and Maximus in *Vis.* 2.3.4), these otherwise unknown persons seem so well known to the readers that their roles need not be emphasized. Of Grapte it is said what she will do with the letter, but she does not have to be reminded that this is her duty. About Maximus there is silence except for the inference that he has betrayed the faith. But it must be stated that Clement's charge is sending letters to other cities—precisely what the author of *1 Clement* does. The author of the *Visions* may be trying too hard to make the connection.

The witness of the Muratorian Canon is anachronistic in its placement

---

[43] Mohrmann, "Origines"; Reiling, *Hermas and Christian Prophecy*, 24; Dibelius (with hesitation), *Der Hirt*, 421–22. The fact that the much later *Liber Pontificalis* confuses Hermas the author with the Shepherd is rightly seen by Dibelius as a separate confusion.

[44] Chadwick ("New Edition," 278-79) suggests that the Muratorian reference is an attempt to discredit a possible defense of prophecy while the Church is in the throes of fighting Montanism. See also Peterson, "Kritische Analyse," 283; Snyder, *Shepherd*, 22–23. Hilhorst (*Sémitismes*, 33) doubts the reliability of just about everything and concludes that the only sure thing is dating to the first half of the second century.

[45] *Pasteur*, 17.

[46] See Hilhorst, *Sémitismes*, 32.

of *Hermas* and the monarchical episcopate together, as Dibelius noted. But anachronism regarding the rise of the Roman episcopate is typical of later writers, beginning in the late second century, so that this factor alone does not disprove the reliability of the text. Hermas the author of the *Shepherd* and Pius the prominent Roman presbyter could still have been brothers, nor is this relationship incompatible with the personal data of *Vis.* 1.1. The Muratorian Canon may still be our most reliable source for dating *Hermas*. If so, the final redaction at least can be situated in the middle of the second century.

Other less definite internal criteria have been proposed for situating the *Shepherd* chronologically. Weinel saw Hermas' ambiguous relationship with the presbyters (*Vis.* 3.1.8–9) as indicative of a struggle of the "prophetic church" over against the church based on authority (*Amt*), which would then mean that *Hermas* represents a period in the development of the Roman Church in which charismatic government was being replaced by institutional.[47] The notion of struggle is overplayed, however. There is no sign of antagonism on Hermas' part, but rather of deference; "there are no traces of a conflict between the prophets and the ordained ministry."[48] Bishops and deacons are mentioned as well as presbyters (*diakonoi*, *Sim.* 9.26.2, though it may be the more general term "ministers" that is meant here; *episkopoi*, *Sim.* 9.27.2; both in *Vis.* 3.5.1; *presbyteroi*, *Vis.* 2.4.3; the more ambiguous *proēgoumenoi*, *Vis.* 2.2.6; *prōtokathedritai*, *Vis.* 3.9.7; *poimenes*, *Sim. 9.31.5–6*), always in the plural, giving evidence of a collegial presbyteral government of the community, which points in the direction of the early and middle parts of the second century.

Another approach is to try to identify the various groups of dissenters and teachers of strange doctrines spoken of by Hermas (e.g., *Sim.* 8.6.5; 8.5; 9.4) and to see in a passage like *Sim.* 5.7 on the sacredness of the flesh a reaction against Gnostic dualism. The frequent suggestion that teachers like Marcion and Valentinus are meant is certainly plausible, especially since most of Hermas' teaching runs a moderate rather than a rigidly ascetic course, but one must then be willing to assign a late date to the *Similitudes*. Without more detail about the nature of the opponents' teachings, it must remain simply a suggestion.

Another possibility for grounding *Hermas* in outside events is the fairly frequent mention of "persecution" or "affliction" (*thlipsis*) for the commun-

---

[47] *NT Apokryphen*, 330–31.

[48] Reiling, *Hermas and Christian Prophecy*, 153. See also *Vis.* 2.4.3. Some even think that elder persons rather than presbyters are meant in *Vis.* 3.1.8; see also Lake, *Apostolic Fathers*, LCL 2.29, n. 1.

ity, seemingly still to come in the *Visions*, at least by apocalyptic convention (*Vis.* 2.2.7; 4.1.1; 4.2.5; 4.3.6; 3.6.5; but already past in 3.2.1 and both past and coming in 2.3.4), and also referred to in the *Similitudes*, where there is talk of denial of the Lord (e.g., *Sim.* 9.21.3; also 8.8 and 8.9, though here the cause is more likely luxury than oppression; the affliction in *Sim.* 5.7 seems to be of a different kind). Some would go so far as to assert that a persecution under Trajan is meant,[49] but except for the isolated instance of Ignatius there is no real evidence for oppression of Christians under Trajan outside Bithynia / Pontus.[50] There is also the good possibility that the "great persecution that is coming" (*hē thlipsis hē erchomenē megalē*) of *Vis.* 2.2.7; 4.1.1; 4.2.5; and 4.3.6 is not historical at all but eschatological.[51] With so many uncertainties it seems safe to conclude only that some kind of oppression or difficulty for Christians occupies the author's concern but offers nothing definitive for placing the book historically.

As for place of origin, only Peterson has raised serious doubts about the Roman, or at least central Italian, provenance of *Hermas*, and even he has not persisted in that objection.[52] It is true that the three locations mentioned in the *Visions* are not in the city but in its environs or farther south: *Vis.* 1.1.2 sets Rhoda's bath "in the Tiber" (*eis ton potamon ton Tiberin*), which is unlikely to be in the city proper; *Vis.* 1.1.3 and 2.1.1 place the author on the road to Cumae; and *Vis.* 4.1.2 takes place in the country just off the Via Campana. The location for *Sim.* 2 is a vineyard.[53] *Man.* 11.8 gives the image of a water pump used to irrigate fields (*ho siphōn*), but the same apparatus was used on fire engines.[54] Both the reference to Clement in *Vis.* 2.4.3 and the Muratorian Canon identify the *Shepherd* with Rome, and the setting of some of the author's visions outside the city is not contradictory. There is no conclusive evidence to place *Hermas* anywhere other than in and around Rome.

This does not mean, however, that *Hermas* need be seen as "typical" or "representative" of Christianity in Rome in this period. Snyder's recollection of the diversity in Roman Christianity in the second century is apropos.[55]

---

[49] E.g., Weinel, *NT Apokryphen*, 330–31; Snyder, *Shepherd*, 20–21, 24.

[50] Pliny, *Ep.* 10.96.

[51] To Dibelius, it is "die . . . offenbar eschatologische Trübsal" (*Der Hirt*, 448).

[52] See Hilhorst, *Sémitismes*, 32 n. 1.

[53] The reference to Arcadia in *Sim.* 9.1.4 is visionary and need not be taken as a claim to geographical localization, despite the suggested emendation to Aricia (see Dibelius, *Der Hirt*, 603). Other allusions to the vineyard image occur in *Man.* 10.1.5 and *Sim.* 9.26.4, but references like these can by this time be considered Christian literary commonplace.

[54] Also *sens. obsc.*; see LSJ and BAG. s.v.

[55] *Shepherd*, 20.

The author may have belonged to one Christian group among many, one probably with a strong Jewish Christian base and a taste for apocalyptic.

Conclusion and Summary of Procedure

The present study is situated within the current pursuit of a social history of early Christianity and a number of recent investigations of specific topics in *Hermas*. It assumes composite authorship and location in Rome in the early to mid-second century and accepts the internal information given about the author and the testimony of the Muratorian Canon as essentially reliable regarding time and place of composition of segments as classified by Giet. It also assumes that even though much of *Hermas* is communicated in traditional literary forms, the content of the book deals with real concerns of the author and his community.

The key question asked here is: What is the actual social situation of Hermas' community, and how does the author use his literary medium to work out a theological understanding of wealth and poverty that will be meaningful to its members?

Chapter II examines the theology of rich and poor in the Hebrew scriptures, in intertestamental literature, and in the two New Testament writings most concerned with the subject, Luke and James. Chapter III documents and interprets all the references to rich and poor in *Hermas* except for the major locus of that theme, the second *Similitude*. Chapter IV further explores the meaning and implications for theology and praxis of two significant expressions in *Man.* 8.10. Chapter V examines the parable of the elm and the vine in the second *Similitude* and shows how it departs significantly from some teaching on wealth elsewhere in *Hermas* but yet is the central point of the final author's synthesis on the subject. Finally, Chapter VI looks at the society in which Hermas and his fellow Christians were immersed. It attempts to ascertain who the "rich" and the "poor" in his experience were likely to have been, to what kind of situation *Hermas* was addressed, and how the author hoped to shape the development of that situation with his message.

II

RICH AND POOR IN THE BIBLICAL TRADITION

No adequate consideration can be given to the theological and social import of the relationship between rich and poor in *Hermas* without first examining the biblical traditions that earlier expressed similar concerns about the interaction of rich and poor and the moral implications of wealth. These traditions form the basis upon which the synthesis of *Hermas* was built.

The theme of rich and poor in biblical literature is vast and can be dealt with here only in abbreviated form. Four questions will be asked about each literary segment that is considered. These questions, suggested by the material itself, help to establish the theological, literary, and social dimensions of the issue: (1) Who are the poor and who are the rich in the eyes of God according to the author? (2) How should rich and poor relate to one another? (3) What are the ethical/theological implications of wealth, considered apart from the question of responsibility to the poor? (4) To which group(s) is the material addressed? In the next chapter the same questions will be asked about the material in *Hermas*.

The Hebrew Scriptures

There is no single position maintained in the Hebrew scriptures regarding rich and poor. Yet certain definite patterns emerge, some of which had considerable influence on the formation of early Christian literature. These patterns are summarized here and documented with a few examples. Others have done the detailed studies on individual texts, traditions, and terminology that underlie this brief presentation.[1]

---

[1] Some of these will appear in the following footnotes. For general articles, see E. Bammel, "*Ptōchos*," *TDNT* 6 (1968) 888–94; J. Dupont, *Les Béatitudes* (EBib; rev. ed.; Paris: Gabalda, 1969) 2.19–90; W. Grundmann, "*Tapeinos*," *TDNT* 8 (1972) 1–26; F. Hauck, "*Penēs*," *TDNT* 6 (1968) 37–40; E. Kutsch, "Armenpflege," *RGG* 1.617–19; "Armut," *RGG* 1.622–23. For further references to more detailed studies, see M. Dibelius, *A Commentary on the Epistle of James* (rev. H. Greeven; Hermeneia; Philadelphia: Fortress, 1972) 39–45.

Who are the poor and who are the rich in the eyes of God?

Under the monarchy, society became increasingly polarized into the land-holding aristocracy and the rural peasantry as the shift from patrimonial (inheritance) to prebendal (royal) domain concentrated economic power in the hands of a small elite group.[2] Thus the poor in the texts are those who are in material need or who depend on the rich for their sustenance—the hired worker, the day laborer, the alien, the beggar, the widow, and the orphan. These people, moreover, are the objects of God's special attention in the law codes, because they are abused by the powerful (Exod 22:23, 27) and because they are a type of the whole nation of Israel in its slavery in Egypt (Lev 19:34; Deut 24:18, 22).

The rich, on the other hand, are generally seen as arrogant, self-sufficient, and—probably on the basis of economic and social experience—oppressors of the poor, especially in the prophetic literature where they are sometimes identified with elders and rulers (Isa 3:14–15; Jer 22:13–17; Amos 2:6–7; 5:11–12; 8:4–6; Micah 2:1–2; 3:1–3).

In the later literature there is an important development that is crucial for understanding the treatment of rich and poor by Christian writers. The prophetic and pentateuchal insistence on justice to the poor and the oppressed found new meaning in the postexilic identification of the whole people with the oppressed. Those who were attentive to the will of God, the "pious," came to see themselves as the "poor" whom God most favors. The development is seen especially in Psalms, while the wisdom literature stresses the sinfulness of excessive wealth and the assurance that those who indulge in it at the expense of the poor will ultimately be punished.[3]

One aspect of this development is the way in which the whole nation is seen as the poor whom God defends (Lev 19:34; Deut 24:18, 22). Isa 41:16–17 occurs in an oracle of Deutero-Isaiah that promises the presence of God over Israel like a protecting parent and the ruin of those who oppose it. The poor

---

[2] R. B. Coote, *Amos Among the Prophets: Composition and Theology* (Philadelphia: Fortress, 1981) 24–32. What is described here in the North was presumably also happening in the South.

[3] On Psalms, see I. Loeb ("La littérature des pauvres dans la Bible," *REJ* 20 [1890] 161–98; 21 [1890] 1–42, 161–206), who takes the position that all the Psalms are postexilic and that their sole theme is the struggle of the poor against the wicked and the final triumph of the poor thanks to divine protection and preference (pp. 162–63). He notes the inherent ambiguity between the poor as the whole nation of Israel and as a distinct group; in some sense the poor are to Israel what the wicked are to the nations—the representation and embodiment (pp. 191–98). On Wisdom literature, see further the excellent discussion of the evolution of the "pious poor" as a religious concept in Dibelius/Greeven, *James*, 39–45 (with literature cited there), 84–88, 134–41.

and the needy will rejoice because God will provide the streams of water which they lack in their thirst. The identification of the poor with Israel, suggested by the development of the passage, becomes clearer by comparison with other Deutero-Isaian passages that speak of the poor protected by God, such as the canticle in chapter 25 where vv. 3–5 proclaim that it is the poor nation and those who are wronged who receive protection and help in time of need (see Isa 3:15; 10:2; 14:32). Even more strongly, Proverbs asserts that what is done to the poor, whether for ill or good, is done to God himself (Prov 14:31; 19:17).

It follows that the "poor" are so no longer by primary reference to their economic status but rather by virtue of their status before God. The extension of the notion of neediness from the literal to the spiritual level makes the needy person one who is aware of dependence on the goodness of God not only for physical sustenance but also for life itself. Such a person therefore makes no pretense of self-importance but rather believes that dispossession in this life, whether of property or of esteem or of life itself, will be rewarded in the next.[4]

The most frequent terms in the MT that are linked to the theology of the "pious poor" are *ᵓebyôn* and *ᶜônî*, frequently used together (e.g., Ps 34:10; 36:14; 39:18; 40:2; 85:1) and usually rendered in the LXX by *penēs* and *ptōchos*, less frequently by *endeēs, epideēs, epideomenos* or the like.[5] The freedom with which these and similar terms are used suggests that both for the MT writers and LXX translators the words in these contexts were generally interchangeable. The meaning of the related word *ᶜānāw* in this literature, more often translated *praüs* or *tapeinos*, is problematic. As the ideas of "poor" and "humble" grew closer together, the distinction between *ᶜônî* and *ᶜānāw* grew less clear, though the use of *ᶜānāw* in context remained different.[6]

---

[4] See Bammel, "*Ptōchos*," 888–901.

[5] The use of the two words *penēs* and *ptōchos* in the LXX for the pious poor is widespread (see E. Hatch and H. A. Redpath, *A Concordance to the Septuagint* [2 vols.; Oxford: Clarendon, 1897] s.vv.). The combination *ptōchos kai penēs* occurs thirteen times, ten in Psalms, the others being Amos 4:1; Ezek 18:12; 22:29. Each time the two terms occur in that order and translate *ᶜônî wĕᵓebyôn*, with the exception of Ps 108 (109):16, where the word order in Greek is reversed, probably with no significance. Compare Deut 15:11 (*penēs kai epideomenos*) and 24:14 (*penēs kai endeēs*), both translating *ᶜônî wĕᵓebyôn*. In both cases *ᶜônî* translates *penēs* as in Ps 108 (109):16, contrary to the usual practice. In Isa 41:17 the phrase *ptōchoi kai endeeis* translates *hāᶜănîyîm wĕhāᵓebyônîm*; here *ptōchos* again translates *ᶜônî* as in most cases. Compare Sir 4:1; 4:8; 34 (31):4, where *ptōchos* translates *ᶜônî*, but in 4:4 it translates *dal*, and in 7:32 and 13:20 it translates *ᵓebyôn*! See Hatch-Redpath, suppl., p. 190.

[6] It is always used in the plural (except in Num 12:3) and not coupled with another similar word; see A. Rahlfs, *ᶜânî und ᶜânow in den Psalmen* (Leipzig: Dieterich, 1892); Bammel, "*Ptōchos*," 892–93.

How should rich and poor relate to one another?

The answer is obvious and one-sided: the rich must not oppress the poor but must treat them justly considering the disparity of economic resources and social power. This comes through clearly in the legal codes and is the subject of many a prophetic denunciation. Interest may not be charged and a mantle may not be kept as a guarantee on a loan (Exod 22:25-27; Deut 24:10-13); gleanings from the harvest must be left for the poor and the alien (Lev 19:9-10; 23:22; Deut 24:19-21); the wages of day laborers may not be withheld (Lev 19:13; Deut 24:14-15; cf. Tob 4:14; Sir 34:22); no partiality may be shown in judgment on the basis of economic status (Lev 19:15; Amos 5:12; Isa 10:1-2; 32:7). Above all, widows and orphans, the classical symbols of the poor and oppressed, must be protected rather than exploited (Exod 22:21; Deut 10:18; Isa 1:17; Jer 5:28; Ezek 22:7, etc.) by members of the covenant community even as they are defended by God (Ps 68:5). The ideal of the sabbatical year calls for the cancellation of debts from fellow Jews, forbidding the refusal of a loan just before (Deut 15:1-11), and the release of Jewish slaves unless they wish to remain (Exod 21:1-6; Lev 25:39-43; Deut 15:12-18).

As for the poor, as members of the covenant community they have a right to expect justice from the powerful. They present the opportunity par excellence for the rich to exercise justice and mercy. They also have a claim on God's special attention since he is their ultimate defender. Apart from the obligations laid down for all Israelites, however, the poor have no special responsibilities or role assigned to them in response to the rich. As the "pious poor" their relationship is more directly with God, who defends and takes care of them and upon whom they depend for everything.

What are the ethical/theological implications of wealth, considered apart from the question of responsibility to the poor?

Here a variety of positions appear. For the legal and sapiential writers economic prosperity is a reward for keeping the Law and therefore a blessing and a sign of God's favor (Lev 26:3-10; Deut 28:3-14; Prov 10:22; 15:6; 28:25; Job 42:10-12; Qoh 5:19). Poverty is a punishment (Deut 28:15-18; Ps 109:10-11; Prov 13:18, 21, 25; Job 15:29; 20:22-23; 27:19). Yet at the same time in the wisdom literature the poor are not always seen as victims: with a kind of incipient capitalist judgment, Proverbs declares that economic misfortune is the result of laziness (Prov 6:6-11; 21:17; 23:21). Still, wealth can also be a corrupting influence, bringing about stinginess, greed, complacency, or worry and sleeplessness (Prov 23:4-7; Qoh 5:10-17; Sir 11:18-19, 23-26; 31:1-3). The time and trouble taken to accumulate it lead nowhere because others will enjoy its fruits (Psalm 49; Qoh 6:1–3; Sir 14:4–5). This later more pessimistic approach provides important background for the New Testament and early Christian literature.

To which group(s) is the material addressed?

Almost universally, discussion of rich and poor in the Hebrew scriptures is aimed at the rich. Legal texts spell out their duties to the economically poor. Even passages that identify the poor with the nation are still aimed at calling the rich and powerful to task (e.g., Lev 19:34). The prophetic literature, while expressing many viewpoints with which the poor can identify, aims its diatribes at the rich, whom it blames for the social abuses that are destroying the covenant community. The wisdom literature is generally recognized as representing the interests of the leisure urban upper classes engaged in commerce and largely living on the income of their country estates.[7] Even the psalms of individual lament and trust in God, which plead the cause of the poor and righteous against the wicked (e.g., Psalms 12, 22, 25, 69) are not necessarily to be taken as speaking for the economically oppressed or even for individual petitioners; they represent as well the whole congregation or nation pleading its cause as the "pious poor" against international enemies.[8] They put forward the perspective of the "pious poor" against their enemies, whoever they might be, and this comes closest to being an exception to the otherwise consistent hammering at the economically and symbolically wealthy.

Summary

There are two very different attitudes toward wealth and poverty set forth in the Hebrew scriptures. On the one hand wealth is part of the prosperity that is a sign of God's blessing, especially in the deuteronomistic and sapiential literature. Yet God champions the cause of the poor. The rich have an important role to play as defenders of the poor, with whom they are to deal in strict justice. Prophetic criticism of the rich calls them to task for failing in these duties.

Later literary traditions evolve the idea of the poor to include all who are humbly dependent on God and trusting in the divine power to save, the

---

[7] See R. Gordis, *Poets, Prophets, Sages: Essays in Biblical Interpretation* (Bloomington and London: Indiana University, 1971) 160–97.

[8] Loeb, "Littérature," 191–98; S. Mowinckel, *The Psalms in Israel's Worship* (Oxford: Blackwell, 1962) 2.18–20; L. Sabourin, *The Psalms: Their Origin and Meaning* (rev. ed.; New York: Alba House, 1974) 95–104.

"pious poor" who are God's righteous ones. While some of the psalms of lament and trust represent the perspective of the "pious poor," most of the literature concerning the poor and the rich is intended as a challenge to the rich to avoid the dangers of wealth but above all to deal justly with the poor.

Intertestamental Literature

There are scattered references to the issue of rich and poor in several intertestamental writings, e.g., that God is the defender of the poor (*Pss. Sol.* 5.2, 11; 15.2; 18.2); that struggle between poor and rich will be one sign of the apocalyptic upheaval (*Jub.* 23.19); that in the eschatological reckoning the poor will be made rich (*T. Judah* 25.4).[9] Two bodies of literature from the period show more interest than others in this language and do so in a way that enhances the theology of the "pious poor", namely, *1 Enoch* and the Qumran writings.

Who are the poor and who are the rich in the eyes of God?

1 Enoch 91–105 represents the perspective of the righteous against the wicked.[10] To those who are victims of violence and oppression, hope is offered for change and the redressing of wrongs.[11] Though the word is not used of them, the "poor" are those who are oppressed, hated, robbed, and devoured (103.9–15) by the rich, who are wicked, unrighteous (94.6–8), foolish ones from whom all their finery will be taken (98.1–3), and sinners who will not be saved because of their unjust deeds (100.6; 102.9).

If the poor are not named as such in *1 Enoch*, by contrast it is the rich who remain unnamed in the Qumran writings, except when they are synonymous with the wicked oppressor, the enemies of the Qumran community. The poor appear among traditional recipients of works of justice to be performed by members of the community (CD 6.16, 21; 14.14), but use of the concept goes far deeper. God's mighty hand is with the poor (1QM 13.14); he delivers the soul of the poor (*nepeš ʾebyôn*), rescues the poor and needy . . . and rescues *my* soul from the mighty (1QH 2.32–35; cf. 3.25; 5.12–18). The

---

[9] See Bammel, "*Ptōchos*," 895–99.

[10] This part of the book is generally dated to the first quarter of the first century B.C.E. (R. H. Charles, *APOT* 2.171; J. J. Collins, *Apocalypse: The Morphology of a Genre* (*Semeia* 14; Missoula, MT: Scholars Press, 1979) 45.

[11] G. W. E. Nickelsburg, "The Apocalyptic Message of 1 Enoch 92–105," *CBQ* 39 (1977) 309–28. In Charles's edition in *APOT* chap. 91 is incorporated in two parts between chaps. 92 and 94 to bring it into sequence in the "Apocalypse of Weeks" (93.1–10; 91.12–17); see p. 260 n. 40.

Teacher of Righteousness preaches good news to the lowly (ʿănāwîm 1QH 18.14) and belongs with all the poor of divine mercy (kôl ʾebyônê ḥesed 1QH 5.22). The Qumran community calls itself God's poor.[12]

How should rich and poor relate to one another?

1 Enoch tells how the wicked see the righteous die with no apparent reward for their innocence and suffering, and so they conclude that righteousness is of no advantage (102.6–11). What they do not realize is that the eschatological reward and punishment will be different for each group (103.3–8; cf. Wis 2:6–5:23). Indeed, the situation here in this "world that is out of kilter"[13] is one of hostility and oppression, but in the eschatological reversal the prayers of the righteous will bring judgment upon the wicked (97.5), and the oppressed will be able to exact violent retribution (98.12).

The same is true in the Qumran writings. The assembly of the poor (ʿădat hāʾebyônîm in 4QpPsa 1–10 ii 10 and iii 10) is persecuted and afflicted now but will be rewarded by heavenly delights. The wicked enemies will be delivered into the hands of the poor (ʾebyônîm),[14] and the hardened heart will be punished by the humble in spirit (bĕʿanwê(y) rûaḥ 1QM 14.7; cf. 11.9, 13).[15] The Wicked Priest will be punished for exploiting and attempting to destroy the poor (1QpHab 12.3, 6, 10).

---

[12] See L. Keck, "The Poor among the Saints in Jewish Christianity and Qumran," *ZNW* 57 (1966) 54–78. Keck's argument is that though the Qumran community used this terminology as a self-description, it was not a technical designation. The difference may be a fine line. As he points out (p. 68), references to the economics of the community and the description of the poor as the community never occur together, which enhances the impression that the terminology is symbolic. See new, mostly fragmentary references in DJD 7.501 1 9; 491 11 i 11; 497 14 2; 508 21 2; 509 8 7; 511 17 2.

[13] Nickelsburg, "Apocalyptic Message," 311. The tension and incongruities between the two groups are expressed through the complementary literary forms of woes to the wicked and exhortations to the oppressed (ibid., 310–12).

[14] A. Dupont-Sommer (*The Essene Writings from Qumran* [Cleveland and New York: World, 1961] 186 n. 1 and 267 n. 4) maintains that ʾebyôn in such passages is a self-designation of the community. Keck ("Poor among the Saints," 70) concedes that they may be so describing themselves, but that it is still not a technical term.

[15] The relationship of this expression to Matt 5:3 is contested. While Keck ("Poor among the Saints," 71–72) would posit no direct connection, D. Flusser ("Blessed Are the Poor in Spirit . . .," *IEJ* 10 [1960] 1–13) would propose historical and literary relationships. See further the discussion and the bibliography in Keck. S. Légasse ("Les pauvres en esprit et les 'volontaires' de Qumran," *NTS* 8 [1961–62] 336–45) establishes that there is no apparent connection between use of this term and voluntary dispossession at Qumran.

What are the ethical/theological implications of wealth considered apart from the question of responsibility to the poor?

In keeping with its complete intolerance of the rich, *1 Enoch* sees the effect of wealth as wholly negative. It leads to forgetfulness of God, blasphemy, injustice, and complacency (94.8–10; 97.8–9; cf. 46.7). The wicked are condemned by their own hearts (96.4). They will lose all their possessions and not be able to escape from the eschatological wrath (97.10; 98.7–10). In summary, the wealthy have acquired their riches unjustly, using their power to oppress the poor, and their luxury stands in sharp contrast to the neediness of the poor. They trust in their wealth to create for them a secure future, but instead they will be condemned to swift and unexpected punishment for their earthly misdeeds.[16]

In the Qumran writings there is no direct discussion of wealth or the wealthy. The impression is given by the Community Rule that dispossession of property carries with it some kind of religious and eschatological advantage. All who enter the community bring their possessions with them (1QS 1.12–13) to be handed over along with wages after passing through the first probationary year; this property and income are kept in trust until the end of the second year, after which they are given over to the common use of the community (6.17–23) under the administration of the priests (5.2). In this discussion of the disposition of property, there is no reference to the poor.[17] As in other ascetic sects in the Greco-Roman world, the obvious difficulties of living a pious life in combination with luxury and wealth led at Qumran to the practice of voluntary dispossession, but the reasons for this are not discussed.

To which group(s) is the material addressed?

The woes addressed to sinners in *1 Enoch* contain explicit condemnations of the rich for their misdeeds and their neglect even of God (e.g., 94.8; 96.4; 97.8–10), but these passages are part of longer harangues in which it becomes clear that "rich" is only one term among many for the enemy. The righteous, however, are addressed in the exhortations, which form the other major pole in the dynamic of the literary unit. They serve to encourage the just, to strengthen them in their resolve, and to assure them that their present

---

16 G. W. E. Nickelsburg, "Riches, the Rich, and God's Judgment in 1 Enoch 92-105 and the Gospel according to Luke," *NTS* 25 (1978-79) 324-44 [332]. See the summary of the discussion of this paper in the same volume, pp. 319-20. The starting point for this paper is one by S. Aalen, "St. Luke's Gospel and the Last Chapters of 1 Enoch," *NTS* 13 (1966) 1-13.

17 Légasse, "Les pauvres en esprit"; Keck, "Poor among the Saints," 68.

suffering will be worthwhile (e.g., 95.3; 102.4–5; 104.6). The author employs the rhetorical technique of addressing the woes to the wicked rich, but his real addressees are the oppressed just ones, who are meant to be encouraged by the exhortations to endurance.[18] Only once is there a hint that repentance may be a possibility for the sinners, and this one fleeting exhortation to them resolves immediately into an assertion that they will do exactly what they are bidden not to do, namely, alter the prophetic word given by this author and others like him (104.9–10).

In a similar way, the language about the "poor" at Qumran is a self-description of the community, spoken for and in the context of the in-group. Whether or not it is technical terminology, certainly the members of the community identify with it as an authentic theological description of themselves before God.

Summary

Though starting from opposite sides, *1 Enoch* 91–105 and the Qumran literature have the same theological perspective on rich and poor. In *1 Enoch* "rich" is one way of designating sinners who engage in all the kinds of wickedness, injustice, and oppression that are known from the prophetic condemnations. The righteous are simply their victims, the sufferers to whom encouragement is addressed. In the eschatological reckoning their lot will be reversed, their suffering avenged, and they will participate in the condemnation and punishment of the wicked, whose course is set and irreversible.

In the Qumran writings "poor" is one term by which the community describes itself as those specially in need of God's help and as recipients of divine protection. There is no terminology of the "rich," but all of the wicked enemies of the community will, as in *1 Enoch*, be turned over to the "poor" in-group in the eschatological battle. In both cases, the literature is addressed to the oppressed and is intended for their encouragement and exhortation to zeal and endurance. The tradition of the "pious poor" continues in both these groups of intertestamental literature.

The theme of poor and rich occurs in a number of places in the New Testament.[19] Because this question is of greater concern in two New Testa-

---

[18] Nickelsburg, "Apocalyptic Message," 324; idem, "Riches," 332. The literary structure is not unlike Luke 6:20–26, and the theological intent may be the same. See the discussion of Luke below.

[19] For a general examination of the theme, see Bammel, "*Ptōchos*," 902–12; M. D. Guinan, ed., *Gospel Poverty: Essays in Biblical Theology* (Chicago: Franciscan Herald, 1977) 25–150; M. Hengel, *Property and Riches in the Early Church: Aspects of a Social History of Early Christianity*, trans. John Bowden (Philadelphia: Fortress, 1974) 23-41.

ment writings, Luke and James, only these will be examined in detail. They represent well the New Testament appropriation and development of the traditions about wealth and poverty and the "pious poor."

The Gospel of Luke[20]

Who are the poor and who are the rich in the eyes of God?

The answer to this question seems to rise with absolute clarity in 6:20–26: Blessed are you who are poor, hungry, weeping, and hated, for yours is the kingdom of God with its reward; woe to you rich, you who are satisfied, who laugh, and who are praised, for you have received your reward and will henceforth experience hunger and sorrow.[21] This judgment is reinforced in the special Lucan material, at least regarding the poor, by Mary's exultation in the God who fills the hungry and sends the rich away empty (1:53); by Jesus' adoption of Isa 61:1 as a description of his own mission to preach the gospel to the *ptōchoi* (4:18; again in Q material in 7:22); by the advice to those who would give a dinner not to invite friends, relatives, or rich neighbors, who can pay back in kind, but rather to invite the poor, the crippled, the lame, and the blind, for whose sake the host will be rewarded in the resurrection of the just (14:12–14); and most perfectly by the dramatized lesson of the parable of the rich man and Lazarus (16:19–31), where the lack of vehemence against the rich man suggests that it is not because he was unmerciful to Lazarus that he suffers torment after death, but simply because he has enjoyed good things in life, including even a proper burial (v. 22).[22] What happens is a simple exchange of states (v. 25), illustrating the

---

[20] Attention is here directed to what can be constructed of the Lucan community and its needs rather than the author's redaction of material stemming from the situation of Jesus. An immense amount has been written on this topic, and it is impossible to do justice to all of it here. See especially the superb study of L. T. Johnson (*The Literary Function of Possessions in Luke-Acts* [SBLDS 39; Missoula, MT: Scholars Press, 1977]), which develops much more thoroughly Luke's use of the theme to express his theology and deals far more with Acts than is possible here. Besides the literature cited in this section, see H.-J. Degenhardt, *Lukas: Evangelist der Armen: Besitz und Besitzverzicht in den Lukanischen Schriften* (Stuttgart: Katholisches Bibelwerk, 1965); T. Hoyt, *The Poor in Luke-Acts* (Ph.D. dissertation, Duke University; Ann Arbor, MI: Xerox University Microfilms, 1975); B. Sanders, "Studies in Luke's Editorial Methods and Their Situations" Ph.D. dissertation, Harvard University, 1975).

[21] Compare *1 Enoch* 46.7; 94.8; 96.4; 100.6; 103.5–6; see also Nickelsburg, "Riches," 340-41. For a recent form critical study of the formation of the beatitudes, see R. Guelich, "The Matthean Beatitudes: 'Entrance-Requirements' or Eschatological Blessings?" *JBL* 95 (1976) 415-34.

[22] Cited by Dupont, *Béatitudes*, 3.60 n. 2.

earlier teaching of the beatitudes and woes in 6:20–26. Added to these is the synoptic narrative of the poor widow who gave most, because she gave all she had, in the face of the wealthy who were giving from their abundance (21:1–4). The biblical tradition of the "pious poor" once more becomes apparent: the poor are objects of God's favor simply because they are poor and their heavenly reward awaits them on that basis; the rich are to some extent identified with the ungodly and therefore with those who will reap a negative reward. The one definite exception to this pattern in Luke is Zacchaeus the publican (19:1–10), who is specifically described as *plousios* (v. 2) and a member of a socially undesirable group besides.[23] Jesus invites himself to Zacchaeus's house, and it is only afterward that the tax collector reveals his monetary generosity, whereupon Jesus replies (v. 9) that today salvation has come to this house, because he [Zacchaeus] too is a son of Abraham. It is on this basis, namely, Zacchaeus's sonship in Abraham, that he can be saved, but he is considered part of what is lost (*to apololos*, v. 10) not because of his wealth, for Jesus sought him out prior to the revelation of his generosity, but because of his social and civil status. The point of the Zacchaeus story is not whether the wealthy can be saved, or how the rich should deal with their possessions, but that even rich *publicans* can be saved, i.e., that salvation cuts across all social barriers.

How should rich and poor relate to one another?

The relationship of rich and poor to one another is a topic that is scarcely developed in Luke. In some instances there seems to be no relationship but simply juxtaposition. In the Lucan story of Lazarus and the rich man, not even after death can communication be established (16:26). The poor widow of the synoptic passage (21:1–4) brushes shoulders with the wealthy, but they and she remain two distinct parties; indeed, the lines drawn in 6:20–26 even recur explicitly in the terminology of this pericope: *tous ballontas eis to gazophylakeion ta dōra autōn plousious* in 21:1 versus *hē chēra hautē hē ptōchē* in 21:3 (in most manuscripts—"the rich who threw their gifts into the treasury box" versus "this poor widow"). In both cases the important term is placed last for emphasis.

In other cases the traditional duty to give to the poor is reinforced. The disciples are encouraged to sell what they have and give alms in order to have theftproof and mothproof treasure in heaven (12:33–34, Q material), and those who give banquets are advised not to invite friends, relatives, or rich

---

[23] The case of the rich official (18:18–23) is really one of moral decision making and discipleship and will be handled as such in the section on the addressees of the material.

neighbors who can repay them, but rather the poor and those reduced to beggary by physical handicaps (14:12–14, Lucan material). In neither case, however, is it altogether clear that the disciples or would-be hosts fall into the classification of "rich." It is only by inference from their ability to give to the poor that this can be surmised. On the other hand, in the synoptic account the official (an *archōn* only in Luke, a *neaniskos* in Matt 19:20, an indefinite *heis* in Mark 10:17) who wished to do something more to attain eternal life (18:18–23) is specifically described, and only by Luke, as extremely rich (*plousios sphodra*, v. 23; Mark 10:22 and Matt 19:22 avoid the term by saying that he had "many possessions" [*ktēmata polla*]). He is given advice similar to that given to the disciples, namely, to sell what he has and this time specifically to give to the *ptōchoi* to acquire heavenly treasure—in view of the pattern of 12:33–34, a clear invitation to a *plousios* to become a disciple, an invitation he is unable to accept. Zacchaeus is also implicitly praised for his generosity to the poor (19:8), and he, like the ruler of 18:18–23, is a *plousios* (v. 2). The obligation of the rich to give to the poor is reiterated by example, but Luke here adds nothing to a long-established theme.

What are the ethical/theological implications of wealth considered apart from the question of responsibility to the poor?

A more complex pattern emerges from the Lucan material. The whole passage 12:15–34 is concerned with possessions and how they are to be handled. The special Lucan saying on avoiding avarice (*pleonexia*, 12:15) warns that life is not to be found in an abundance of possessions. The saying supposedly completes the pericope on the division of inheritance begun at v. 13, but it really serves better to introduce the parable of the rich fool (vv. 16–20), which is completed in v. 21 by the instruction that the rich man's folly was to place his treasure elsewhere than in God—a new adaptation of the traditional theme of acquiring heavenly treasure (cf. Mark 10:21 par. Matt 6:21; Luke 18:22; Matt 6:20–21 par. Luke 12:33–34).[24] The next thirteen verses contain instruction from Jesus to his disciples on virtuous lack of concern about material necessities, ending with the admonition to sell what one has, give alms, and collect heavenly treasure instead of earthly (vv. 33–

---

[24] He complacently took pleasure not only in his success but also in bodily enjoyment (v. 19), traditionally an inevitable evil result of wealth. This is perhaps what Luke had in mind in adding "the pleasures of life" (*hēdonai tou biou*) to the application to thorns in the synoptic parable of the sower (Luke 8:14 par. Mark 4:19; Matt 13:22). Just before, Luke omits the Marcan (and Matthean) "deceit" of wealth (*apatē*), perhaps because in Luke's eyes wealth itself is deceit enough.

34). In spite of the actual encouragement in v. 33 to sell possessions, a pattern is already forming: it does not seem to be wealth itself that is the problem but rather the concentration of energy and concern on one's possessions. Even in vv. 21 and 33, a substitute (heavenly) treasure is offered. The warning of 16:13 (Q material) about the inability to serve God and *mammō-nas* reinforces the case against divided loyalties, one's possessions and God, and it is significant that the Pharisee listeners according to Luke miss the point and respond with mockery, since they are *philargyroi*.[25]

Consequently, the abrupt saying of 14:33 comes as a surprise and seems to be out of context. After two special Lucan parables about foresight and planning (vv. 28–32), the declaration is made that thus (?) anyone who does not renounce all his possessions cannot be Jesus' disciple. It is the puzzling *houtōs* that is the key. Previously in vv. 25–27 the hearers are told (from Q material) that discipleship demands a priority of personal loyalty and the bearing of the cross. Then come the Lucan parables on careful planning for building and warfare, then the passage on renunciation of possessions. The injunctions of vv. 25–27 are to be understood as requisites for discipleship. And just as the builder of a tower must be certain of having the proper materials, and just as a king waging war must be certain he has an army that can measure up to the foe, so the one who wishes to be a disciple of Jesus must be certain that he is *willing* to give up his possessions for the sake of discipleship (e.g., 12:33–34) or for the use of the community and those in need (Acts 4:31c–35).[26]

It is significant that thus far there has been discussion of possessions and what to do with them as a Christian but no actual use of the terms *ploutos* and *plousios* except in the case of the Lucan foolish barn-builder of 12:16–20, who serves as a negative example. But the official who seeks the one thing more for the kingdom (18:24–27) is, according to Luke, a *plousios*.

---

[25] Dupont (*Béatitudes* 2.196; 163–72) would include the parable of the "unjust" steward (16:1–9) among the Lucan material on riches, as the exact opposite of the rich fool (12:16–21). The clever steward is praised for his ingenuity, and he teaches the proper use of money, namely, giving it away, so that the poor recipients of his generosity will receive him into life eternal when money fails (as in 14:14?). However, the parable itself, independent of applications, seems intended to emphasize cleverness more than disposal of money; the fact that the master of the story is a *plousios* (v. 16) would then have no bearing on the interpretation.

[26] Seen by R. J. Karris ("Poor and Rich: The Lukan Sitz im Leben," in *Perspectives on Luke-Acts*, ed. C. Talbert [Special Studies Series 5; Danville, VA: Association of Baptist Professors of Religion, 1978] 121) in dependence on Dupont (*Béatitudes*, 2.262–72 and "Renoncer à tous ces biens [Luc 14,33]," *NRT* 93 [1971] 561–82). The story of Ananias and Sapphira (Acts 5:1–11), discussed by Karris in the same context, is not as immediately relevant except insofar as it illustrates Luke's belief in a primitive Christian communal sharing of goods—albeit voluntary.

Indeed, he is a test case for the principle laid down in 14:33. He is offered the moment in which further discipleship asks of him the renunciation of his goods, but he fails the test. The saying about the camel and the eye of the needle (18:24–27) follows immediately—and in his presence (contrary to the setting in Mark or Matthew). A rich man has been invited into the circle of disciples and cannot accept because he is unwilling to pay the price. Still there are no *plousioi* counted among the disciples, but the call to remain independent of the snares of wealth is clear. The salvation of the rich is difficult for that very reason, but it is not impossible because salvation is in God's hands (18:27).

Once again Zacchaeus seems to be an exception: he is a *plousios* who clearly and explicitly receives the gift of salvation (19:9–10). Zacchaeus, however, exhibits that justice and generosity in the use of money and that straightforwardness which Jesus demands. Moreover, he is part of what is despised, the *apolōlos*, and hence not one of the privileged members of society. In Luke's eyes, the possession of wealth carries with it no clear condemnation but rather a stern warning that it is laden with difficulties for the one who wishes to follow Christ singleheartedly. But what of the "woes" against the rich in 6:24–26?

Other occurrences of the "woe" literary pattern in the synoptics, i.e., against the Pharisees (e.g., Matt 23:4–29 with loose parallels in Luke 11:42–52) suggest that the "woe" form of speech denotes a proclamation of condemnation. On the contrary, the Greek *ouai* as well as its Semitic and Latin counterparts was primarily an "exclamation of pain and anger," perhaps originating in funerary lamentation.[27] It is, in other words, an expression of dismay, lament, and in that context, of anger. It need not imply a prophetic pronouncement of imminent catastrophe. Rather, it may be as if to say "you are unfortunate because. . . ." If this is true, then Luke 6:24–26 is not necessarily a condemnation nor even a call to conversion or renunciation, but may be simply a descriptive statement of eschatological misfortune. As such, its parallelism and contrast with the beatitudes of vv. 20–23 are heightened.[28]

---

[27] LSJ and BAG, s.v.; C. T. Lewis and C. Short, *A Latin Dictionary* (Oxford: Clarendon, 1879) s.v.; Dupont, *Béatitudes*, 3.28–30. The Latin *vae* is common in literary texts; the Greek *ouai* is attested outside biblical literature (where it usually translates *ʾôy* or *hôy*) only in Epict. *Disc.* 3.19.1 and 3.22.32 (but cf. *oimoi* in 3.5.4) and POxy.413.184-85, where it is more likely under the influence of the Latin than the Hebrew cognate. For further background, see A. D. Lowe, "The Origin of *ouai*," *Hermathena* 105 (1967) 34-39.

[28] Though blessing and woe sayings are here associated, W. Janzen points out ("ʾAŠRÊ in the Old Testament," *HTR* 58 [1965] 220-21) that through the prophetic literature, Psalms, and as late as Sirach, they are not.

In Luke, 6:24–26 is the only locus of *ouai* that is not either in a common synoptic passage (Luke 21:23 par. Matt 24:19, Mark 13:17; Luke 22:22 par. Matt 26:24, Mark 14:21)[29] or with wording common enough with Matthew to be assigned to Q (Luke 10:13 par. Matt 11:21; Luke 11:42 par. Matt 23:23; Luke 11:43 par. Matt 23:6; Luke 11:44 par. Matt 23:27; Luke 11:45 par Matt 23:4; Luke 11:47 par. Matt 23:29; Luke 11:52 par. Matt 23:13; Luke 17:1 par. Matt 18:7).[30] The "woe" form is not original but is borrowed by Luke. There is a good possibility that the substance of 6:24–26 is not Lucan material but was taken by Luke from the same source as its correlate 6:20–23 (i.e., Q) because of his concern with the question of wealth; Matthew omitted it for his own reasons. If 6:24–26 can be interpreted not as a condemnation of the wealthy and those who enjoy life now but as a lament over them because of a belief that their fate, like that of the poor, will be reversed, then the passage may not deviate from the tone presented by the other Lucan passages discussed above: the possession of riches carries difficulties and disadvantages from which poverty delivers.

To which group(s) is the material addressed?

The simplest answer to this difficult question would be that such passages in Luke are addressed literally to the poor and the rich in the community. In this case there is in the texts a definite warning to the rich that, far from being a sign of divine favor as they suppose, their wealth puts them at a disadvantage with regard to the kingdom.[31] On the other hand, poverty is not an end in itself but is certainly an easier means to the kingdom. The reasons for the renunciation of goods are the cultivation of personal detachment and the sharing of goods for the common benefit. In this case the "woes" against the rich in 6:24–26 are as interpreted above, i.e., solemn warnings of the ultimate difficulties of the wealthy and the prosperous.

Against this interpretation is the difficulty that those designated as *plousioi* seem always somehow to be outsiders. The rich fool of 12:16–21 is a negative example. The practical advice of 14:12 suggests *not* to invite rich neighbors (which does not at all imply that the would-be host sees himself as

---

[29] Of these two common passages, the second might imply condemnation ("Woe to the one by whom the Son of Man is betrayed"); the first surely does not ("Woe to those who are pregnant or nursing in those days") but is rather an eschatological lament.

[30] It is to be noticed that six of the eight Q references given above occur within the same chapter in both Luke and Matthew, though not in the same order. In the case of Luke 11:43 and 45, the word *ouai* is not present in the Matthean parallel.

[31] This is the conclusion of R. Karris, "Poor and Rich," esp. p. 124.

rich—the whole point is "getting ahead" in society).[32] The parable of the rich man and Lazarus (16:19–31) casts the rich man as alienated from any reward or consolation, while Lazarus is the protagonist. The synoptic story of the rich (young) man (in Luke, *archōn*) in 18:18–23 features a man who hears spoken before him, in the third person, the saying of vv. 24–27 implying that he can scarcely be saved—and he still turns away. Once again the exception is Zacchaeus (19:1–10), who is proclaimed saved more as a social outcast than as a wealthy man.

There is one other exception to this pattern: the direct address in the beatitudes and woes of chapter 6. Contrary to Matthew's construction, Luke's beatitudes (vv. 20–23) and woes (vv. 24–26) are in the second person plural, grammatically direct address. But to whom are they actually spoken? If the woes against the Pharisees and the lawyers in Luke 11 were intended as spoken directly to those parties in the time of Jesus, the same could be assumed of the woes against the rich in 6:24–26. It would be difficult, however, to envision the woes of Luke 11 as intended for their most obvious recipients in the situation of the Lucan community; yet the direct address is retained for dramatic effect. The same can be assumed regarding the woes against the rich in 6:24–26. In other words, paraenetic direct address for the purpose of lament or excoriation cannot be used to prove that such a category of recipients actually existed in the Lucan community.

Moreover, peculiar phrasing in vv. 24 and 27 cannot be overlooked. The conjunction *plēn* at the beginning of v. 24, whether it comes from Luke or an earlier redactor, sets what follows in juxtaposition to the preceding verse (cf. Luke 10:11; Luke 10:14 par. Matt 11:22; Matt 18:7).[33] This alone would be inconclusive; the very shift of reference from poor to rich would be sufficient to warrant usage of the expression. More striking is the opening of v. 27 immediately after the close of the last woe saying: *Alla hymin legō tois akouousin· agapate tous echthrous hymōn* ("But to you who are listening I say: love your enemies . . ."). What follows is explicitly addressed to the hearers of Jesus within the literary setting of his preaching. As such it stands in contrast to what preceded it, namely, the woes to the rich, which have been cast grammatically in the second person because that is the traditional style in which they are to be delivered.[34]

It can be concluded that the woes of Luke 6:24–26 need not have been

---

[32] The master of the "dishonest steward" is described as rich (16:1) for narrative effect only.

[33] Dupont (*Béatitudes*, 3.30–34) documents the discussion and concludes that the *plēn* of v. 24 comes from Luke, to emphasize the opposition between the beatitudes and woes.

[34] Compare especially the break in thought of Luke 11:41, also introduced by *plēn* and followed by *alla*. See Dupont, *Béatitudes*, 3.34–37.

addressed either to rich Christians in Luke's community (and therefore the passage in itself gives us no indication that such a group existed there) nor even to actual hearers of Jesus' sermon within the literary context of Luke 6.

Who then are "the rich" in Luke? If they are not members of the community, they are in some way outsiders—perhaps inimical outsiders. The thesis that "the rich" in the situation of Luke's community are really the Jews who are antagonistic to Christianity has much to commend it.[35] Luke, for instance, alters Mark's young man (Mark 10:17–22) to an *archōn*[36] (Luke 18:18) and precedes the story with the parable of the Pharisee and the publican; the story of the rich man and Lazarus is preceded by criticism of the Pharisees as greedy (*philargyroi*, 16:14) and hypocrites (16:15); while Jesus is at table with an official of the Pharisees (14:1) he suggests by way of contrast to the host's present position that he invite the poor to dine with him (14:13); the rich man of the Lazarus parable considers himself on close terms with Abraham (16:24).[37] The ominously distant "they" spoken by Abraham of the rich man's surviving relatives in v. 29 could simply be maintaining the dramatic effect of dialogue among the dead about the living, but when it is seen alongside "their fathers" (*hoi pateres autōn*) of 6:23 and 26 the possibility arises that in both cases the dramatic context has been eluded and real opponents are indicated.[38] Once again, the story of Zacchaeus is significant, for Zacchaeus the publican is the only *plousios* in Luke's Gospel who is proclaimed saved (19:9), and by his open response to Jesus he is the counterpart of the rich *archōn* of the previous chapter (18:18–23). That the "rich" in Luke's Gospel are the opponents of Jesus and therefore quite possibly of Luke's community is a feasible supposition.

Who then are the poor? They are precisely those who are addressed, i.e., the Christians of Luke's community. Since questions regarding the disposition of possessions are raised (e.g., 12:33–34; 14:33; 18:28–30; Acts 2:41–47; 4:31–35, etc.) and are apparently intended for disciples, it does not seem likely that the poor to whom the Gospel is generally addressed are economi-

---

[35] Proposed by F. Hauck and W. Kasch (*"Ploutos,"* TDNT 6 [1968] 328) and adopted cautiously by Dupont (*Béatitudes*, 3.55–64 and passim).

[36] A word connected by Luke with Jewish responsibility for the death of Jesus (23:13, 35; 24:20; Acts 3:17; 13:27) and with Jewish persecution of the apostles (Acts 4:5–8); see also Luke 14:1 and Dupont, *Béatitudes*, 3.49–58.

[37] Some of these examples and others are given by Hauck and Kasch ("*Ploutos,"* 328) and Dupont (*Béatitudes*, 3.55–64). Some of the arguments given by Hauck and Kasch are too sweeping but are refined and developed by Dupont.

[38] The implication in vv. 23 and 26 is that their sons will do the same to you! (Dupont, *Béatitudes*, 3.34–40).

cally impoverished. They are rather the poor of the prophetic tradition, the "pious poor" who are oppressed by the powerful but upheld by God.[39]

Summary

As presented by Luke, the rich are those who have their reward in this life and hence are not objects of God's favor or mercy. The poor, because of their suffering, are the beloved objects of God's favor. Luke has little to say about how poor and rich are to relate to one another except to repeat the traditional duty of the rich to give to the poor. The implications of wealth are complex: the possession of riches causes many difficulties for the Christian, whose life is better off without them, but ultimately it is detachment and generosity that are important rather than actual poverty. Luke carefully distinguishes the question of riches from the category of rich people, a title he seems to reserve, Zacchaeus excepted, for opponents of Jesus and the community or those who cannot meet the requirements for entrance into the kingdom.

The Epistle of James[40]

The relevant passages in the epistle are 1:9–11; 2:1–7; and 4:13–5:6.

Who are the poor and who are the rich in the eyes of God?

The concise statement in Jas 2:5 leaves no doubt that the poor are favored:

[39] This is also the conclusion of Dupont (*Béatitudes*, 3.205–6 and passim). It is somewhat surprising that he accepts this interpretation in view of his general resistance to the interiorization of the theological terminology of the Gospel. He does stress however (2.15–16) that the essence of spiritual poverty is not inner dispositions but the nature of the coming kingdom.

[40] While the position that the author of the epistle was James of Jerusalem has not been entirely abandoned (witness recently T. W. Leahy, "The Epistle of James," *JBC*, 2.369-70), most modern scholars would place it at least in a second-generation milieu, perhaps Jewish Christian, perhaps merely under the literary influence of Diaspora Judaism (see Dibelius/Greeven, *James*, 11-21; B. S. Easton, "The Epistle of James," *IB* 12.3–18; J. H. Ropes, *A Critical and Exegetical Commentary on the Epistle of St. James* [ICC; New York: Scribner's, 1916] 43-52; S. Laws, *The Epistle of James* [HNTC; San Francisco: Harper and Row, 1980] 38–42). Dibelius/Greeven's conclusion (p. 20) that what can be learned from the text about the actual author of the epistle is "next to nothing" is not encouraging. Laws (pp. 22–26) posits a Roman origin for James, basing this in part on *Hermas'* apparent familiarity with it, which she argues convincingly, and the appearance of the term *dipsychos* in early Christian literature only in James, *1* and *2 Clement*, and *Hermas*. For the development of later traditions about James of Jerusalem see Dibelius/Greeven, pp. 12–16; Ropes, pp. 53–74; R. B. Ward, "James of Jerusalem," *Restoration Quarterly* 16 (1973) 174–90.

οὐχ ὁ θεὸς ἐξελέξατο τοὺς πτωχοὺς τῷ κόσμῳ πλουσίους ἐν πίστει καὶ κληρονόμους τῆς βασιλείας ἧς ἐπηγγείλατο τοῖς ἀγαπῶσιν αὐτόν;

Has not God chosen the poor in regard to the world[41] to be rich in faith and heirs of the kingdom which he has promised to those who love him?[42]

This epitome of the spiritual and hidden identity of the "pious poor" carries on the biblical tradition of the despised outcasts in the world who are in reality the favored ones who will triumph when the true divine order is revealed.[43]

The rich do not come off well in James. The juxtaposition of the exaltation of the humble brother with the humiliation of the rich man in 1:9–10 and the expectation that each is to boast in the fact result in an ironic play on words at the expense of the rich: *Kauchasthō de ho adelphos ho tapeinos en tō hypsei autou, ho de plousios en tē tapeinōsei autou.*[44] All he can boast about is his humiliation, his "being laid low." The process is spelled out in 5:1–6 in a vindictive proclamation, "the ancient verdict of the 'pious' regarding the rich,"[45] who can only weep and wail at their eschatological destruction because of their unjust dealings with their laborers (v. 4), here symbols of the "poor," who are then identified with the just (*ho dikaios*) in v. 6. In

---

[41] Dibelius/Greeven (*James*, 137-38) rules out the "dative of respect ' because it would have to mean "those poor in worldly goods" and opts for a "dative of advantage" (*dativus commodi*), "those who are poor before the world." This sense fits poorly the usual use of the dative of advantage. Given the further use of the word *kosmos* by James (1:27; 3:6; 4:4) as a conglomeration of evil forces opposed to God, the word need not mean "worldly goods" in 2:5, but rather something closer to "worldly values," and thus the dative of respect is a smoother explanation. Ropes seems to concur, with "dative of reference, or 'interest'" (*James*, 193). The minor variants *en tō kosmō* (passim) and *tou kosmou* (Koine text) do not alter the meaning of the phrase and are to be rejected on grounds of insufficient evidence.

[42] See 1 Cor 2:9. Ropes points out (*James*, 194) that this is James's only mention of the "kingdom."

[43] See Dibelius/Greeven, *James*, 39–40; 84-85; E. Bammel, "*Ptōchos*," 888-901; 1QM 13.13–14; 1QH 18.14; *T. Gad* 7.6; Matt 5:1–12; Luke 1:46–55; *1 Clem.* 59.3. Perhaps Paul's way of approaching the same idea is expressed in 1 Cor 6:2 through Rom 15:26.

[44] Dibelius/Greeven (*James*, 84–85) rightly chooses between the "heroic" and "ironic" alternatives in favor of the ironic, for the continuing analogy of withered grass applied to the rich (v. 11) bespeaks nothing but humiliation and doom, of which it can only be ironic that the rich should boast (See Luke 14:11; Jer 9:22). For background usage of *tapeinos* in the literature of the poor see Dibelius/Greeven, *James*, 84 n. 74. It is true that in the quotation in 4:6 the word has ethical significance; however, its use in 1:9 is not without ethical significance, as he implies. As the counterpart of *plousios* it principally connotes the theological category of "pious poor." But given the negative ethical load carried by the word *plousios* elsewhere in James, a positive ethical connotation to its counterpart can be implied. In *Hermas* only an ethical and not a theological or a social connotation can be attached to the *tapeinos* word group (see *Vis.* 3.10.6; *Sim.* 5.3.7; 7.4, 6; 8.7.6; *Man.* 4.2.2; 11.8).

[45] Dibelius/Greeven, *James*, 235.

James the lines are clearly drawn: the poor are those preferred by God; the rich are those whom the divine wrath awaits.

How should rich and poor relate to one another?

The epistle can answer only in negatives. The negative paradigm for the rich, i.e., how they should *not* deal with the poor, lies in 5:4, 6, simply echoing a long line of prophetic complaints about treatment of the poor by the rich—withholding of just wages, inordinate luxury not shared with the needy, exploitation, and murder of the helpless.

A more important passage for the consideration of this question is 2:1–7. Here the exhortation against *prosōpolēmpsia* or social discrimination is supported by a practical example. A well-dressed man wearing a gold ring[46] and a poor man in shabby clothes enter the assembly.[47] The well-dressed man is seated in an honorable position, while the poor man is disdainfully told to stand or else to sit on a footstool. This is the negative paradigm for the poor *if* they are considered the addressees of the letter in the light of 1:9 and 2:5–7,[48] i.e., preferential treatment of the rich is condemned. Moreover, the feeling of the poor for the rich erupts into hostility in 2:6, 7: it is the rich who exploit you and drag you into court, who blaspheme the good name by which you are called.[49] The rich will perish like grass (1:10–11), while the poor who endure will receive the crown of life (v. 12; cf. 2:5). James sets no patterns for a relationship between rich and poor. He simply echoes the traditional enmity felt between the two groups in earlier literature of the "pious poor."

---

[46] B. Reicke's assumptions (*The Epistles of James, Peter, and Jude,* [AB 37; Garden City, NY: Doubleday, 1964] 27-28) that the "splendid garment" is a Roman citizen's white toga and the gold ring indicates senatorial or equestrian status are unfounded; see R. B. Ward's criticism of the latter claim ("Partiality in the Assembly," *HTR* 62 [1969] 88 n. 4) by citing Epict. *Disc.* 1.22.18. To this could be added Lucian *Demonax* 17, where a lost gold ring is claimed by an adolescent boy who becomes the subject of a vulgar joke because he cannot accurately describe it. But Ward's assumption that the ring of Luke 15:22 is of gold is also perhaps unfounded. At least one other type, the wedding ring, was made of iron.

[47] The *synagōgē* might just as well be a Christian assembly as a Jewish one and may not be a specifically cultic gathering (Dibelius/Greeven, *James*, 132-34) or a Jewish judicial setting, i.e., a story of two men who come to an assembly for judgment, applied to a worship situation (R. B. Ward, "The Communal Concern of the Epistle of James," Th.D. thesis, Harvard University, 1966; and idem, "Partiality in the Assembly," 87-97).

[48] But see the section below on the addressees of the letter.

[49] Dibelius/Greeven (*James*, 140-41) takes the expression *to kalon onoma to epiklēthen eph' hymas* as a Christian phrase, because the rich do not also bear the name as they would in the Jewish literature of the poor.

What are the ethical/theological implications of wealth considered apart from the question of responsibility to the poor?

A quick glance at 1:10–11 and 5:1–6 yields the judgment that the implications of wealth, even apart from obligations toward the poor, are devastating. Moreover, these passages are not calls to repentance but sure proclamations, partly in the prophetic past tense, of an inevitable disaster for the rich.[50] Those immersed in business concerns are caught up in the same judgment (4:13–17), because they plan their business ventures (v. 13) and boast in their arrogance (v. 16) instead of being aware of their contingency and dependence on God from day to day.[51] In this section (4:13–17) there is no suggestion of injustice to the poor, only of neglect of piety, but the rhetorical linking of the passage with the following by the repetition of the introductory *age nun* (4:13 and 5:1) links them also in theological import. Besides, the connection of business and wealth is a natural one: the first presumably produces the second and both engender the same love of gain and luxury. There is, however, a distinction being worked here: those who engage in business are told that their arrogant and presumptuous attitude is evil, while the rich in 5:1–6 are being thrust headlong into punishment. But this difference of degree cannot be pushed too far; it may exist only for the literary effect of building up to a climax in the second section.

To which group(s) is the material addressed?

It would seem that the perspective is that of the poor. In 1:9 the *tapeinos* is spoken of as *adelphos*, and in its juxtaposition against *plousios* the word *tapeinos* carries the ethical/theological symbolism of the poor.[52] Because of an obvious preference for the poor and the identification of the rich with those who oppress *you*, 2:5–7 could also be so interpreted, but then v. 5c remains a problem.

Ward has pointed out that the richly dressed, gold-ringed man of 2:2 is never called a *plousios* even though his counterpart is a *ptōchos*.[53] It has been argued above that Luke deliberately alters synoptic material to avoid

---

[50] Compare *1 Enoch* 94.6–95.7. In spite of several similarities between James's treatment of the rich and that of *Hermas*, this is the most striking dissimilarity; see also *Vis.* 3.9.5,6.

[51] See Jer 9:22; Prov 27:1. A reading of Rev 18:11–17 reveals that at this point James is being remarkably restrained. The anomalous saying of v. 17 that sin consists in not doing the good one might do fits loosely as a correlate to boasting in the previous verse, but its relationship to its context is tenuous. It does, however, belong to a history of search for sins of omission in Jewish moral tradition (see Dibelius/Greeven, *James*, 235).

[52] See above, n. 44.

[53] "Communal Concern," 106, and "Partiality in the Assembly," 96-97.

using the term *plousios*, which, with the exception of the Zacchaeus story, he reserves for the opponents of Jesus and his followers. By omitting *plousios* in the example of 2:2–3, James too preserves "a remarkable degree of consistency" by restricting the term to opponents (vv. 6–7) and outsiders, so that the community can remain cast as God's poor ones.[54]

The *age nun* of 4:13 and 5:1 is a rhetorical device, and it need not suggest, especially in the case of the consequences following 5:1, that the "rich" themselves are the actual addressees of the epistle. Yet neither is there a direct address to the "poor"; in fact, in 2:1–7 both poor and rich are described in the third person. This leads to a consideration of the nature of the short narrative of 2:2–3, and here Dibelius is correct in asserting that we are dealing with a fictitious example and not a special case drawn from the life of the community, that this is an example "narrated without any concern for its reality" or consideration of the circumstances or possibility under which such an incident could have happened. Consequently, the example "cannot be used as a historical source for actual circumstances within the Christian communities."[55] This interpretation becomes more certain when, in reading further in chapter 2, one realizes that the tension in the ongoing discussion is not so much about variant treatment of different social classes as about how to put faith into practice in the exercise of good works. The story in 2:2–3 functions as an introductory negative example from which instruction can develop.[56]

It cannot be said that 2:14 really addresses either group, rich or poor. Yet the "poor" are favored, both here and elsewhere, and the blessedness of

---

[54] Ward, "Partiality in the Assembly," 97. Thus according to Ward's interpretation of the entire passage as a judicial court scene instead of an assembly of worship (see above, n. 47), both the richly dressed man and the poor man can be members of the congregation. Whether or not this factor is significant, however, depends on the interpretation of the function of the entire scene, which will be discussed below.

[55] *James*, 125, 129. See the corresponding example from Epictetus cited on pp. 129–30. If this is so, then whether or not both men in the narrative can be construed as Christians becomes irrelevant (see above, n. 54). But a further warning (ibid., p. 135) should be heeded: the example would be useless if some relevant situation were not envisioned as at least being possible.

[56] The relation of the faith-works theme in James to that in the Pauline writings, a major problem in interpreting James, need not be developed here. See Easton, "The Epistle of James," 40–41 (James does polemicize against Paulinists but misunderstands Paul); Ropes, *James*, 35–36 (the substance of James is contained in Paul; the distinctiveness and originality of Paul are lacking in James; but there is substantial agreement between the two); Dibelius/Greeven, *James*, 174–80 (James is in a tradition not directly derived from Paul, yet remarks like 2:14 or 17 are inconceivable before Paul's slogan "faith, not works"); Laws, *Epistle of James*, 128–33 (James is reacting to paulinists who have misunderstood Paul). Dibelius/Greeven's conclusion (p. 180) that James, in contrast to Paul, was a Christian who found his God without a "shaking of his soul" and thus wrote for the masses is somewhat patronizing.

the poor is to be assumed throughout the epistle. If implicitly the poor are the community and therefore the hearers, then 2:5c (*hymeis de ētimasate ton ptōchon*) could be, as Ward sees it, the highest irony: you (poor) have dishonored the poor, you the just have played the role of the oppressor.[57] The phrase may be understood as the completion of the rhetorical question posed in v. 4: (If you do this) have you not made distinctions among yourselves and become judges with evil designs . . . and (if you do this) you have dishonored the poor. If this is true the phrase poses less of an interpretive problem than if it referred to an actual situation.

Summary

James, like Luke, remains in the theological world of the "pious poor." The literary tradition acceptable in his community still identifies "the poor" as those chosen by God, while the rich are more vehemently condemned than in Luke. This hostility of the community to the rich leads to the conclusion that the community and the chosen poor are identical, just as the rich are identified as their oppressors and persecutors. To this extent it can be construed that the epistle is directed to those who understand themselves to be the poor of God who are chosen to inherit the kingdom.

Conclusion

We have traced the development of the theme of rich and poor from the Hebrew scriptures through illustrative intertestamental writings to its best proponents in the New Testament. In the vast material of the Hebrew scriptures the theological tendencies are varied, but in the later literature the theology of the "pious poor" begins to emerge—the blessedness of those whose lowliness and helplessness draw the special attention and protection of God. Much of the literature seems intended to admonish the rich to do their duty to the poor; however, in the literature of the "pious poor" the perspective of the poor is also represented and much of the writing seems to be addressed to them.

1 Enoch 91–105 and the Qumran literature in the intertestamental period take the perspective of the "pious poor" as their own. Though *1 Enoch* does not use the terminology traditionally connected with the poor and Qumran does not speak specifically of the rich, still the perspective is the same: the powerful (= the rich) and the oppressed (= the poor) are now engaged in an

---

[57] "Communal Concern," 100-106.

unequal confrontation in which the rich seem to have the advantage. In the eschatological reckoning, when God's justice triumphs, the situation will be reversed and the wrongs righted.

The Gospel of Luke carries the dichotomy between rich and poor into the New Testament with some major modifications. The stylized division is continued in the beatitudes and woes of chapter 6, and the mission of Jesus is portrayed symbolically as addressed to the poor. Yet the realistic question of riches as a hindrance to Christian life is tackled in a new way that leaves no doubt that there are members of Luke's community who have considerable possessions. Luke retains the traditional symbolic language of poor holy ones and rich oppressors, but at the same time, by distinguishing ownership of possessions from the category of "the rich," he addresses a practical and radical challenge to those who are prosperous to share their affluence with the whole community, especially the needy, and to be prepared to renounce all possessions for the sake of the kingdom.

The Epistle of James carries on the tradition of the "pious poor" by identifying the poor as God's chosen ones and the rich as oppressive perpetrators of injustice. While 2:1–4 presents a strong plea for impartiality regarding rich and poor, the other passages concerned with the theme do not follow this lead but rather indicate God's partiality to the poor for the traditional reasons.

III

HERMAS' TREATMENT OF RICH AND POOR

Having seen the literary and theological background of the "pious poor" tradition in biblical literature, we can now look at *Hermas'* use of the theme of rich and poor. It will be helpful to first classify the references according to genre before asking of the material the four questions that have been asked of the biblical literature. Because the two relevant expressions in *Man.* 8.10 and the whole of the second *Similitude* will be treated in the following chapters, they will be mentioned only in passing in the discussion in this chapter.

Terms Associated with Rich and Poor in *Hermas*

The overriding concern of *Hermas* is the call to repentance.[1] Repentance from what? The answer to this question is frequently, repentance from abuse stemming from wealth and business affairs. There is but one obvious exception—*dipsychia*.[2]

---

[1] The theme of repentance is ubiquitous in *Hermas*. BAG (s.vv.) lists fifty-two uses of the verb *metanoeō* and forty of the noun *metanoia* (the second list is not claimed to be complete). For discussions of the repentance theme in *Hermas*, see M. Dibelius, *Der Hirt des Hermas* (HNT Ergänzungsband; Die Apostolischen Väter 4; Tübingen: J. C. B. Mohr (Paul Siebeck), 1923) 510-13; R. Joly, *Hermas le Pasteur* (SC 53; Paris: Editions du Cerf, 1958 and 1968) 22-30; G. Snyder, *The Shepherd of Hermas* (Apostolic Fathers 6; Camden, NJ: T. Nelson and Sons, 1968) 69-72; S. Giet, *Hermas et les pasteurs: les trois auteurs du Pasteur d'Hermas* (Paris: Presses Universitaires de France, 1963) 125-34, 174-78, 189-94, 230-34; A. Benoît, *Le Baptême Chrétien au second siècle: La Théologie des Pères* (Etudes d'Histoire et de Philosophie Religieuses; Paris and Strasbourg: Presses Universitaires de France, 1953) 115-35.

[2] The word group *dipsychia, dipsycheō, dipsychos* occurs about fifty times in twenty-four loci in *Hermas*. The idea is associated with excessive business concerns in *Sim.* 8.8 and with wealth in *Sim.* 8.9. Snyder (*Shepherd*, 15) notes two important concerns common to James and *Hermas*. The first is *dipsychia* (Jas 1:8), though Hermas "connects it with repentance in a way quite unrelated to Jas." But actually it would be difficult to say that *dipsychia*, mentioned only once by James, is a major concern of his. The second common concern given by Snyder is the debate "with those who believe in faith without works." As evidence for this issue in *Hermas* he cites *Vis.* 3.6.1-4; *Man.* 10.1.4; *Sim.* 8.9.1; 8.10.3; 9.19.2; 9.21.2. To this list could be added *Vis.* 3.5.4; Man. 6.1.2; 6.3.7-8; 6.3.5-6; *Sim.* 8.9.2-4; 9.26.8. The focus in *Hermas*, however, is

The word group *ploutos, plousios, plouteō* occurs seventeen times in a literal sense outside *Sim.* 2 (and again thirteen times in *Sim.* 2 alone): *Vis.* 1.1.8; 3.6.5 (twice), 6 (three times), 7; *Man.* 8.3; 10.1.4; 12.2.1; *Sim.* 1.8, 9, 10; 8.9.1; 9.20.1 (twice), 2. Added to these terms are *divitiae* (*Sim.* 9.30.4), *opes* (*Sim.* 9.30.5), and *vanitates opum* (*Sim.* 9.31.2), where the Greek text is not extant; *polyteleia* (in the same sense three times,[3] *Sim.* 1.10; *Man.* 8.3; 12.2.1), *hoi echontes* (*Vis.* 3.9.4), and *hoi hyperechontes* (*Vis.* 3.9.5). Concern about business affairs is equally prevalent, referred to as *pragmateiai* (ten times,[4] *Vis.* 2.3.1; 3.6.5; *Man.* 3.5; 10.1.4; *Sim.* 4.5; 8.8.1, 2; 9.20.1 (twice), 2), *praxeis* (five times,[5] *Vis.* 1.3.1; *Man.* 6.2.5; 10.1.5; *Sim.* 4.5, 7), *pragmata* (twice,[6] *Vis.* 3.11.3; *Man.* 5.2.2), and *lēmma* (*Sim.* 9.19.3). On three occasions *ploutos* and *pragmateiai* are linked (*Vis.* 3.6.5; *Sim.* 9.20.1-2; *Man.* 10.1.4).

There are fewer terms for the poor and the needy than for the rich in *Hermas*, and the terms are not used consistently. The common terms *ptōchos* and *penes* do not occur outside *Sim.* 2; the word *endeēs* occurs meaning economically poor or needy only once (*Man.* 8.10); *peinōntes* occurs once (*Vis.* 3.9.5); the *psychai thlibomenai* of *Sim.* 1.8 may be the needy.[7]

---

entirely different: there is no debate over a theological problem of faith versus works, as there is in Jas 2:14-26. Rather, the issue is joined at the ethical level. Hermas takes it for granted that faith must be supported by good works. On *dipsychia*, see J. Reiling, *Hermas and Christian Prophecy: A Study of the Eleventh Mandate* (NovTSup 37; Leiden: Brill, 1973) 32-33; O. Seitz, "The Relationship of the Shepherd of Hermas to the Epistle of James," *JBL* 63 (1944) 131-40; idem, "Antecedents and Signification of the Term *DIPSYCHOS*," *JBL* 66 (1947) 211-19; idem, "Afterthoughts on the Term 'Dipsychos,'" *NTS* 4 (1957-58) 327-34; Dibelius/Greeven, *James*, 31, 83.

[3] The first use of *polyteleia* in *Sim.* 1.10, which is figurative, and its use in *Man.* 6.2.5, which is restricted to food, are not considered.

[4] The use of *pragmateia* in *Sim.* 8.8.2 considered alone need not refer to business (see 2 Tim 2:4). In the context, however, it follows immediately upon the linking of the same word with the participle *empephyrmenos* in 8.8.1, an association which in other contexts can most easily be understood as embroilment in business affairs (*Sim.* 9.20.1, 2; *Man.* 10.1.4). In a similar way, the use of *pragmateia* in *Man.* 3.5 does not necessarily mean "business", but, given the use of the word elsewhere in *Hermas*, that meaning seems to make the best sense in the context. The second use of the word in *Man.* 10.1.4 is probably more general.

[5] *Praxis* is also a deceptively general word, and it is not always easy to decide when it is used in such a restrictive sense. Doubtful cases like *Sim.* 8.9.4 or 6.3.5 are excluded, the latter against the classification given by BAG (s.v. N5) because of its immediate identification with *ponēra erga* (which could mean anything) in the same sentence.

[6] The two uses of *pragmata* may be understood more generally as "concerns," "affairs," or "issues" of ordinary life (*biōtika pragmata*), i.e., "worldly affairs," especially earning a living; cf. 2 Tim 2:4.

[7] It is followed immediately by a typical "widows and orphans" clause. Too much emphasis should not be put on the verb *agorazō*, since the image of purchasing land is the predominant metaphor of vv. 8-9.

Tapeinophrōn and related words never have an economic meaning in *Hermas*.[8] The more common term for the poor is *hysteroumenoi*, used seven times (*Vis.* 3.9.2, 4, 6; *Man.* 2.4; 8.10; *Sim.* 5.3.7; 9.27.2). If widows and orphans are to be included among the poor, they are mentioned four times as objects of charity[9] (*Man.* 8.10; *Sim.* 1.8; 5.3.7; 9.27.2) and once as victims of abuse (*Sim.* 9.26.2). In four of these five passages (all except *Sim.* 9.26.2) they are linked to the poor and the needy.

List of References and Classification by Literary Genre

References to Wealth and the Wealthy outside Sim. 2

Revelatory Discourse

> *Vis.* 1.1.8 Those who obtain this world and rejoice in their wealth (οἱ τὸν αἰῶνα τοῦτον περιποιούμενοι καὶ γαυριῶντες ἐν τῷ πλούτῳ αὐτῶν) (repent but have no hope).

Paraenesis

> *Vis.* 3.9.4 This lack of sharing is harmful to you who have . . . (αὕτη οὖν ἡ ἀσυνκρασία βλαβερὰ ὑμῖν τοῖς ἔχουσι).
>
> 5 Let those with abundance seek out the hungry (οἱ ὑπερέχοντες οὖν ἐκζητεῖτε τοὺς πεινῶντας).
>
> 6 (See to it) you who rejoice in your wealth (οἱ γαυρούμενοι ἐν τῷ πλούτῳ ὑμῶν) (that the needy not groan against you).
>
> *Sim.* 1.8 Spend your wealth on (τὸν πλοῦτον ὑμῶν . . . δαπανᾶτε) (charitable works).
>
> 9 This is why the master has made you rich (εἰς τοῦτο γὰρ ἐπλούτισεν ὑμᾶς ὁ δεσπότης) (so that you might help the needy).
>
> 10 Do not imitate the wealth of the heathen (τὴν οὖν πολυτέλειαν τῶν ἐθνῶν μὴ πράσσετε).

Catalog of Vices

> *Man.* 8.3 Refrain from abundance of wealth (ἀπὸ . . . πολυτελείας πλούτου).

---

[8] See BAG, s.v., and below, chap. IV, n. 27.

[9] Excluding *Vis.* 2.4.3, where they are merely recipients of Hermas' letter through Grapte.

12.2.1 desire . . . for an abundance of wealth (ἐπιθυμία . . . πολυτελείας πλούτου)

Allegory

Sim. 8.9.1 (sticks two-thirds dry, one-third green)—these are they . . . who are faithful . . . but have become wealthy and notable among the heathen (οὗτοι . . . πιστοὶ . . .*πλουτήσαντες* δὲ καὶ γενόμενοι ἐνδοξότεροι παρὰ τοῖς ἔθνεσιν).

9.30.4–5 (round, bright stones)—those whose *divitiae* have alienated them somewhat from the truth, but they have remained faithful. God cut away their *opes* so they could do something good with what is left (see below, *Vis.* 3.6.6–7).

9.31.2 (stones left on the ground)—those from whom this world and *vanitates opum* must be cut away.

References to Business and Worldly Affairs

Revelatory Discourse

Vis. 1.3.1 [Because Hermas loves his family, he is corrupted] by daily concerns (ἀπὸ τῶν βιωτικῶν *πράξεων*).

2.3.1 You have become entangled in your evil undertakings (ταῖς *πραγματείαις* σου συνανεφύρης ταῖς πονηραῖς).

3.11.3 You have been weakened by daily concerns (ὑμεῖς μαλακισθέντες ἀπὸ τῶν βιωτικῶν *πραγμάτων*).

Paraenesis

Man. 5.2.2 Bad temper makes the heart bitter because of daily affairs (ἕνεκεν βιωτικῶν *πραγμάτων*) or food or other trifles.

Catalog of Vices

Man. 6.2.5 desire for many affairs (ἐπιθυμία *πράξεων* πολλῶν)

Allegory

Sim. 8.8.1 (sticks half-green, half-dry)—those embroiled in their businesses and not committed to the saints (οἱ ταῖς *πραγματείαις* αὐτῶν ἐμπεφυρμένοι καὶ τοῖς ἁγίοις μὴ κολλώμενοι)

2 [no repentance for those who] blasphemed and denied the Lord because of their business affairs (διὰ τὰς *πραγματείας* γὰρ αὐτῶν ἐβλασφήμησαν τὸν κύριον καὶ ἀπηρνήσαντο αὐτόν)

Commandment

Man. 3.5 [Keep the commandments of truth] so that the former lies you spoke in your business may become trustworthy (ἵνα καὶ τὰ πρότερα ἅ ἐλάλησας ψευδῆ ἐν ταῖς *πραγματείαις* σου, τούτων εὑρεθέντων ἀληθινῶν).

Sim. 4.5 Abstain from much business and do not sin. For those involved in much business also sin much, being pulled away by their business (ἀπέχου δὲ ἀπὸ πολλῶν *πράξεων* καὶ οὐδὲν διαμάρτῃς. οἱ γὰρ τὰ πολλὰ πράσσοντες πολλὰ καὶ ἁμαρτάνουσιν, περισπώμενοι περὶ τὰς *πραγματείας* αὐτῶν).

7 Anyone involved in one business can still serve the Lord (ἐὰν δὲ μίαν τις *πρᾶξιν* ἐργάσηται, δύναται καὶ τῷ κυρίῳ δουλεῦσαι).

Prophetic Pronouncement

Sim. 9.19.3 [repentance offered to those who did not blaspheme nor betray] but because of the lust after profit they were hypocrites (διὰ δὲ τὴν ἐπιθυμίαν τοῦ *λήμματος* ὑπεκρίθησαν) . . . they will receive judgment, yet repentance is open to them.

References to Wealth and Business Combined

Allegory

Vis. 3.6.5 (round white stones that do not fit the building)—those with faith but also worldly riches (*πλοῦτον* τοῦ αἰῶνος τούτου) . . . in persecution, because of their wealth and business, they deny the Lord (διὰ τὸν *πλοῦτον* αὐτῶν καὶ διὰ τὰς *πραγματείας* ἀπαρνοῦνται τὸν κύριον αὐτῶν).

6 They will be useful when their wealth which seduces them is cut off (ὅταν . . . περικοπῇ αὐτῶν ὁ *πλοῦτος* ὁ ψυχαγωγῶν αὐτούς, τότε εὔχρηστοι ἔσονται τῷ θεῷ) . . . Those rich in this world cannot be useful unless their wealth is cut off from them (οὕτω καὶ οἱ *πλουτοῦντες* ἐν τούτῳ τῷ αἰῶνι, ἐὰν μὴ περικοπῇ αὐτῶν ὁ *πλοῦτος* οὐ δύνανται τῷ κυρίῳ εὔχρηστοι γενέσθαι).

7 Know this from your own case: when you were rich you were useless, but now you are useful (ἀπὸ σεαυτοῦ πρῶτον γνῶθι· ὅτε *ἐπλούτεις* ἄχρηστος ἦς, νῦν δὲ εὔχρηστος εἶ).

Sim. 9.20.1 (From the third mountain of thorns and thistles come) the wealthy who are embroiled in business affairs (οἱ μὲν *πλού-*

σιοι, οἱ δὲ *πραγματείαις πολλαῖς ἐμπεφυρμένοι*). The thistles are the rich, the thorns are those embroiled in varied businesses (οἱ μὲν *τρίβολοί εἰσιν* οἱ *πλούσιοι*, αἱ δὲ *ἄκανθαι* οἱ ἐν ταῖς *πραγματείαις* ταῖς *ποικίλαις ἐμπεφυρμένοι*).

2 Those who are mixed up in many and varied businesses do not mix with the servants of God, but wander astray, choked by their affairs. Thus the rich . . . will with difficulty enter the kingdom of God (οὗτοι [οὖν, οἱ ἐν πολλαῖς καὶ ποικίλαις *πραγματείαις ἐμπεφυρένοι*, οὐ] κολλῶνται τοῖς δούλοις τοῦ θεοῦ, ἀλλ' ἀποπλανῶνται πνιγόμενοι ὑπὸ τῶν *πράξεων* αὐτῶν· οἱ δὲ *πλούσιοι* . . . *δυσκόλως εἰσελεύσονται εἰς τὴν βασιλείαν τοῦ θεοῦ*).

Paraenesis

Man. 10.1.4 Those mixed up in business and wealth and pagan friendships and many other worldly occupations do not understand the parables (οἱ . . . *ἐμπεφυρμένοι* δὲ *πραγματείαις* καὶ *πλούτῳ* καὶ *φιλίαις ἐθνικαῖς* καὶ ἄλλαις πολλαῖς *πραγματείαις* τοῦ αἰῶνος τούτου).

5 Even when they listen to [teaching about] God and truth, their mind is taken up with their business, and they really understand nothing (ἀλλὰ καὶ ὅταν ἀκούσωσι περὶ θεότητος καὶ ἀληθείας, ὁ νοῦς αὐτῶν περὶ τὴν *πρᾶξιν* αὐτῶν καταγίνεται, καὶ οὐδὲν ὅλως νοοῦσιν).

References to the Poor and the Needy

Catalog of Virtues

Man. 8.10 not to oppress debtors and the needy (χρεώστας μὴ θλίβειν καὶ *ἐνδεεῖς*)

Paraenesis

Vis. 3.9.2 Give to the needy (μεταδίδοτε καὶ τοῖς *ὑστερουμένοις*).

4 This lacking of sharing is harmful to you who have and do not share with the needy (αὕτη οὖν ἡ ἀσυνκρασία βλαβερὰ ὑμῖν τοῖς ἔχουσι καὶ μὴ μεταδιδοῦσιν τοῖς *ὑστερουμένοις*).

5 Let those who have an abundance seek out the hungry (οἱ ὑπερέχοντες οὖν ἐκζητεῖτε τοὺς *πεινῶντας*).

6 See to it . . . lest the needy groan . . . to the Lord (βλέπετε οὖν . . . μήποτε στενάξουσιν οἱ *ὑστερούμενοι* . . . πρὸς τὸν κύριον).

Man. 2.4 Give simply to all in need (πᾶσιν ὑστερουμένοις δίδου ἁπλῶς).

Reference to Widows and Orphans Alone (As Victims of Abuse)

Allegory

Sim. 9.26.2 Those with spots from the ninth mountain are ministers . . .
who devoured the living of widows and orphans (διάκονοι
. . . διαρπάσαντες χηρῶν καὶ ὀρφανῶν τὴν ζωήν).

References to Widows and Orphans Associated with the Needy

Catalog of Virtues

Man. 8.10 to minister to widows and look after orphans and the needy
(χήραις ὑπηρετεῖν, ὀρφανοὺς καὶ ὑστερουμένους ἐπισκέπτεσθαι)

Paraenesis

Sim. 1.8 Instead of lands buy afflicted souls . . . and look after widows
and orphans and do not neglect them (ἀντὶ ἀγρῶν οὖν ἀγο-
ράζετε ψυχὰς θλιβομένας . . .καὶ χήρας καὶ ὀρφανοὺς ἐπισ-
κέπτεσθε καὶ μὴ παραβλέπετε αὐτούς).

Commandment

Sim. 5.3.7 You shall give the proceeds of your fast to a widow or orphan
or someone in need (δώσεις αὐτὸ χήρᾳ ἢ ὀρφανῷ ἢ ὑστερουμένῳ).

Allegory

Sim. 9.27.2 (from the tenth mountain)—bishops who always sheltered the
needy and widows by their services (οἱ δὲ ἐπίσκοποι πάντοτε
τοὺς ὑστερημένους καὶ τὰς χήρας τῇ διακονίᾳ ἑαυτῶν ἀδια-
λείπτως ἐσκέπασαν)

See also *Vis.* 2.4.3, where widows and orphans are a group to be
instructed.

Theological and Paraenetic Tendencies

In order to explore the theological and paraenetic tendencies in these
passages, the same four questions will be asked that were asked above of the
biblical material: (1) Who are the poor and who are the rich in the eyes of
God according to the author? (2) How should rich and poor relate to one

another? (3) What are the ethical/theological implications of wealth considered apart from the question of responsibility to the poor? (4) To which group(s) is the material addressed?

Who are the poor and who are the rich in the eyes of God?

Outside *Sim.* 2 the rich are called by many names: *hoi plousioi* (*Sim.* 9.20.1);[10] *hoi gauriōntes en tō ploutō* (*Vis.* 1.1.8; 3.9.6; cf. *Ps.-Phoc.* 53, Μὴ γαυροῦ σοφίῃ, μητ' ἀλκῇ, μητ' ἐπὶ πλούτῳ, "Do not be haughty over wisdom, or strength, or wealth"); *hoi echontes* (as opposed to *hoi hysteroumenoi*, *Vis.* 3.9.4); and *hoi hyperechontes* (as opposed to *hoi peinōntes*, *Vis.* 3.9.5). They are objects of condemnation in *Vis.* 1.1.8, the first general group against whom the apparition of the Church levels such a condemnation, because they are too caught up in the enjoyment of their earthly wealth to care about heavenly goods. They are likewise called to task by the same Church in *Vis.* 3.9.2–6 for their insensitivity to the needy.[11] But condemnation is not absolute. *Vis.* 1.1.9 holds out the lingering call to repentance, as does *Vis.* 3.9.6, in contrast to Jas 5:4, of which the earlier part of the verse is reminiscent (cf. Jas 4:9; *Sim.* 8.8; 9.19.3). Indeed the sense of condemnation consistently resolves into a prophetic call to repentance. Nor are the rich considered to be of no value as they are. In spite of the triple mention of their potential usefulness only when their wealth is removed from them (*Vis.* 3.6.6–7; *Sim.* 9.30.4–5; 9.31.2), *Sim.* 1.8–11 develops a strong case for the usefulness of their wealth for accomplishing good deeds in the present.[12] Nowhere in the *Shepherd* is it suggested that the rich are without hope.

The poor are not frequently mentioned in *Hermas* outside *Sim.* 2, but when they are it is as objects of oppression by church officials (*Sim.* 9.26.2), as counterparts of the general readership of the book (*Man.* 8.10; *Vis.* 3.9), or as objects of charity (*Vis.* 3.9.2; *Man.* 8.10; *Sim.* 1.8; 5.3.7; 9.27.2, in the last case on the part of church officials).[13] The only indication outside *Sim.* 2

---

[10] This obvious designation, *hoi plousioi*, occurs only here in *Sim.* 9.20.1, 2.

[11] It is not to be inferred from the shift to addressing church leaders in v. 7 that these are included among the rich. The *nyn oun* with which the sentence opens indicates a change of focus, and the church leaders are accused on different charges—dissension and schism.

[12] This explanation leads immediately into *Sim.* 2. The theme of the value of the wealthy with and without their wealth will be discussed below in the section on the removal of wealth.

[13] See the list of references above. The almost unanimous association of widows and orphans with the poor in the texts would seem to justify treating them together. As noted above, the one exception to this pattern is *Vis.* 2.4.3, where widows and orphans seem to be an organized group in the community, though probably as recipients of charity (see also Jas 1:27; Arist. *Apol.* 15.7; Justin *Apol.* 1.67).

that the poor stand in any special relation to God is *Vis.* 3.9.6, where those who blindly enjoy their wealth are warned that the cries of the afflicted poor are capable of reaching God and influencing him to shut the wealthy out of the tower that is under construction, i.e., out of the eschatological salvation afforded by membership in the Church (see *Vis.* 3.3.3; 3.5; 3.8.8).[14]

How should rich and poor relate to one another?

The rich are castigated in *Vis.* 3.9 for insensitivity to the poor and for selfishness. Readers are encouraged in other paraenetic passages to give to the poor, the needy, widows, and orphans (*Man.* 2.4; *Sim.* 1.8). The commandment regarding fasting includes a directive to give the money saved by fasting to a widow, an orphan, or someone needy (*Sim.* 5.3.7).[15] In no instance outside *Sim.* 2 is anything said about the relationship of rich and poor that does not simply depict the traditional duty of the rich to give to the poor. The poor and the needy are spoken of only as foils for elaborating on the responsibilities of the rich (sometimes specifically, e.g., *Vis.* 3.9.1–6; *Sim.* 1.8-9) or at least of those for whom such paraenesis is appropriate (*Sim.* 5.3.7; *Man.* 2.4; 8.10). Outside of *Sim.* 2 the relationship between the rich and the poor is one-sided.

What are the ethical/theological implications of wealth, considered apart from the question of responsibility to the poor?

The ethical and theological implications of wealth go far beyond the traditional responsibility of giving to the poor and the traditional danger of being too intent on the things of this world to notice those in need.

Wealth and Entanglement in Business Affairs

The themes of wealth and entanglement in business affairs are closely associated throughout *Hermas*, and in three passages they are explicitly connected (*Vis.* 3.6.5; *Man.* 10.1.4; *Sim.* 9.20.1). In the first of these passages,

---

[14] For the power of the poor to get vengeance from God on their oppressors or reward for their benefactors, see Exod 22:21–27; Deut 24:13 (poor debtor), 24:15 (wage-earner); Sir 4:6; 35:13–24; Jas 5:4, etc. For the significance of the building of the tower, see Dibelius, *Der Hirt*, 462–71, esp. pp. 465–66.

[15] In the allegory of the twelve mountains of Arcadia, church officials who misuse funds destined for the needy are singled out (*Sim.* 9.26.2). This need not imply that they are the rich, or are included among the rich. As in *Vis.* 3.9.7–10, they constitute a different case (see above, n. 11). Likewise, church officials in *Sim.* 9.27.2 are praised for caring for the needy, which is simply part of their traditional duty (see Justin *Apol.* 1.67; Ign. *Pol.* 4.1).

Vis. 3.6.5, Hermas asks his female revealer what group in the community corresponds to the round white stones that do not fit into the tower of his vision. He is told that they are those having faith but also worldly riches, who, when persecution (*thlipsis*) arises, deny their Lord because of their wealth and their business (*tas pragmateias*).

The second passage, *Man.* 10.1.4, comes in the first part of a treatise on grief (*lypē*) that includes *Man.* 10.1-3. Those who only believe but do not take the trouble to seek the understanding of divine things (*peri tēs alētheias . . . peri tēs theotētos*[16]) because they are involved in business, wealth, heathen friendships (*philiais ethnikais*), and other worldly affairs do not understand the divine parables (*tas parabolas tēs theotētos*). In the following verse (1.5) the same idea is repeated and reinforced by the metaphor of a vineyard in which thorns and weeds have been allowed to run wild.

The third passage in which wealth and business are associated is *Sim.* 9.20.1-2. Here, on the third of the twelve allegorical mountains of Arcadia, are found thorns and thistles, which represent those entangled in business and the rich, respectively:

1 Ἐκ δὲ τοῦ ὄρους τοῦ τρίτου τοῦ ἔχοντος ἀκάνθας καὶ τριβόλους οἱ πιστεύσαντες τοιοῦτοί εἰσιν· ἐξ αὐτῶν οἱ μὲν πλούσιοι, οἱ δὲ πραγματείαις πολλαῖς ἐμπεφυρμένοι. οἱ μὲν τριβολοί εἰσιν οἱ πλούσιοι, αἱ δὲ ἄκανθαι οἱ ἐν ταῖς πραγματείαις ταῖς ποικίλαις ἐμπεφυρμένοι.

2 οὗτοι (οὖν, οἱ ἐν πολλαῖς καὶ ποικίλαις πραγματείαις ἐμπεφυρμένοι, οὐ) κολλῶνται τοῖς δούλοις τοῦ θεοῦ, ἀλλ᾽ ἀποπλανῶνται πνιγόμενοι ὑπὸ τῶν πράξεων αὐτῶν· οἱ δὲ πλούσιοι δυσκόλως κολλῶνται τοῖς δούλοις τοῦ θεοῦ, φοβούμενοι μή τι αἰτισθῶσιν ὑπ᾽ αὐτῶν· οἱ τοιοῦτοι οὖν δυσκόλως εἰσελεύσονται εἰς τὴν βασιλείαν τοῦ θεοῦ.[17]

1 But from the third mountain having thorns and thistles are such believers: some of them are rich while others are involved in many business affairs. The thistles are the rich and the thorns are those mixed up in various affairs.

2 Now those who are involved in many and various businesses do not continue to associate with the servants of God, but wander astray choked by their works; for the rich with difficulty stay with the servants of God, fearing lest they ask something of them. People like these will therefore with difficulty enter the kingdom of God.

As an allegory, vv. 1-3 are poorly constructed, making this passage one of the least exemplary of literary quality in *Hermas*. In the first sentence the

---

[16] *Theotēs* is an unusual word in early Christian literature before *Hermas*; it is used in the *Shepherd* only here and in *Man.* 11.5, 10, 14. See also Col 2:9 and BAG under *theiotēs*.

[17] The words in parentheses are restored from Latin and Ethiopic manuscripts.

believers about to be discussed are said to be *from* or *out of* (*ek*) the mountain which has thorns and thistles. In the second sentence some of them (i.e., the believers) are rich, and some are involved in much business. In the third sentence the thorns and thistles of the mountain are *identified* with the two types of believers but in reverse order: the thistles are the rich; the thorns are those involved in business. In the first sentence of v. 2, those in business are castigated for not associating with the rest of the community, but instead they go astray choked by their deeds.[18] The metaphor has been switched: they are choked by the thorns they themselves were supposed to be in the original allegory. In the next two sentences the rich are described as associated with the community only with difficulty because they fear to be asked for a contribution. Here either the allegory has broken down or irony is intended, for those who are identified above as thistles or burrs—the rich—can only with difficulty "stick to"[19] the servants of God! The verse ends with an allusion to a synoptic theme, probably connected through the key word *dyskolōs* (see Mark 10:23–24; Matt 19:23–24; Luke 18:24–25).[20] Thus far the rich have retained their allegorical identification with the thistles, even if they do not behave like thistles. In v. 3 their identification breaks down just as did that of those in business in the first sentence of v. 2. The simile of walking with naked feet among thistles now identifies the rich with the walkers who are subjected to thistles, just as those involved in business were subjected to thorns.

The distinction maintained throughout the passage between the rich and those in business is a literary device.[21] Both classes come from the same allegorical mountain and are subjected to the same difficulties. In the light of their identification in *Vis.* 3.6.5 and *Man.* 10.1.4, it can be assumed that here in *Sim.* 9.20 they are also considered as one type of problematic person in the community. The association of the wealthy and those involved in business affairs therefore spans the three divisions of *Hermas: Visions, Mandates,* and *Similitudes.*

---

[18] Compare the parable of the sower (Mark 4:18–19 par. Matt 13:22; Luke 8:14).

[19] "Stick to" is the original meaning of the verb *kollaō*, "to glue or cement"; see LSJ, s.v.

[20] See H. Koester, *Synoptische Überlieferung bei den Apostolischen Vätern* (TU 65; Berlin: Akademie-Verlag, 1957) 245-46.

[21] Dibelius (*Der Hirt,* 629) calls it a *Deutungskunststück.* The identification of the two groups is strengthened by the inclusion of both ideas in Mark 4:18–19 and parallels, to which 20.1 probably alludes: the seeds that fell among thorns are those in whom the word is choked by the cares of the world and the deceit of wealth and the lusts for the other things. Mark is similar, but the descriptions in Matt 13:22 and Luke 8:14 are less elaborate.

Dipsychia

In two closely connected and similarly constructed passages wealth and business are joined with the overriding ethical concern of *Hermas*, *dipsychia*, which at least in this context seems to mean the inability to decide and act one way or the other, for or against the Lord. In both *Sim.* 8.8 and 9, three responses of the business-ridden or wealthy are presented: repentance, apostasy, and double-mindedness—from which there is still a chance of repentance.

> *Sim.* 8.8: Sticks half-green and half-dry are those embroiled in business and so not remaining in association with the saints (οἱ ἐν ταῖς πραγματείαις αὐτῶν ἐμπεφυρμένοι καὶ τοῖς ἁγίοις μὴ κολλώμενοι)—v. 1
>> (a) many repented (*metenoēsan*)—v. 2
>> (b) some ultimately apostatized (*apestēsan*)
>> (c) many were double-minded (*edipsychēsan*)—v. 3
> (Vv. 4–5 exhibit the same structure for those two-thirds green and one-third dry, i.e., those who have made multiple denials.)
> *Sim.* 8.9: Sticks two-thirds dry and one-third green are the faithful who are rich and honored among the heathen and therefore do not associate with the just (πλουτήσαντες δὲ καὶ γενόμενοι ἐνδοξότεροι παρὰ τοῖς ἔθνεσιν . . . καὶ οὐκ ἐκολλήθησαν τοῖς δικαίοις)—v. 1
>> (a) many repented (*metenoēsan*)—v. 2
>> (b) others apostatized (*apestēsan*)—v. 3
>> (c) others were double-minded (*edipsychēsan*)—v. 4

According to *Sim.* 8.8.3 and 8.9.4 *dipsychia* flows from business involvements and wealth rather than vice versa. *Sim.* 8.9.4 gives one of the clearest insights in the whole of *Hermas* into what the author intends by *dipsychia*: *heteroi. . . edipsychēsan mē elpizontes sōthēnai dia tas praxeis, has epraxan* ("they had given up hope of salvation because of what they had done").[22]

---

[22] This despair of the ultimate mercy of God and the hesitation and doubt about acting well that it inspires (see also *Vis.* 3.7.1; *Man.* 9.1–11; 11.4; *Sim.* 9.21.1; Reiling, *Hermas and Christian Prophecy*, 32-33) are the opposite of another expression that is used exclusively in Hermas, the adverb *adistaktōs*, which with its verb *distazō* encourages asking (*Man.* 9.2, 4, 6), giving (*Man.* 2.4; *Sim.* 2.5; 9.24.2), and repentance (*Sim.* 8.10.3) without doubting or hesitating (see BAG s.v.). Snyder's description (*Shepherd*, 82-83, 87) of *dipsychia* as that which "stands for the condition of man caught between the spirits" in the two-spirit system is another way of characterizing the same thing.

Removal of Wealth

In the greater part of *Hermas* the wealth of those who possess it is taken for granted, and the problems treated are its positive or negative value and how it should be used. In three passages, however, it is suggested that the wealth of the rich must be removed from them before their full usefulness for God can be realized.

In the first of these passages, *Vis.* 3.6.5–7, wealth and business are blamed for denial of the Lord in time of persecution (*hotan genētai thlipsis, dia ton plouton autōn kai dia tas pragmateias aparnountai ton kyrion autōn,* v. 5). Therefore they can be useful (*euchrēstoi*) for the construction of the tower only when their seducing wealth is cut off from them (*hotan . . . perikopē autōn ho ploutos ho psychagōgōn autous*). As surely as round stones cannot be square unless something is cut off from them, so the wealthy cannot be useful to the Lord unless their riches are cut away from them (v. 6). In v. 7 a puzzling personal application to Hermas completes the passage: when he was wealthy, he was useless (*hote eplouteis achrēstos ēs*), but now he is useful and helpful for the Christian life[23] (*nun de euchrēstos ei kai ōphelimos tē zōē*). Then the text reverts to the paraenetic plural (*euchrēstoi ginesthe tō theō*) and immediately back to the singular with an obscure statement: *kai gar sy autos chrasai ek tōn autōn lithōn.* The implication is that Hermas was once rich but is no longer so. Yet there is no other suggestion in the biographical information of the *Visions* that Hermas has suffered a reversal of fortune. The final statement could be understood as a warning through literary convention to Hermas and thus to every reader that all stones that do not fit the building will be dealt with in the same severe manner. The historicity of the application to Hermas and the exact meaning of the closing statement are not of direct relevance to the present discussion.[24] What is relevant is that the removal of all or part of one's wealth is set in the context of persecution (*thlipsis*), a recurrent theme in the *Visions.*[25] It is because of their wealth and business that these Christians cannot sustain their faith in time of persecution; therefore, if they are to be useful in the Church, their wealth must be wholly or partly removed from them, possibly by ordinary economic reversals or possibly by official confiscation. That they are described in v. 5 as having faith but also riches and that they can eventu-

---

[23] Or for eternal life. As Dibelius remarks (*Der Hirt*, 469), *zōē* is here substituted for the tower.

[24] For a characterization of Hermas' familial situation as a portrayal of the entire community, see Dibelius, *Der Hirt*, 419-20.

[25] See 2.2.7–8; 4.1.1; 4.3. Note the similar theme of purification and consequent usefulness for the tower in 4.3.4.

ally be part of the tower when the obstacle of wealth is removed indicate that the author does not have in mind a group of people who have apostatized under stress. Rather, the passage is a warning to wealthy Christians and also a comfort to any who may have had property confiscated but have remained faithful.

The other two passages that speak of the necessary removal of riches from the wealthy are in that section of *Sim.* 9 which again takes up the allegory of the round white stones that do not fit into the tower.[26] In *Sim.* 9.30 such stones have remained white because, though their wealth has darkened them a little (*pusillum . . . obfuscaverunt*), they have remained in truth without doing evil (vv. 3-4). Still they are round because of their riches, and therefore their wealth must be only partly cut away so that they can still do some good with the remainder (*dominus . . . iussit et opes eorum circumcidi, non enim in totum tolli, ut possint aliquid boni facere de eo, quod eis relictum est*, v. 5). *Sim.* 9.31.2 repeats the same theme, that the vanities of wealth must be cut off the stones that have remained round, this time because they have not received the seal (*sigillum*, v. 1) of baptism (*oportet autem circumcidi saeculum illorum cum illis vanitatibus opum suarum*).

While the third passage, *Sim.* 9.31.2, is a simple restatement in a slightly different context, the second, *Sim.* 9.30.5, is a significant development of the original theme of *Vis.* 3.6.6. The straight statement as found there and in *Sim.* 9.31.2, that the wealth of the rich must be removed from them, is different from the treatment of wealth elsewhere in *Hermas.* In most contexts the wealthy are reminded of the dangers into which they may fall and of their failure to live up to the ideals of Christian life (e.g., *Vis.* 3.9.3–6; *Man.* 10.1.4; *Sim.* 9.20.1–4), but the purpose is exhortatory: in each case those addressed are invited or warned to change and to repent, but there is no suggestion that they cannot remain rich. *Sim.* 1.9 and 2.10 affirm the usefulness of wealth for helping those in need—apparently in direct contrast to *Vis.* 3.6.6–7, where usefulness comes only with the loss of wealth. *Sim.* 9.30.5 is a compromise that bridges the gap between these two apparently contradictory opinions: here the removal of wealth is divinely directed, but not of all of it. Rather, some is to be left to them so that they can do some good with it (*ut possint aliquid boni facere de eo, quod eis relictum est*; cf. *Sim.* 2.10, *diakonēsai ti agathon*, and 9.20, *agathon ti poiēsōsin*).

---

[26] The reworked image of the building of the tower runs throughout *Sim.* 9, from 3.1 through 32.1, interlaced with the image of the twelve mountains of Arcadia, which extends from 1.4 through 29.1.

The Ideal of Autarkeia

There is yet another kind of theological treatment of wealth in *Hermas* besides the critique of its dangers, the traditional responsibility to share with the needy, and the infrequent theme of the usefulness of riches. It is the ideal of simplicity in self-subsistence, *autarkeia*, as an invitation to freedom from possessions and the correlate encouragement to acquire spiritual wealth.

The first *Similitude* presents a metaphor of dual residence. The servants of God live in the world as if they were migrants in a foreign country (*epi xenēs katoikeite*, *Sim.* 1.1). The foreign country in which they are dwelling has its own law; at any time the lord of the city can expel those who do not keep that law (vv. 3, 4). If the transients have amassed fields, expensive arrangements, buildings, and extravagant houses (*agrous kai parataxeis polyteleis kai oikodomas kai oikēmata mataia*), what will they do with them when expelled from that city (vv. 1, 4)? If they attempt to retain these possessions, they will not be able to keep the law of their own city or return to it (vv. 2, 5).[27] Because of this precarious situation, the Christian is to take no more than what is sufficient (*mēden pleon hetoimaze seautō ei mē tēn autarkeian tēn arketēn soi*) in order to be prepared for expulsion from the city in which he is living, when its master (*ho despotēs*) wishes to cast him out for not keeping the law (v. 6).[28] The danger lies in amassing wealth and, in particular, property (vv. 1, 4). Instead, surplus money is to be spent on

---

[27] The metaphor of temporary residence in a foreign land is already a common one in Stoic philosophy, Diaspora Judaism, and early Christianity before *Hermas*. Dibelius (*Der Hirt*, 550-51) gives an abundance of references. Particularly noteworthy are Epict. *Disc.* 3.22.38 and *Enchir.* 1.1-3; Philo *De agr.* 65; *De cherub.* 120; Phil 3:20; Gal 4:26; Heb 11:13; 13:14; 1 Pet 1:1; 2:11; *2 Clem.* 5.1, 5-6; *Diogn.* 5.4, 9 (but cf. v. 10); 6.8; Lucian *Philosophies for Sale* 17. The stress on the law of the city of residence over the law of one's own city (not found in the related texts cited below) may stand in deliberate proximity to the completion of the twelve *Mandates* or *Commandments*, expressly so-called in *Man.* 12.3.2, the beginning of the concluding section or epilogue of the *Mandates* (see Dibelius, p. 546). On *autarkeia* already as a Christian ideal, see Phil 4:11-13 and 1 Tim 6:6-8.

[28] Whether the master of the city is thought to be the Roman emperor, the devil, or someone else is irrelevant, since we are here dealing with a parable and not an allegory. Thus, Dibelius is correct in rejecting an allusion to persecution by the Roman state (though compare the connection of law with what is more probably a reference to persecution in *Sim.* 8.6-7). The conflict lies rather in the Christian's own tendency to compromise his true citizenship by overinvolvement in this world through material possessions (see Dibelius, *Der Hirt*, 551-52). For further notes on the idea of *autarkeia* in Hellenistic philosophical usage, see M. Hengel, *Property and Riches in the Early Church: Aspects of a Social History of Early Christianity*, trans. John Bowden (Philadelphia: Fortress, 1974) 54-59; BAG and LPGL, s.v. The idea of having only one business in *Sim.* 4.7 is possibly related.

"buying afflicted souls," widows, orphans, and the needy—in short, on traditional Christian (and Jewish) works of charity (v. 8).[29]

A shift occurs in the second part of the chapter, beginning after the transitional exhortation of v. 7. Vv. 1–6 have developed the ideal of detachment from earthly wealth. V. 8 gives a concrete proposal for what to do with the money one does have to spend.[30] V. 9 states unambiguously the value of earthly wealth in a way that could lead directly into the second *Similitude*: *eis touto gar eploutisen hymas ho despotēs, hina tautas tas diakonias telesēte autō*.[31] The very reason for the possession of wealth by individuals is that it might be used to accomplish charitable deeds. The metaphor of ownership of property is taken up again in v. 9b: it is better to buy the kinds of fields, property, and houses that will be found in one's own true city, i.e., spiritual goods.[32] V. 10a describes this spiritual wealth as beautiful (*kalē*), joyful (*hilara*), without sadness (*lypē*) or fear (*phobos*).[33] Vv. 10b–11 complete the chapter with an exhortation not to follow after pagan wealth but after one's own, i.e., spiritual wealth.[34] The whole of the first *Similitude* is thus divided into two related but distinct themes: vv. 1–6 emphasize detachment from the earthly city and its goods for the sake of mobility; vv. 8–11 show how to amass another superior kind of wealth, that which belongs to the city of the Christian's true citizenship.[35] The firm statement of divine purpose behind

[29] It makes more sense to read as Dibelius did (*Der Hirt*, 553) the detached and final relative clause of v. 8 (*has elabete para tou theou*) as belonging to the material possessions and not to the figurative "fields and houses" immediately preceding it.

[30] The change from a singular to a plural verb is not significant. The chapter begins in the plural (v. 1) and switches to the rhetorical singular in vv. 3–6, then back to the paraenetic plural until the end.

[31] The meaning of this plain statement is clear in spite of the fact that *despotēs* has occurred immediately above as the title of the opposing lord (v. 6) and is not a usual title for God in *Hermas* (but cf. *Vis.* 2.2.4–5).

[32] Because of the continued metaphor of purchasing spiritual fields and property in v. 9b, the allusion to purchasing "afflicted souls" (*agorazete psychas thlibomenas*) in v. 8 cannot be interpreted to mean primarily ransoming slaves or prisoners (against S. S. Bartchy, *MALLON CHRĒSAI: First-Century Slavery and the Interpretation of 1-Corinthians 7:21* [SBLDS 11; Missoula, MT; Scholars Press, 1973] 101).

[33] In *Man.* 2.4 the adjective *hilaros* is connected with the idea of giving to the needy, and *lypē* is associated with business and wealth in *Man.* 10.1.1-4 (see also Mark 10:22; Matt 19:22; Luke 18:23).

[34] V. 11 would seem to be an extraneous paraenesis against greed were it not for the associations with Stoic popular philosophy recalled by the juxtaposition of *idios* and *allotrios*. What is alien is everything not immediately under the control of one's attitude—for Epictetus, the body, property, one's reputation, authority (*Enchir.* 1.1). See also Dibelius, *Der Hirt*, 550; Epict. *Disc.* 2.6.8, 24; 4.5.7, 15.

[35] See Matt 6:19–21; Luke 12:33–34; 12:21; 1 Tim 6:18–19.

the possession of wealth by some Christians (found only in *Sim.* 1.8–9 and *Sim.* 2) stands in evident conflict with the proclaimed uselessness of the wealthy as long as they are in possession of their wealth (found only in *Vis.* 3.6.6–7 and *Sim.* 9.30.4–5; 31.2), though *Sim.* 9.30.5 may be an attempt to work out a compromise between the two positions.

With the affirmation of the usefulness of wealth for the work of God, the stage is set for the second *Similitude.*

To which group(s) is the material addressed?

Though the implications of wealth in *Hermas* are extremely complex, by contrast the question of who is being addressed in the material on rich and poor is quite simple. Indeed, its simplicity stands in contrast not only to the complexity of the previous question but also to the similar problem of determining the addressees of this type of material in Luke and James. While in both of these writings—though certainly far more in Luke—there is evidence on both sides, in *Hermas* the evidence is unilateral. Direct address is used only to the rich (*Vis.* 3.9.4, 6; *Sim.* 1.9); the poor are referred to in the third person as recipients of the neglect or attention of the rich (*Vis.* 3.9.4, 6; *Sim.* 1.8–9). The ambiguous personal reference to Hermas in *Vis.* 3.6.7 (*hote eplouteis, archrēstos ēs, nun de euchrēstos ei*) need not mean that Hermas now qualifies as poor or needy, even with the most literal interpretation.[36]

There is no example of a complementary address to the poor in *Hermas.* When the needy, orphans, and widows are mentioned (*Vis.* 3.9.2–6; *Man.* 2.4; 8.10; *Sim.* 1.8; 5.3.7; 9.26.2; 27.2),[37] they are those *about* whom something is said, not those *to* whom the message is directed.

Passages like *Vis.* 3.9 and *Sim.* 1 are clearly paraenesis for the rich. The final section of the *Mandates, Man.* 12, opens with an exhortation to put away all *epithymiai*, which are named at 12.2.1—lust for the wife or the husband of another (stressed only in *Vis.* and *Man.* 4), desire for much wealth, and extravagance of food, drink, and luxury. Thus, the closing exhortation of the *Mandates* concerns sexual sin and covetousness centered around wealth and luxury. There is no doubt that the rich are members of the community (see *Vis.* 3.9.6; *Sim.* 8.8.1; 9.20.2), in contrast to the situations reflected in Luke and James.

---

[36] See above, nn. 23 and 24.

[37] *Vis.* 2.4.3 is excluded because there widows and orphans are not considered recipients of material goods.

Comparison with Luke and James

The theology of rich and poor developed in *Hermas* can be better understood in the light of other major early Christian documents that give serious consideration to the topic. The invitation to self-sufficiency (*autarkeia*) in *Sim.* 1 can be compared with the spirit of detachment seemingly intended in Luke 14:33. While for Luke the *plousioi* cannot be demonstrated to be members of the Christian community but rather are cast as opponents and those unable to grasp the message of salvation, the *plousioi* of *Hermas* are often called to task for their transgressions—but always with the hope of their repentance and consequent salvation. Moreover, in *Sim.* 2 they have an integral part to play in the life of the community precisely *as* wealthy.

So also in James it cannot be proved that the rich are members of the community. Once more the evidence seems to indicate that they are opponents who are not offered a chance for salvation. The three passages in *Hermas* that suggest the necessity of removing the wealth of the rich before they can be useful (*Vis.* 3.6.7; *Sim.* 9.30.4–5; 31.2) may create a bridge to James's hostility toward the rich, but the position in *Hermas* is compromised in *Sim.* 9.30.5 and de-eschatologized in *Vis.* 3.6.6, where Hermas does become useful by shedding his wealth. The judgment pronounced on the rich coupled with the groans of the needy in *Vis.* 3.9.5–6 bears some similarity to James's condemnation of the rich in 5:1–6; yet in *Hermas* the judgment is conditional (e.g., v. 6, *blepete . . . mēpote*) and thus is essentially a call to repentance, not a condemnation to destruction. The uncompromising hostility toward the rich that is shown by James is simply not present in *Hermas*.

If this interpretation is correct, both Luke and James represent the theological world in which their own group of Christians can be characterized as the "pious poor," while the rich are at least symbolically the opponents or those unable to answer the call of discipleship. The privilege of the poor before God remains a factor in the social theology of *Hermas*, as the next two chapters will show more clearly, but the poor are by no means coextensive with the community. Rather, the focus shifts and the wealthy receive a large amount of attention as members of the community who need to be called to repentance but are nonetheless full participants in the life of the community.

The passages in *Hermas* (apart from *Sim.* 2) that mention the poor give them no particular role except the traditional one of receiving abuse or charity. In one case the poor are those sufficiently protected by God that their cries of affliction will get his attention (*Vis.* 3.9.6). Spiritual poverty or lowliness appears as an element of Christian virtue in *Man.* 8.10; 11.8, but it is presented as an ideal, not as a divine favor. Nor does it seem to have any relationship to social grouping.

Conclusion

Wealth and the wealthy are discussed frequently throughout *Hermas*. The rich are at times severely criticized, but they are never condemned without hope. Their traditional obligation to give to the needy is reinforced, but outside of *Sim.* 2 the poor have no role of their own. Wealth is closely connected with overinvolvement in business and worldly affairs and is associated with *dipsychia* at two points (*Sim.* 8.8 and 9). Three passages in the *Visions* and the ninth *Similitude* (*Vis.* 3.6.5–7; *Sim.* 9.30.4–5; 31.2) propose that the wealthy are not useful for the work of God until their wealth is removed from them, while *Sim.* 1 and 2 teach a contradictory theology of the usefulness of wealth spent for charitable purposes. *Sim.* 9.30.5 is perhaps intended as a compromise between the two positions. The ideals of detachment from worldly wealth and preference for acquisition of spiritual wealth form the substance of *Sim.* 1. The poor and needy are never addressed and are mentioned only as recipients of charity, while the rich are addressed several times and it is their perspective to which appeal is consistently made. Consequently, there can be no doubt that the paraenesis of *Hermas* about wealth and poverty is intended for the rich, who are presented as insiders called to repentance.

IV

A STUDY OF *MANDATE* 8.10

Man. 8.10 contains several phrases that are indicative of the theology and praxis of Hermas' community regarding wealth and poverty. Their function within the tradition and their own literary contexts reveal their contribution to an understanding of Hermas' social theology in its own situation. In spite of the author's concern for the religious problems of the rich, demonstrated in the previous chapter, *Hermas* still draws considerably on the traditional theology of the "pious poor."

Context in Book and Chapter

In *Man*. 8, there are vices and evil deeds from which one must refrain (vv. 3–6) and virtues and good deeds from which one should *not* refrain (vv. 9–10).[1] By this latter extension of the idea of "restraint" Hermas affords himself the opportunity of including a whole new list of virtues that have no conceptual relation to the initial idea of *enkrateia*. The phrase *mē enkrateuesthai ap' autōn* at the end of v. 9, reiterated at the end of v. 11 and again in v. 12, is inserted in all three cases as the middle term of the familiar "if you do this . . . you will live" pattern in order to extend this applied negative use of *enkrateia* as a complement to its usual use in vv. 4, 6 and 12. A further subdivision of the basic categories yields two lists for both, a primary series of items of conduct (vv. 3, 9) and a second list introduced as *ta akoloutha* (vv. 5, 10), concluded in both instances with the generalizing expression "and whatever is like these." *Enkrateia*, the main theme of *Man*. 8, is in turn the third virtue of the trilogy *pistis, phobos, enkrateia* of *Man*. 1. The literary structure of this material can be diagrammed thus:

---

[1] See Dibelius (*Der Hirt*, 525-28) for the major points of the exposition of this schema and further detailed analysis.

Man. 1

Man. 6—*pistis*	*Man.* 7—*phobos*	*Man.* 8—*enkrateia*
	things from which to refrain—first list, v. 3	things from which not to refrain—first list, v. 9
	conclusion, v. 4	
	second list, v. 5—*ta akoloutha*	second list, v. 10—*ta akoloutha*
	reinforcement, v. 6	reinforcement, v. 11
	conclusion, v. 12	

Interpretation

In order to understand *Hermas'* theology, its Sitz im Leben, and its social implications, the folowing question must be considered: Given what we know of the history and style of the literary form known as the "catalog of virtues" (or "vices"), can we expect that such a passage will be consistent with an author's theology and will reflect real social concerns? It can safely be assumed that such lists usually lie closer to a philosophical ideal than to practical expectations.[2] Of the first list of virtues in *Man.* 8.9 (faith, fear of the Lord, love, harmony, righteous speech, truth, patience) this conclusion can be applied with reasonable certainty, in view of the abstractness of the behavior enjoined and the frequency with which the terms occur in paraenetic literature. These are exhortations to those qualities of life suitable to the Christian. So also in the two lists of vices (vv. 3, 5) the evils are those condemned again and again in early Christian literature.[3]

The fourth list, *Man.* 8.10, is the one of greatest interest.

εἶτα τούτων τὰ ἀκόλουθα ἄκουσον· χήραις ὑπερετεῖν, ὀρφανοὺς καὶ ὑστερουμένους ἐπισκέπτεσθαι, ἐξ ἀναγκῶν λυτροῦσθαι τοὺς δούλους τοῦ θεοῦ, φιλόξενον εἶναι (ἐν γὰρ τῇ φιλοξενίᾳ εὑρίσκεται ἀγαθοποίησίς ποτε), μηδενὶ ἀντιτάσσεσθαι, ἡσύχιον εἶναι, ἐνδεέστερον γίνεσθαι πάντων ἀνθρώπων, πρεσβύτας σέβεσθαι, δικαιοσύνην ἀσκεῖν, ἀδελφότητα συντηρεῖν, ὕβριν ὑποφέρειν, μακρόθυμον εἶναι, μνησικακίαν μὴ ἔχειν, κάμνοντας τῇ ψυχῇ παρακαλεῖν, ἐσκανδαλισμένους

---

[2] E.g., the qualities sought after in a general (Onosander *De imp. off.* 1) or in a dancer (Lucian *Salt.* 81); see M. Dibelius and H. Conzelmann, *The Pastoral Epistles* (ed. H. Koester; Hermeneia; Philadelphia: Fortress, 1972), applications 3, 4, pp. 158–60, esp. the application to bishops, pp. 158-59 n. 2.

[3] E.g., Rom 1:29–31; 1 Cor 5:11; 1 Tim 6:4; esp. *1 Clem.* 35.5; *Herm. Man.* 12.2.1.

ἀπὸ τῆς πίστεως μὴ ἀποβάλλεσθαι, ἀλλ' ἐπιστρέφειν καὶ εὐθύμους ποιεῖν, ἁμαρτάνοντας νουθετεῖν, χρεώστας μὴ θλίβειν καὶ ἐνδεεῖς, καὶ εἴ τινα τούτοις ὅμοιά ἐστι.

Then hear what follows: to minister to widows, to look after orphans and the needy, to ransom from distress the servants of God, to be hospitable [for in hospitality is found the doing of good], to resist no one, to be gentle, to become poorer than all, to reverence the aged, to practice justice, to preserve brotherhood, to bear with insult, to be courageous, not to bear a grudge, to comfort those burdened in spirit, not to reject those who have been made to stumble from the faith but to convert and encourage them, to admonish sinners, not to oppress debtors and the needy, and anything else similar to these.

Although it is reasonably certain that the lists of vices in *Man.* 8.3 and 5 and the list of virtues in 8.9 reflect traditional values preached in the Christian community, the same can be said only with qualification of the selection of virtues found in 8.10. The verse has a natural place in the structure of the chapter, but its inner structure is different from that of the three lists that have gone before.[4] This is the only one of the four catalogs in which the items are not simply nouns or noun phrases.[5] Rather, they are extended clauses, which are common in early Christian literature. These, however, are not the usual imperative and participial clauses of paraenetic commentary (e.g., 1 Pet 2:13–3:9; *Barn.* 20.2), but infinitive clauses.[6]

---

[4] See above, n. 1. Dibelius comments (*Der Hirt,* 527) that there is no difference in *importance* between the first and second lists of virtues, as if the first were commandments and the second merely counsels for the Christian life. The point is well taken; the question raised here is whether every item is from "tradition" in the same way.

[5] Compare *1 Clem.* 35.2, 5 (nouns); *Barn.* 20.1 (nouns); Rom 1:29-31 (adjectives).

[6] These are unusual but not unknown; see Rom 12:15; Jas 1:27; 1 Tim 6:17–18. However, such a series of seventeen infinitive-imperative clauses is unprecedented. For the use of participles and to some extent infinitives as imperatives in paraenesis, see the discussion of E. Lohse ("Paränese und Kerygma im 1. Petrusbrief," *ZNW* 45 [1954] 68-89, esp. 75-76) and the study of D. Daube, which is summarized by Lohse ("Participle and Imperative in 1 Peter" in E. G. Selwyn, *The First Epistle of St. Peter* [London: Macmillan, 1947] 467-88). Daube's argument is that the use of participles as imperatives, common only in the NT in general rules for Christian conduct, developed not from Hellenistic usage but from Tannaitic Hebrew moral codes. Lohse provides an earlier connection by producing several similar examples from Qumran that use infinitive, imperative, and participle. Daube successfully shows that alleged Hellenistic analogies in the papyri are not convincing and that use of the participle and occasionally the infinitive to describe ideals of conduct is common in Tannaitic Hebrew analogies to the NT genre, i.e., compilations of series of exhortations with similar grammatical structure.

Sources

The material in *Man.* 8.10 derives from three different literary traditions: traditional lists of virtues, or vices, church order material and the *Haustafel*, and the paraenesis of the "pious poor."[7] The catalog of virtues, which can be traced to earlier Hellenistic models,[8] is the predominant literary form of the first three lists (vv. 3, 5, and 9), and traces of it remain in v. 10. Though they are clothed in infinitive clauses, the terms *philoxenia, hēsychia, dikaiosynē*, and *makrothymia* are common catalog elements.[9] The noun *mnēsikakia*, meaning generally "bearing a grudge," "vengefulness," is not attested in early Christian usage in an actual catalog outside of *Hermas*, but it appears in the LXX, in Hellenistic texts, in Christian paraenetic texts, and elsewhere in *Hermas*.[10]

The church order material included here is expressed not in the form of regulations but as ideals of duty and right conduct, directed largely toward particular groups and particular cases in the community. Its similarity to the *Haustafeln*, or duties of members of a household to one another, is evident;

---

[7] The three are not mutually exclusive but overlap at some points, e.g., the rules for a bishop in Titus 1:7–9 and the *Haustafeln* in 2:1–10 are based on lists of virtues and vices. See Dibelius and Conzelmann, *Pastoral Epistles*, 132–33, 139–41. The liturgical prayer of *1 Clem.* 59.3–4 contains many elements of the theology of the "pious poor."

[8] See the examples in Dibelius and Conzelmann, *Pastoral Epistles*, 159–60.

[9] *Philoxenia* is a frequent ideal of Christian conduct, having Jewish prototypes in Heb 13:2; *1 Clem.* 10.7 (Abraham), 11.1 (Lot), 12.1 (Rahab). It appears in catalogs of Christian virtues (Rom 12:13; 1 Pet 4:9; *1 Clem.* 1.2; Arist. *Apol.* 15.7) and as a quality expected of bishops (1 Tim 3:2; Titus 1:8; *Herm. Sim.* 9.27.2—but the role of *episkopos* in *Hermas* is less clearly defined than that in the Pastorals, see Dibelius *Der Hirt*, 634-35). In both *Man.* 8.10 and Heb 13:2 *philoxenia* is the only virtue accompanied by an explanatory note answering the question "why"—though the answers differ. Dibelius (*Der Hirt*, 528) limits his comments about *hēsychia* to the realm of reaction to civil authority and performance of civic responsibility as expressed in 1 Tim 2:2 (see also Rom 13:1, 2). It is possible that in Christian paraenesis the word *hēsychios* had come to mean something equivalent to "not creating a scene"; consider especially the contexts of 1 Tim 2:2 (of women in church) and *Man.* 11.8 (of the true prophet). *Dikaiosynē* probably alludes to fairness in personal and business dealings (Dibelius, *Der Hirt*, 528; see also BAG s.v., esp. #1, 4). For *makrothymia* see 2 Cor 6:6; Gal 5:22; *1 Clem.* 62.2; see also BAG s.v.).

[10] It appears in the first list of vices, *Man.* 8.3; also (though not in a list) in *Vis.* 2.3.1; see BAG s.v. Though the phrase *mnēsikakian mē echein* does not appear in the Latin manuscripts of *Man.* 8.10 and is altered to the single adjective *amnēsikakon* in the Athous manuscript, the major texts have it as given. The verb *mnēsikakeō* is found in sections of extended Christian commandment material based on ethical lists, in future-as-imperative form, in *Did.* 2.3; *Barn.* 19.4; also *Barn.* 2.8 in a quote from Zech 7:10 LXX. It is denied of God in *Man.* 9.3; *Sim.* 9.23.4; *Diogn.* 9.2. The adverb *amnēsikakōs* appears in a list of virtues in *1 Clem.* 62.2. The noun is adequately attested elsewhere though not in ethical lists, e.g., Philo *De Jos.* 261; Jos. *Ant.* 16.9.3 §292; Plut. *Mor.* 860A. See LSJ s.v.

the whole community is by extension one household.[11] "To preserve brother-hood" *adelphotēta syntērein* is the most general admonition, yet it may actually mean, besides preserving bonds of mutual charity, something akin to group loyalty.[12] "To minister to widows" and "to look after orphans and the needy" are the supreme works of charity and are the major objectives of prophetic preaching.[13] "To ransom from distress the servants of God" is common Christian paraenesis (see Matt 25:36, 43; Heb 13:3; *1 Clem.* 59.4; Ign. *Smyrn.* 6.2). "To reverence the aged" is common *Haustafel* advice (see 1 Pet 5:5; *1 Clem.* 1.3; cf. Lev 19:32). "To comfort those who are burdened in spirit" is a simple and general Christian exhortation reminiscent of Matt 5:7.[14] "Not to reject those who have been made to stumble from the faith but to convert them and encourage them" and the similar directive "to admonish sinners" are to be expected in a treatise on Christian repentance, but here they belong more to the common paraenetic tradition than to the central theme of the book.[15] They occur frequently in passages on church order. "Not to oppress debtors and the needy" will be discussed below.[16]

The third major source for the moral exhortations of *Man.* 8.10 is the theology of the "pious poor" (Dibelius's *Armenfrömmigkeit*), already discussed at length in chapter II. Two different themes are interwoven in this

[11] See 1 Tim 3:15; Dibelius and Conzelmann, *Pastoral Epistles*, 35, 60.

[12] Cf. 1 Pet 2:17, where the word *adelphotēs* could simply mean mutual charity or broth-erly love, and throughout its history this is one of its two root meanings. But the other is a "brotherhood" to which one belongs and on behalf of which one labors; see 1 Pet 5:9; *1 Clem.* 2.4; BAG s.v. LSJ (s.v.) gives a third usage in a form of address (not relevant here) and cites both 1 Pet 2:17 and 5:9 as examples of the second meaning, which is not quite correct.

[13] See Dibelius (*Der Hirt*, 527) and Dibelius/Greeven (*James*, 121) for references in the OT; see also CD 6.16; Sir 4:10; Philo *De spec. leg.* 1.308-10, etc. For Christian sources see Jas 1:27 (as one true way to worship); *Barn.* 20.2 (negatively in a catalog of vices); Arist. *Apol.* 15.7; *Herm. Sim.* 1.8 (linked with redemption of those in affliction—see below), 5.3.7 (as an appro-priate use for money saved from fasting); *Vis.* 2.4.3 (widows and orphans as a social category in the church).

[14] Compare its transposition, along with many other phrases from this passage, into the context of intercessory liturgical prayer in *1 Clem.* 59.4.

[15] So Dibelius, *Der Hirt*, 528. See Gal 6:1; Matt 18:15-16; Ign. *Pol.* 6.1; also Jas 5:19-20 and the commentary in Dibelius/Greeven, *James*, 257, esp. n. 94; *1 Clem.* 59.4 (*tous planōmen-ous tou laou sou epistrepson*). *T. Benj.* 4.5 (longer reading) uses both terms *epistrephō* and *noutheteō*. *Skandalizō* often bears a meaning similar to *astheneō*, "to fall through weakness," rather than "to take offense." The former is probably closer to the meaning here, and Lake's translation "offended in the faith" is therefore inexact (LCL 2.107). See *Vis.* 4.1.3 and M. Barré, "Paul as 'Eschatologic Person': A New Look at 2 Cor 11:29," *CBQ* 37 (1975) 513-14.

[16] See below, pp. 68–76. Lake's translation (LCL 2.107) "not to oppress poor debtors" is misleading. Two types of victims are being (at least grammatically) distinguished: *chreōstas mē thlibein kai endeeis.* Debtors have rarely been limited to the poor in any society, nor creditors to the leisure classes!

kind of Christian teaching. The first is a strict sense of community justice because the community belongs to God. In *1 Clem.* 59.4 a catalog of works of mercy is converted into a liturgical prayer of petition to illustrate this point: God is the ultimate rescuer of the oppressed, the one who has mercy on the needy. All Christian exercise of virtue toward those in need becomes an imitation of his action. The second theme is the advantage for the individual Christian of resembling as closely as possible the attitude of the poor since it is they who are blessed by God. In the context of this theology of the "pious poor," "to resist no one" and "to bear with insult" appear as virtues in *Man.* 8.10 (see Rom 12:13; 1 Pet 2:19).[17] "To become poorer than all" (*endeesteron ginesthai pantōn anthrōpōn*) will be discussed below (pp. 64–67).

Out of these three theological-paraenetic sources—traditional lists of virtue or vices, church order material, and the paraenesis of the "pious poor"—the seventeen exhortations of *Man.* 8.10 are composed. Within the structure of the eighth *Mandate*, the list in v. 10 comes as the second catalog of virtues, parallel to the second catalog of vices in v. 5 (see the diagram above, p. 59). In both cases the list is reinforced in the following verse (vv. 6 and 11) by a short exchange in which the Shepherd elicits Hermas' agreement about the wickedness or goodness of the attitudes and practices just mentioned.[18] But this dialogue does not intend to give greater importance to the second list in either case, any more than the label *ta akoloutha* at the beginning of both second lists implies that they are less important than the first lists.[19] Though the list in *Man.* 8.10 uses infinitive clauses rather than single adjectives or two-word adjectival phrases, it can hardly be said that the virtues in v. 10 would have been considered more important than *pistis*, *phobos kyriou*, or *agapē* of the first list in v. 9. Nor can a distinction be made in terms of "inner" and "outer" virtues, i.e., virtues of internal attitude and virtues with active or social dimension. *Hēsychion einai . . . hybrin hypopherein, makrothymon einai* of v. 10 do not differ radically from *agapē*, *homonoia, hypomonē* of v. 9. The same must be said of the two lists of vices in vv. 3 and 5: nothing listed in v. 5 could be considered a graver sin than *moicheia . . . porneia . . . blasphēmia* of v. 3. Moreover, the *katalalia* from

---

[17] Compare Jas 5:6, where the just one is unable to resist the onslaught of the exploiting rich; but God the avenger opposes the arrogant and favors the lowly in Jas 4:6 (quoted from Prov 3:34), a favorite theme repeated in 1 Pet 5:5; *1 Clem.* 30.2; and Ign. *Eph.* 5.3 to prove a different point—submission to ecclesiastical authority.

[18] The concluding section, *Man.* 8.12, is a summary reinforcement, in rough chiastic structure, of the whole eighth *Mandate*: Keep *this commandment*, that of *enkrateia* (8.1). The play on the word that has characterized the whole discussion in every verse of *Man.* 8 except v. 10 continues to the conclusion.

[19] See above, n. 4.

v. 3, to take just one example, is more "socially oriented" than the *keno-doxia* of v. 5.

It cannot therefore be said that in the two sets of virtues and vices in *Man.* 8 either the first or the second grouping of either category is more important ethically, rhetorically, or socially than its counterpart. What can be affirmed of the second list of virtues (*Man.* 8.10) vis-à-vis the first line (v. 9) (but *not* of the second list of vices vis-à-vis the first) is that some of the exhortations are more expanded and specific. Some are expressed in terminology different from that of the traditional early Christian paraenesis and may refer to definite behavior in concrete situations. In this light, two of the exhortations in v. 10 warrant further investigation: to become poorer than all (*endeesteron ginesthai pantōn anthrōpōn*) and not to oppress debtors and the poor (*chreōstas mē thlibein kai endeeis*).

Exhortations

Endeesteron ginesthai pantōn anthrōpōn

Endeesteron ginesthai pantōn anthrōpōn (to become "poorer" than everyone else) in *Man.* 8.10 is by any standard an unusual expression, and it is further complicated by a different use of *endeēs* later in the same verse. The phrase is paralleled only by the nearly verbatim expression *heauton endeesteron poiein pantōn tōn anthrōpōn* (to make oneself "poorer" than everyone else) in *Man.* 11.8. The adjective *endeēs* (from *endeō, endeēsō*) is common enough in ancient literature, normally with the meaning "needy," "wanting," "insufficient," "lacking," etc., either economically or figuratively.[20] It occurs in the economic sense at the end of *Man.* 8.10. It is, however, an uncommon word in other early Christian literature, appearing only once before *Hermas*,[21] in Acts 4:34, where it retains the same meaning, "in need of the means of sustenance," and is probably influenced by the utopian description of life in the sabbatical year in Deuteronomy 15 (see vv. 4, 7, 11). It is nearly as uncommon in biblical literature. Of the twenty-three occurrences in the LXX, nine of them in Proverbs are in expressions meaning lack of sense (7:7; 9:4, 16; 11:12; 12:11; 13:25; 15:21; 18:2; 24:45); five others refer to a lack or deficiency of some kind (Prov 9:13; 11:16; 28:16; Wis 16:3; Ezek 4:17); four

---

[20] See LSJ s.v.

[21] I.e., in that literature indexed by BAG (s.v.). The related participial noun, *ho endeomenos*, is used in *Did.* 4.8; 5.2 par. *Barn.* 20.2 in admonitions not to turn away the needy. The connotation of the word is still negative, depicting an undesirable condition open to amelioration. See too the use of a similar word, *epideisthai*, in *Diogn.* 10.6 and Ign. *Mag.* 14. *Endeēs* appears in Justin as "weak," "miserable," "needy" (*Apol.* 2.5.4; *Dial.* 22.1, 11; 87.2, 3; 88.1, 4).

others probably mean "poor" or "needy" but not as representative of "pious poor" theology (Tob 2:2; Prov 3:27; 21:17; 27:7—in the last case, more exactly "hungry," *roʿēb*). The five occurrences of *endeēs* in Deut 15:4, 7, 11; 24:15; and Isa 41:17 all contain the warning of God's protection of the poor and vengeance upon those who oppress them, a familiar element of "pious poor" theology.

There is another use of *endeēs* in *Hermas* that may shed light on its meaning in *Man.* 8.10. In *Vis.* 3.1.2, Hermas is waiting impatiently for a further revelation promised through the aged woman. In her introductory speech she tells him that since he is *endeēs . . . kai spoudaios eis to gnōnai panta*,[22] he will see what he should see if he follows her directions. Here *endeēs* cannot mean economic need—Hermas' financial situation would be incongruous with *spoudaios* and would have nothing to do with whether or how he will see his next vision.[23] The word is being used figuratively, and there are three possible interpretations that could shed light on the use of *endeēs* in the comparative in *Man.* 8.10 and 11.8.

(1) "insistent" (Lake's "importunate"). This integrates well with its companion term *spoudaios* ("eager"[24]) and is certainly descriptive of Hermas' behavior throughout the *Visions*. The woman is saying that since Hermas keeps asking so intently, she will tell him. This interpretation does not clarify the use of *endeesteros* in *Man.* 8.10 and 11.8; to make oneself more insistent than anyone else is hardly consonant with being *praüs* and *hēsychios* (8.10 and 11.8).

(2) "needy." If "insistent" describes behavior, "needy" describes the actual condition underlying the behavior. Economic need would hardly be relevant in *Vis.* 3.1.2, but a need to know, to be informed about the meaning of the vision, would be a possible interpretation.[25]

(3) "humble," "self-effacing." This interpretation is an extension of "poor and needy," the original meaning of the word. In this case it is Hermas' penitence (*Vis.* 1.2.1, etc.) and simplicity (2.3.2) that characterize him, and in 3.1.2 the elderly woman of his vision recalls his humble attitude and rewards him for it. "To know everything" then modifies only eager (*spoudaios*). This

---

[22] Lake translates, "importunate and zealous" (?); see LCL 2.27.

[23] The cryptic reference in *Vis.* 3.6.7 that Hermas was once rich but is no longer so need not mean that he is a pauper, no matter how much historicity one wishes to attribute to the autobiograpical statements in the *Shepherd.*

[24] Or "quick," "in haste" (LSJ s.v.); "zealous," "earnest," "diligent" (BAG s.v.). Cf. 2 Cor 8:22; Ign. *Pol.* 3.2. For an example of encouraging insistence in dealing with God, see Luke 18:3–8.

[25] The suggestion in BAG (s.v.), "poorly instructed," may point in the same direction but is less clear. Compare the LXX phrase *endeēs phrenōn*, "in need of good sense," in Prov. 7:7; 9:4, 16; 11:12; 12:11; 13:25; 15:21; 18:2; 24:45.

interpretation fits well with the *endeesteros* of *Man.* 8.10 and 11.8. The word has acquired a positive connotation. The behavior of being *endeēs* is to be encouraged and rewarded; it is not an unfortunate condition to be alleviated. This interpretation of the word fits the "pious poor" theology. In *Vis.* 3.1.2 this is not so obvious, but it can be assumed by comparison.

Why is *endeēs* or its comparative used four times in *Hermas* (while the more common *ptōchos* and *penēs* are completely avoided except in *Sim.* 2), only once in earlier Christian literature (but with a different implication), and only twenty-four times in the whole LXX (fifteen of them in Proverbs)? Was it simply a favorite term for Hermas or his community, as it seems to have been with a different meaning for the compiler of Proverbs?[26] But Hermas had many opportunities to use *endeēs* that he did not take, and this word competes with another favorite term, *hysteroumenos*, a word with similar origins.[27] It is also possible that *Man.* 8.10 was influenced by Deuteronomy 15. This will be dealt with further below in the discussion of *chreōstas mē thlibein kai endeeis.*

The use of the comparative *endeesteros* in a positive sense is a unique phenomenon in *Herm. Man.* 8.10 and 11.8. The comparative form is well attested in classical and Hellenistic literature, but always with the sense of being more in need or more inferior than someone or something else.[28] It is unattested in biblical and early Christian literature. Its occurrence in both places in the *Mandates* is in a catalog of virtues. In both instances the idea of humility has been amply covered by other terms, in 8.10 by *mēdeni antitassesthai* and *hēsychion einai*, in 11.8 by *praüs, hēsychios,* and *tapeinophrōn.* But it must be remembered that eclecticism and repetition in the choice of ethical motifs are common characteristics of paraenetic style.[29] If it can be

---

[26] See Hatch-Redpath, s.v., and the discussion above.

[27] *Hysteroumenos*, from the verb *hystereō*, also originally meant one who is inferior or lacking. It occurs seven times in Hermas, frequently linked with widows and orphans (*Vis.* 3.9.2, 4, 6; *Man.* 2.4; 8.10; *Sim.* 5.3.7; 9.27.2). It is not used as a noun in the LXX (see BAG s.v.). The adjective *tapeinos* and its related words also have a double meaning; the idea of being of low social position is extended to being humble of heart. Hermas does not use the simple adjective *tapeinos*, and the meaning of the related words *tapeinophroneō* (*Sim.* 5.3.7; 7.4, 6), *tapeinophronēsis* (*Sim.* 8.7.6), *tapeinophrosynē* (*Sim.* 5.3.7; *Vis.* 3.10.6), *tapeinophrōn* (*Man.* 11.8), and *tapeinoun heauton* (*Man.* 4.2.2) is decidedly different from that of *endeēs*. There are no socio-economic overtones; for Hermas these terms unambiguously describe a humble attitude, often connected with repentance and fasting. This word group has for him moved completely into the category of ethical terminology (see BAG s.v.). *Tapeinos* in the LXX translates *ʾebyôn* (Amos 8:6); *ʿānî* (Ps 17[18]:28; 81[82]:3; Prov 24:37 [30:14]); *ʿānāw* (Amos 2:7; Isa 61:1 Sin.; Sir 3:20). It is the ambiguity of *endeēs* in its various contexts in *Hermas* that is the problem.

[28] E.g., Hdt. 7.48; Thuc. 1.10; 2.11; 4.65; Isoc. *Pan.* 105; Sop. *Philoc.* 524; Plut. *Cic.* 35 (see LSJ s.v.).

[29] Dibelius/Greeven, *James*, 5–11.

assumed that "pious poor" theology is behind the use of *endeesteros* in this way, then the Christian reader of *Man.* 8.10 is enjoined to be more humble than all others, i.e., not to put himself forward, to "take a back seat."[30] This is similar to *tē timē allēlous proēgoumenoi* in Rom 12:10, setting an example of respect for each other, or *mē ta hypsēla phronountes alla tois tapeinois synapagomenoi* in Rom 12:16, not caring about lofty (snobbish?) things but associating with the lowly (i.e., the socially less desirable).[31] Similarly in 11.8, one of the criteria by which an authentic prophet can be known is that he does not throw himself forward, filled with a sense of his own importance, to initiate prophetic utterance; nor, as the next lines go on to say, does he accept requests for oracles but waits for the Spirit to speak through him.[32] In both cases, that of the prophet and that of the ordinary Christian, the suggested attitude is that of God's poor and lowly ones who depend entirely upon him and therefore have no claim to public notice by which they can be preferred to others.

Summary

The unusual choice of words in these passages shows that the author is expressing the theology of the "pious poor," which reflects one of the biblical attempts to grapple theologically with the mystery of the weakness and the misfortune of believers. This places *Hermas* in the Christian tradition represented in some ways by the beatitudes and the Epistle of James. But there is

---

[30] See BAG s.v. and esp. Bauer's German ed. (Berlin: A. Töpelmann, 1958) 519: *mangelhafter werden als jmd. = jmdm. gegenüber zurücktreten.* This is also how Dibelius understands it (*Der Hirt*, 527–28) translating *sich allen gegenüber erniedrigen* at *Man.* 8.10. The Latin translation *humilior*, which Dibelius points out, does not help since it has even stronger socioeconomic overtones than *endeēs* has.

[31] These references are suggested by Dibelius (*Der Hirt*, 527–28). The social overtones of *tapeinos* in Rom 12:16 are not present in Hermas' use of its derivatives (see above, n. 27). What is being encouraged—associating with those (i.e., other Christians) socially inferior to oneself— is just the opposite of what the Shepherd is complaining about against the wealthy elsewhere, in *Sim.* 8.9.1 and 9.20.2. Reiling's suggestion that *endeesteron* in 8.10 and 11.8 refers to voluntary poverty is not without its difficulties (*Hermas and Christian Prophecy*, 49 n. 5). The *endeēs* of *Vis.* 3.1.2 could not be interpreted in this way. To make oneself voluntarily poorer in order to share one's goods with those in need is a Christian ideal of long standing (Acts 4:34–35; *Did.* 4.8, etc.). To put oneself voluntarily in need of support from others is an ideal only for the Christian who seeks the heroic extra (Mark 10:21 pars.) and not even for the prophets in general (*Did.* 11.6, 12; 12.3; 13.1, 2), who must work physically or for the spiritual welfare of the community to earn their food. Voluntary poverty is not encouraged for general Christian conduct and would besides be inconsonant with (and not "suggested by"—so Reiling) the injunction in *Man.* 8.10 not to oppress debtors and the *endeeis*.

[32] See the interesting collection of texts on the self-exaltation of "false" Christian "prophets" in Dibelius, *Der Hirt*, 540.

ambiguity on these points for Hermas. From other important issues raised in the book it is clear that he is not exclusively addressing the dispossessed. Neither social nor religious status should make any difference for the Christian's behavior. Yet in some instances it does, and a type of conflict born of the search for deepened understanding ensues. This will be apparent later in the examination of the second *Similitude.*

Chreōstas mē thlibein kai endeeis

There remains the last exhortation of *Man.* 8.10, not to oppress the debtors and the needy. Are those who virtuously assume a humble attitude being classed with debtors? The word *endeēs* must certainly be understood here primarily in one of its basic senses, namely, one who is economically in need.

While exhortations to generosity are ubiquitous in early Christian literature,[33] commands to resolve unjust economic situations are rare. The Matthean story of the unforgiving debtor (Matt 18:23–35) is a parable on forgiveness in general, not on releasing debtors (cf. vv 21–22); the rich young man (Matt 19:16–26 and pars.) is not accused of wrongdoing; the narrative of the expulsion of the merchants from the temple by Jesus (Matt 21:12–13 and pars.) contains no suggestion that their shady involvements are paradigmatic for Christians; the sins of the goats in the eschatological discourse (Matt 25:41–46) are all sins of neglect. Even in the parable of the rich man and Lazarus (Luke 16:19–31) the rich man in torment after death is not reproached for having dealt harshly with Lazarus; it is simply explained to him that this is the way things are because they were reversed on earth! In the parable of the unjust judge and the insistent widow (Luke 18:1–8) the application given in vv. 6–8 casts the judge as God, the widow as one of his *eklektoi,* the sufferer of injustice whom he will avenge. 1 Tim 6:17–19 warns in nearly Lucan style against the danger of riches but does not criticize the wealthy for any social abuses except an arrogant attitude. No early Christian catalog of virtues before *Hermas* contains a definite admonition against oppressing the poor,[34] and even exhortations to deal fairly with other Christians are rare.[35]

---

[33] E.g., Matt 5:7; 25:31–46; 1 Tim 6:18; Jas 1:27; *Did.* 4.5–8 par. *Barn.* 19.9, 11; *1 Clem.* 38.2; *Herm. Sim.* 1.8; 5.3.7; Ign. *Smyrn.* 6.2 (in the form of a catalog of vices practiced by the heterodox); etc.

[34] In fact, the author of *2 Clem.* 4.3 has an excellent opportunity to do so since the passage contains several injunctions to virtue in negative infinitival clauses. 1 Tim 5:10 includes *helping* the oppressed among the duties of a widow, but that is quite another angle.

[35] A possible exception is 1 Thess 4:6: *to mē hyperbainein kai pleonektein en tō pragmati,*

Notable exceptions to the absence of polemic about oppression of the poor are *Did.* 5.2 par. *Barn.* 20.2, and Jas 5:4–6. The *Didache-Barnabas* passage is part of a "two-way" polemic in which the Way of Death is characterized in part (and in the third person plural) by those who, besides being unmerciful to the poor and refusing those in need, place burdens on the afflicted and are advocates of the rich and lawless judges of the poor. Their counterparts in the Way of Life (addressed in the second person singular) are told to give just judgment and to favor no one in refuting transgressions (*Did.* 4.3 par. *Barn.* 19.11 in part). From the use of a traditional literary form of paraenesis, from the shift from homiletic address for the Way of Life to narrative description for the Way of Death, and from the relative length of the two literary units (*Didache*: four chapters on the Way of Life versus one chapter on the Way of Death; *Barnabas*: the Way of Light passage three times longer than the Way of the Dark One), it can be inferred that the behavior comprising the Way of Death (or the Way of the Dark One in *Barnabas*) is not being presented to the readers as a realistic part of their lives but by way of contrast.[36] The ideals presented in the Way of Life are standard Christian virtues after which the readers are exhorted to strive; the vices listed in the Way of Death are understood as attitudes and practices removed from the readers' experience and meant to stay that way. This situation stands in sharp contrast to classical prophetic condemnations of injustice as found in passages like Isa 58:6.

Jas 5:4–6 is part of a scathing denouncement of the vices of "the rich." Withholding the wages of laborers, living in luxury in spite of the depriva-

---

possibly meaning "that no man . . . defraud his brother in business" (*RSV* note, ad loc.) or "in lawsuits" (*NEB* note, ad loc.). The interpretation hinges on the possible meanings of *pragma* ("lawsuit" in 1 Cor 6:1, frequently "business" in the plural but not in the singular) and the context, itself far from clear, including the controversial *skeuos* in v. 4. Opting for some kind of sexual offense are *RSV* text; *JB*; *KVJ*; *NEB* text; E. Best, *The First and Second Epistles to the Thessalonians* (HNTC; New York: Harper and Row, 1972) 166. R. Beauvery ("*Pleonektein* in 1 Thess 4, 6a," *VD* 33 [1955] 78-85) opts for complementary vices, lust and greed in business dealings, on the basis of the juxtaposition of *porneia* and *pleonexia* elsewhere in the Pauline corpus, e.g., 1 Cor 5:10–11; 6:10; Eph 5:5. For the most complete treatment of the problem see B. Rigaux, *Saint Paul: Les épîtres aux Thessaloniciens* (Paris: Gabalda, 1956) 510-11. The rather frequent occurrence of *pleonektēs* and *pleonexia* in the New Testament should not be overlooked. But the reference in Luke 12:15 is concerned with personal attitude only; 1 Thess 2:5 and 2 Cor 9:5 are nonapplicable personal references of Paul; Eph 4:19 and 5:3 do not ascribe it to Christians; and all other uses of the terms occur in traditional lists of vices (see BAG s.v. and below, n. 43).

[36] For further discussion of the "two-way" genre, especially of the confluence here of Deuteronomic and sapiential traditions, see J.-P. Audet, *La Didachè: Instructions des apôtres* (Paris: Gabalda, 1958) 252-60. For the relationship between *Barnabas* and the *Didache*, see ibid., pp. 122-63; between *Hermas* and the *Didache*, pp. 163-66.

tions suffered by others, causing the death of the helpless just one—these are all themes familiar from the legal and prophetic denunciations of the Hebrew scriptures. But again, a consideration of context and literary form suggests that the criticism is not levelled at the readers but, for their enjoyment, at their perceived opponents. The use of traditional paraenetic language and images, the abrupt shift from condemnation in v. 6 to an exhortation to patience in v. 7, and the treatment of the theme of poor and rich throughout the letter of James indicate that this material is designed "to revive anew all the accusations which the pietism of the Poor had for centuries raised against 'the Rich'" in a situation in which "the Poor" are Christians and "the Rich'" are their opponents.[37]

In Christian literature before *Hermas*, admonitions against unjust treatment of the poor or even expressions of concern that Christians are not living up to ideal standards in this regard are scarce, except in the stylized treatments discussed above. The same is true about the more specific function of moneylending and the creditor-debtor relationship.[38]

The term *chreōstēs* found in *Herm. Man.* 8.10 is not attested elsewhere in early Christian literature, but its cognates *chreo(ō)-pheiletēs* and *ophei-*

---

[37] Dibelius/Greeven, *James*, p. 240. See the whole discussion of the passage Jas 5:1–6 (ibid., pp. 235–40) and of the equally problematic 2:1–9, which deals with partiality to the rich and snubbing of the poor (ibid., pp. 124–44, esp. 137–41). The interpretation of the categories "rich" and "poor" in James have been discussed above in chapter II.

[38] Moneylending is spoken of frequently in the Jewish legal codes and in the prophetic and sapiential literature. On the question of taking securities for loans, see Hatch-Redpath and LSJ s.vv. *enechyrasma, enechyron, enechyrasmos, enechyrazō*, words usually translating *ḥābāl* or one of its substantive derivatives; G. A. Barrois, "Debt, Debtor," *IBD* 1.809-10; R. de Vaux, *Ancient Israel, Its Life and Institutions* (London: Darton, Longman and Todd, 1961) 171-73; G. E. Wright, "Deuteronomy," *IB* 2.474-75; R. North, *Sociology of the Biblical Jubilee* (AnBib 4; Rome: Pontifical Biblical Institute, 1954) 135-39. For the time of the Second Temple and later, see E. E. Urbach, "The Laws Regarding Slavery As a Source for Social History of the Period of the Second Temple, the Mishnah and Talmud," *Papers of the Institute of Jewish Studies, London* (ed. J. G. Weiss; Jerusalem: Hebrew University, 1964) 1.1-95. On the cancellation of debts in the sabbatical year, see S. R. Driver, *A Critical and Exegetical Commentary on Deuteronomy* (3d ed.; ICC; Edinburgh: T. and T. Clark, 1951) 178-79; M. Weinfeld, *Deuteronomy and the Deuteronomistic School* (Oxford: Clarendon, 1972) 223-24; J. Blenkinsopp, "Deuteronomy," *JBC* 1.111; J. Morgenstern, "Sabbatical Year," *IDB* 4.141-44; B. Z. Wacholder, "Sabbatical Year," *IDBSup*, 762-63. For evidence of the continuation of the custom in Palestine even into Roman times, see Urbach, "The Laws Regarding Slavery," 7-8. On usury in the ancient world and the early Church, see R. Maloney, "Usury in Greek, Roman and Rabbinic Thought," *Traditio* 27 (1971) 79-109; idem, "The Teaching of the Fathers on Usury," *VC* 27 (1973) 241-65; also de Vaux, *Ancient Israel*, 171; Barrois, "Debt, Debtor," 809-10. In spite of repeated legal prohibitions and prophetic condemnation, passages like Neh 5:6-13, Prov 28:8, and Sir 29:28 show that the charging of interest on loans by Israelites to Israelites was never eradicated.

letēs do occur.[39] The social reality of the creditor-debtor relationship is utilized in parabolic material twice in Luke and once in Matthew. In the parable of the two debtors (Luke 7:41–43) the reader is meant to identify with the debtors, not the creditors. In the parable of the clever steward who cancelled out his master's loans in order to get a better reception for himself (Luke 16:1–8), the focus of attention is the brash action of the steward himself, who is not directly involved in the loans. The first conveys the obvious lesson that gratitude is in proportion to the amount of indebtedness (or guilt) forgiven; the second extols worldly wisdom and has no bearing on the social burden of debt. The parable of the unmerciful servant (Matt 18:23–35), who is released from his debt but who will not do the same for his own debtors, envisions a "middleman," probably a slave with a mismanaged *peculium*, who is indeed castigated for not being merciful to his debtors; he is the antithesis of Matt 6:12. But the context of fraternal forgiveness and the spiritual application in v. 35, as well as in 6:12, suggest that what is at stake here as well as in the Lucan passage is not so much financial intricacies as personal wrongs and grudges, for which the cancellation of debts is simply a metaphor.

The difference is that in Luke 7:41-42 the plan of action is between God and the people involved, whereas in the case of the unmerciful servant (Matt 18:23–35) the dimension of brother to brother becomes a heavy factor in the implications of the parable. It is important to emphasize in both cases (and less certainly in Luke 16:1-8) that the creditor is a God figure rather than a human one and that the parables are metaphorical rather than literal examples.[40] While they are rich in conveying the horizontal dimension of Christian righteousness, they contribute very little to an early Christian teaching or even concern about the treatment of debtors except insofar as general principles of love, justice, and forgiveness apply. The reader can infer social values from the behavior attributed to God and apply them to one's own situation.

This does not mean, however, that moneylending is not mentioned at all

---

[39] *Chreōstēs* is unattested in the LXX but is used by Philo in his discussion of Exod 22:25-27 (*De somn.* 1.92–101) and by Josephus regarding the sabbatical cancellation of debts (Deuteronomy 15), attributed by him to the jubilee year (*Ant.* 3.12.3 § 282). BAG s.vv. Noteworthy is the figurative use of *opheiletēs* (esp. Matt 6:12 par. *Did.* 8.2, and Luke's specification of the spiritual debt in 11:4). Discussion of debts and debtors is notably absent from the Qumran literature with the exception of CD 10.18, which forbids lending or discussion of wealth and profit on the sabbath.

[40] For the problems of interpretation on the parable of the unjust steward, see C. H. Dodd, *The Parables of the Kingdom* (rev. ed.; New York: Scribner, 1961) 17–18; J. Jeremias, *The Parables of Jesus* (rev. ed.; New York: Scribner, 1963) 45-48.

in the synoptic Gospels. Matt 5:42, part of the repudiation and reversal of the "law of talion," exhorts the reader to give to whoever asks, to loan to whoever wishes to borrow (see Deut 15:7–8). Luke 6:34–35, part of the Lucan "Sermon on the Plain," holds up as part of the ideal of generosity the willingness to lend even to those from whom one cannot be certain of receiving back one's investment! Matthew and Luke speak from a community in which moneylending is certainly practiced; the parables discussed above show this. But the two paraenetic sayings function as parts of ethical formulas which on this point take up the spirit of Deuteronomy 15. The paraenetic language remains informal (i.e., "give to whoever wants to borrow" rather than "establish just terms on loans" or something similar) and there is no complaint against abuses and mistreatment of debtors.

Rom 13:8 in the context of a paraenesis of social duties admonishes the reader to owe no one anything except mutual love, i.e., to contract no obligation apart from the religious commitment of loving one another, for the one who does this has fulfilled the law. Though the ideal of contracting no financial debts to a fellow Christian (and probably to no one at all) is undoubtedly included in the meaning, that is not the only or even the most obvious level at which the statement is meant.[41] In any event, the paraenesis is against contracting debts—against borrowing—not loaning. No concern about creditors' treatment of debtors is raised.

There are no other passages in early Christian literature that deal with the creditor-debtor relationship before *Hermas*—with the exception of two references to the practice of usury, one positive and one negative.[42] In the Q parable of the talents (Matt 25:14–30; Luke 19:11–27) the king upon his return upbraids the lazy slave for burying or hiding rather than investing the money entrusted to him as did the others—with returns of 100 to 1000 percent! According to Matt 25:27 and Luke 19:23 he states that the slave should have invested it with the bankers, from whom he upon returning would have been able to reclaim it with interest, *syn tokō*, which presupposes usury as the normal way of investing money. Yet the second-century *Apocalypse of Peter* indicates that at least one Christian moral code kept the Jewish prohibition against charging interest; it places in the torments of hell

---

[41] For a discussion of the play on the double meaning of *opheilō* (debt and duty), see O. Michel, *Der Brief an die Römer* (MeyerK 4; 10th ed., Göttingen: Vandenhoeck and Ruprecht, 1955) 4.288–89; also C. K. Barrett, *A Commentary on the Epistle to the Romans* (Black's NT Commentaries; London: Adam and Charles Black, 1957) 249–50; J. A. Fitzmyer, "The Letter to the Romans," *JBC* 2.326–27; and the sensitive interpretation of C. H. Dodd, *The Epistle of Paul to the Romans* (MNTC; New York and London: Harper, 1932) 205–6.

[42] Phlm 18 probably refers to financial debt (or theft!) but represents a practical situation that is immaterial here.

those who have lent money at interest (Ethiopic translation, 10) or at compound interest (*tokoi tokōn*, Akhmim frag., 31).[43]

By the time of the writing of the *Shepherd* traditional Christian paraenesis had already developed its own customary sets of terms and phrases. *Chreōstas mē thlibein* was not among them. As a paraenetic unit it arises from the world of Leviticus and Deuteronomy. It may be significant that in all Greek biblical and early Christian literature the occurrence of the theme of lending money to the needy is found together with the unusual word *endeēs* only in Deut 15:3–4, 7–8, 10–11 and *Herm. Man.* 8.10. However, the circumstances represented by Deuteronomy and *Hermas* are very different. The Deuteronomic description of the sabbatical year is largely an idealized picture, created late in the period of the monarchy.[44] According to this admittedly semi-idyllic scene, it seems to be only poor Jews who need to borrow, and they are kept poor by the fact that they are in debt. The remission of debts will release them from their condition of need (v. 4), so that, in characteristic Deuteronomic language, the creditor may be blessed in the land and obedient to all the commandments laid down to be observed. Deut 15:11 adds a note of realism—*ou gar mē eklipę endeēs apo tēs gēs*—which is no doubt closer to the actual situation.

By contrast, *Hermas* reflects the financial world of imperial Rome, where moneylending and borrowing were enterprises undertaken on a broad scale among every class and *ordo*. Seneca (*Ep.* 41.7) considered it part of the investments of a good agricultural businessman to loan money at interest:

---

[43] Eng. trans. in E. Hennecke, *New Testament Apocrypha* (ed. W. Schneemelcher; Philadelphia: Westminster, 1965) 2.676. *Apoc. Pet.* is usually dated to the first part of the second century. See the introduction by Ch. Mauer, p. 664. It is also possible that the common derogative term *pleonektēs* in 1 Cor 5:11 and 6:10 means "usurer" (so translated by *JB*, but see *RSV* et al. "greedy"). Neither LSJ nor BAG lists "usurer" as a possible meaning, nor "usury" for the equally common vice of *pleonexia* (Rom 1:29; 2 Cor 9:5; Eph 4:19; *1 Clem.* 35.5; *Barn.* 10.4; *Did.* 5.1; *Herm. Man.* 6.2.5; 8.5 etc.) but rather the more general "greediness," "avarice," etc. But Eph 5:5 and Col 3:5 connect the concept with idolatry, and in Luke 12:15 and 2 Pet 2:14 a more general quality is surely meant. While the taking of usury could easily have been interpreted as pure greed by those who opposed it, the *JB* interpretation seems justified. In view of the evidence, it is more likely that *pleonexia* includes usury but is not limited to it. For a later Christian condemnation of usury, see *Didasc.* 18 = *Ap. Const.* 4.6.5. Here it occurs in a long "blacklist" of illicit ways of gaining profit; such money cannot be contributed to the Church for the relief of widows and orphans. That the prohibition of usury was a traditional formula not completely taken seriously by the faithful is indicated by the fact that earlier (*Didasc.* 15 = *Ap. Const.* 3.7.3) enterprising widows are criticized for engaging in business transactions themselves, among other things, charging too much interest!

[44] There is no consensus either about the dating or about the form and the structure of the individual parts of Deuteronomy. See Blenkinsopp, "Deuteronomy," 101–2 and the bibliography given there. See also Weinfeld, *Deuteronomy*, 7 and passim.

multum serit, multum fenerat. The younger Pliny stated openly (*Ep.* 3.19.8) that he invested some of his estate *aliquid tamen fenero.* Cicero did the same and also borrowed, even from professional moneylenders or *faeneratores* (*Ad amic.* 5.6.2; *Ad Att.* 5.4.3; 7.2.11; 7.85), in spite of his opinion (*De Off.* 1.150–1) that the occupation of *faenerator* ranked among the *sordidi* because it required dishonesty and incurred ill-will (*odia hominum.*).[45] Nevertheless, moneylenders were necessary to society, and he did not hesitate to draw on their services.[46] Cicero would by no means have considered himself a *faenerator*, nor would any of his senatorial colleagues. Even though they may have engaged in lending money at interest on a large scale, they felt no contradiction or embarrassment about it. The social structure prevented their formal membership in such low occupations; moreover, they were engaged primarily in the noble pursuits of politics and agriculture.

Yet the *ordines* were vulnerable to financial crises from both ends. i.e., as lenders and as borrowers. Cicero's vigorous objections to legislation that cancelled debts in moments of economic crisis centered on his demand that the state protect the proprietor's unhindered use of his property (*De Off.* 2.78–84), including outstanding loans. In 33 C.E. growing discontent with "widespread irregularities" by moneylenders caused a crisis in which the creditors recalled their loans. The mortgaged property of the aristocracy was sufficiently threatened that Tiberius provided a floating fund of one hundred million sesterces for interest-free loans to save those whose *dignitas* and *fama* as well as their fortunes were at stake (Tacitus *Ann.* 6.16–17; Dio Cass. 58.21.1–5; Suet. *Tib.* 48.1).[47]

---

[45] In the same classification he includes tax collectors; wage-earners because they are paid for labor instead of skill; retailers because they could not make a profit without lying; craftsmen; cooks, butchers, etc. who cater to sensual pleasures; perfumers and entertainers. If small-scale traders can work their way up into a business that is *magna et copiosa* and therefore presumably without the need of deceit, they are grudgingly removed from the *sordidus* category. However, the higher professions that require higher intelligence or bring benefit to society are medicine, architecture, and the teaching of higher things (*doctrina rerum honestarum*), but he adds with typical old Roman senatorial idealism that nothing is better or more dignified than agriculture. Cicero's aristocratic snobbery about the baseness of those occupations whose products he enjoyed is not surprising given the rigidity of theoretical social divisions in the first centuries of the empire. See too the elder Cato's pejorative remarks about *faeneratores*, *De agr.*, Introd. 1.

[46] See M. I. Finley, *The Ancient Economy* (Berkeley and Los Angeles: University of California, 1973) 54–55; R. Duncan-Jones, *The Economy of the Roman Empire: Quantitative Studies* (Cambridge: Cambridge University, 1974) 21.

[47] See Finley, *Ancient Economy*, 143, 187 n. 47; C. Rodewald, *Money in the Age of Tiberius* (Manchester: Manchester University, 1976) 1–17. Though in this case many senators were also moneylenders. The creditors were often people without the same *dignitas* to lose. Trimalchio's ten million sesterces, accumulated in one day at his estate in Cumae and stored away because it was unable to be invested (*Satyr.* 54.3), is no doubt a fanciful sum; yet

Roman debt laws had by imperial times undergone considerable reform. The original right of a creditor to seize and even kill a debtor was modified and restricted as early as the Law of the Twelve Tables (ca. 450 B.C.E.), which specified a procedure of imprisonment and public notification over a period of sixty days before capital punishment or, more likely, the sale of the debtor—but beyond the Tiber. According to Livy (8.28) a *Lex Poetelia Papiria* of 326 B.C.E. abolished the formal legal power of the *nexum*, the ability of the creditor to exercise the right of personal seizure as security. However, the right of *addictio* or temporary bondage of the debtor or a dependent continued to be exercised with the consent of magistrates; it apparently involved personal confinement or forced labor with the suspension of legal rights but no permanent loss of original legal status.[48]

Beyond the practice of debt-bondage and sale, laws and customs of forfeiture of property for debt naturally developed. A *Lex Julia de bonis cedendis*, probably supplemented by a later Antonine law and expanded in the legal codes, provides for such an official procedure, a *cessio bonorum*, in which the debtor admitted insolvency before a praetor or magistrate and with official permission ceded land or goods in settlement to the creditor(s), keeping a sum sufficient to support himself. The advantage of such a legal process was that the amount of property subject to seizure was restricted and

---

Trimalchio, for all the exaggeration of the author, is to be understood as a type of a powerful rising class of moneyed merchants and investors whose financial prowess was a serious threat to the traditional landed aristocracy. In spite of the evidence of prodigious commercial and banking activity in the late republic and early empire, the modern concepts of a "money-market" or a real estate market do not apply: the absence of a system of credit, the lack of understanding of the long-range effects of taxation and price control, and the absence even of common Greek or Latin words for "land-seller," "house-seller," "property-seller," or "broker" indicate a very limited level of economic development in a society whose economy remained essentially agrarian in spite of increasing urban agglomerates. See Finley, *Ancient Economy*, esp. pp. 23, 118, 141, and the author's rejection of the LSJ rendering of *propōlēs* as "broker," pp. 203-4 n. 63.

[48] Scholarly interpretations of the Roman debt laws are abundant and by no means unanimous. See W. L. Westermann, *The Slave Systems of Greek and Roman Antiquity* (Philadelphia: American Philosophical Society, 1955) 59; M. W. Frederiksen, "Caesar, Cicero, and the Problem of Debt," *JSR* 56 (1966) 128-29; H. J. Roby, *Roman Private Law in the Times of Cicero and of the Antonines* (Aalen: Scientia, 1975) 2.296-310, 424-25; A. G. A. Leist, "Addictus," *PW* 1.352-53. In Greece, the sale of oneself or one's wife or child for private debt was supposed to have been abolished by Solon in 594 B.C.E. (Plutarch, *Solon* 13.2-3; cf. 15.3-5); there is evidence from Ptolemaic Egypt of the pledging of children as security and their consequent enslavement (Westermann, *Slave Systems*, 4-5, 30, 44, 50-51). The readers of Matt 18:23-35 must have been familiar with the sale of a debtor and his family and property as well as imprisonment. Westermann (p. 135) points out that as late as Constantine an edict of 329 C.E. limited the legal sale of a son or daughter to cases in which the sale was for the purpose of providing support for them, and the right to redemption was retained by the parents (*Cod. Just.* 3.43, 2).

supervised by officials, and so the debtor could not be left destitute. Further provisions were that the debtor did not suffer the social degradation of *infamia* and could not be prosecuted again for the same debts unless he meanwhile acquired new means of paying them. In spite of the equitable and protective aspects of such a law, however, it seems not to have been generally applied but was rather considered an unusual concession granted to a debtor for a special reason. It easily became yet another way of exercising social or political privilege and was not of much help to the poor debtor.[49] For him the laws of debt remained "uniformly harsh and unyielding," and compulsory labor, the sale of children, and the seizure of property were the usual results of insolvency.[50]

Summary

In the Deuteronomic and prophetic traditions, "the poor one" is a member of a religious category, the ʾebyôn, and is heard precisely because of his poverty and helplessness at the hands of his human oppressors. In Deuteronomy 15 the debtor forms part of the group of God's poor ones. In *Herm. Man.* 8.10 the same religious concept is at work but in a different social and religious setting. Here the poor or needy one and the debtor are still objects of human exploitation and therefore of God's special care. The pattern of debt-bondage and seizure of goods still prevails, especially for the socially powerless, as it did nearly everywhere in the ancient world in spite of periodic attempts at restrictive legislation. Hermas, however, speaks out of an economy heavily dependent on immediate cash-flow loans and investments at all levels of society.

There is almost no precedent in Christian literature for an expression of concern about Christian oppression of the poor or in particular of debtors, i.e., literature that casts the Christian as one in a position to be unjust or harsh to (not necessarily Christian) paupers and debtors. To speak theologically of his own situation Hermas therefore reaches back into the Hebrew scriptures and finds a theme that reflects similar circumstances for the believing community. Thus, *chreōstas mē thlibein kai endeeis* is another example of traditional paraenesis taken out of its original context in the Hebrew

---

[49] Though one papyrus document of mid-second-century C.E. Egypt shows the judgment of *cessio bonorum* given to an *aporos*. For the whole discussion, see Frederiksen, "Caesar," 135-36; Roby, *Roman Private Law*, 2.440.

[50] See Finley, *Ancient Economy*, 40. A senate ruling of 51 B.C.E. fixed maximum interest rates at 12 percent, a rate that held throughout the first centuries of the empire for sound investments, and rates were often lower. Loans in kind and bottomry loans were not subject to these regulations; interest on the former could go as high as 50 percent. See Duncan-Jones, *Economy*, 33 n. 3, and 133; F. Heichelheim, "Interest, Rate of," *OCD* s.v.

scriptures and used in a new context. In this new setting, economic life has changed considerably, but for some believers the challenge to function justly from a position of power is much the same.

Conclusion

Man. 8.10 is an integral part of the literary structure of the eighth *Mandate.* Its inner structure, however, is significantly different from its three parallel lists in vv. 3, 5, and 9. While these verses contain traditional lists of vices or virtues found in earlier Christian literature, v. 10 is unusual in its extended paraenetic clauses and their grammatical structure. Two of those clauses are significant for an investigation of the social constitution of Hermas' community.

Endeesteron ginesthai pantōn anthrōpōn, which occurs only in *Man.* 8.10 and 11.8, reflects the theology of the "pious poor" and indicates that for Hermas, as for many earlier Christian authors, "the poor" are to some degree synonymous with "the faithful." Poverty is a religious ideal for all, not a condition of certain segments of the community. Yet *chreōstas mē thlibein kai endeeis* sets off the debtor and the poor as just such segments of the population, subject to oppression by some Christians. For this situation there is hardly any precedent in Christian literature. Even if the supposition that debtors are classifiable with the needy may not be warranted for second-century Rome, the expression of concern that Christians are in a position to oppress them both is unavoidable. If the text of *Hermas* reflects a real situation—and there is sufficient evidence to conjecture that it does—then its religious concept of the "poor" and the social reality of Hermas' milieu do not coincide. Christians find themselves not cast exclusively or perhaps even predominantly in the role of the poor. As Dibelius remarks, "die Aufnahme der sozialen Mahnungen an Besitzende zeigt, dass das Christentum nicht mehr reine Armenreligion ist."[51]

---

[51] *Der Hirt*, 528.

V

THE SECOND *SIMILITUDE*

The second text in the *Shepherd of Hermas* to be considered with regard to the theme of rich and poor is the second *Parable*, or *Similitude*, according to traditional titles. The passage is, as Dibelius remarks, that in which the author's Christianity most appears as that of the "pious poor."[1] Yet it is the passage that also most clearly reveals the author's conflicting interests and departure from *Armenfrömmigkeit* theology.

The setting is a walk in the country, where Hermas sees an elm and a vine growing together. While he ponders the sight, the Shepherd appears, announces that the scene is a good parable of the "servants of God," and explains why: though the elm does not bear fruit and though the vine left to grow on the ground produces only poor fruit, when the vine is supported by the elm it not only bears good fruit but also provides a way for the elm to be fruitful through it. Likewise the rich one is without spiritual fruit and the poor one without material resources, but, when the wealthy one provides for the poor out of his riches and the poor in turn provides for the wealthy prayer and intercession that are powerful before God, both together accomplish the work of the Lord. Moreover, in time of drought the elm retains water and nourishes the vine with it so that the vine can continue to bear fruit both for itself and for the elm. In a similar fashion do rich and poor complete what is lacking in each other.

The accounts of contemporary agriculturalists show that Hermas was describing not the romantic vision of a lone, stately elm with an equally lone, gnarled wild grapevine wending its way gracefully up the massive trunk.[2] On the contrary, what Hermas was contemplating was no doubt an *arbustum*, a whole field, possibly sown in grain, with elm trees neatly arranged at twenty- or forty-foot intervals. The trees were lopped off at a maximum height of twenty feet and carefully trimmed so that they spread their few branches

---

[1] *Der Hirt*, 555: "Es ist die Stelle unseres Buches, an der sein Christentum am meisten als *Armenfrömmigkeit* erscheint."

[2] This is what is usually imagined; see the modern illustrations in P. Demetz, "The Elm and the Vine: Notes Toward the History of a Marriage Topos," *Proceedings of the Modern Language Association* 73 (1958) 521—32; L. Alfonsi, "La vite e l'olmo," *VC* 21 (1967) 81—86.

widely into a latticework that received anywhere from three to ten vines planted closely around the base of the tree. The vines were strung up to the first level of branches like vertical garlands and then horizontally across the width of branches and up to the next level, forming a patchwork of elm foliage (trimmed and therefore kept to a minimum), vine foliage, and grape clusters, apparently woven together and hardly distinguishable except at close range.

The parable is a carefully constructed use of a common sight well known to the author's contemporaries as a viticultural method. The image was frequently used by Latin writers for erotic and marital symbolism. Its use to describe the relationship of social groups to one another, however, is unknown elsewhere either before or after *Hermas* except by a few later Christian writers, who are probably dependent on the account in *Sim.* 2.[3]

Comparison with *1 Clem.* 38.2

There is a brief passage in *1 Clement* that uses language strikingly reminiscent of that of the second *Similitude* of *Hermas*:

ὁ πλούσιος ἐπιχορηγείτω τῷ πτωχῷ, ὁ δὲ πτωχὸς εὐχαριστείτω τῷ θεῷ, ὅτι ἔδωκεν αὐτῷ δι' οὗ ἀναπληρωθῇ αὐτοῦ τὸ ὑστέρημα.

Let the rich one supply what is needed to the poor and let the poor one give thanks to God that he has given him one through whom what he lacks may be furnished.[4]

Twice in *Sim.* 2 the same verb, *epichorēgeō* is used of the rich toward the poor: ὅταν . . . ὁ πλούσιος καὶ χορηγῇ αὐτῷ τὰ δέοντα ("when . . . the rich one supplies for him his needs," v. 5c) and ἐπιχορηγεῖ οὖν ὁ πλούσιος τῷ πένητι ("the rich person supplies for the poor," v. 5d). Once, both of the verbs that are used in *1 Clem.* 38.2 occur in the same relationship in *Sim.* 2: ὁ πένης οὖν ἐπιχορηγούμενος ὑπὸ τοῦ πλουσίου ἐντυγχάνει τῷ θεῷ εὐχαριστῶν αὐτῷ, ὑπὲρ τοῦ διδόντος αὐτῷ ("the poor one, supplied by the rich, prays to God thanking him for the one who gives to him," v.6).[5]

The passage in *1 Clement* is part of a paraenesis on mutual responsive-

---

[3] For further detail, see Appendix C.

[4] *1 Clem.* 38.2. For critical texts and commentaries, see J. B. Lightfoot, *The Apostolic Fathers*; Part 1. *S. Clement of Rome* (2 vols.; 2nd ed.; London and New York: Macmillan, 1890); R. Knopf, *Der erste Clemensbrief* (TU 20,1; Leipzig: J. C. Hinrichs, 1901); A. Jaubert, *Clément de Rome: Epître aux Corinthiens* (SC 167; Paris: Editions du Cerf, 1971).

[5] For the full translation of *Sim.* 2, see Appendix A.

ness that begins at 37.1. Just before, at 36.5, a brief exegesis of Ps 110:1 leads to the identification in 36.6 of the "enemies" of the psalm verse as the wicked and those who oppose the will of God. Then follows a chain of key-word connections. Seemingly as a response to the warfare image suggested by "enemies" (*echthroi*), 37.1 exhorts the reader to serve wholeheartedly in the militia of Jesus Christ. From there vv. 2-3 focus on Christian leaders as analogous to a variety of military officers each of whom carries out his duties according to his rank.[6] But not all can be officers. Hence the theme of interdependence in v. 4: the great (*hoi megaloi*) cannot live and function without the insignificant (*hoi mikroi*) and vice versa, and this is to their mutual usefulness.[7] The presentation in v. 5 of the body as an example is reminiscent of 1 Cor 12:14-21 in ideas if not in language.[8] The analogy ends, however, with the conclusion that all the parts of the body function together in a common submission for the good of the whole—an idea foreign to 1 Corinthians 12 (though not to Eph 1:22-23 and 4:11-12) but quite useful to Clement's general purpose of bringing about peace in a community torn by an authority crisis.[9]

The transition from 37.5 to 38.1 is made by catchwords: all the members work together in a common submission (*hypotagē*) to save the whole body (37.5). The exhortation follows in 38.1 to let the whole body be saved in Christ Jesus and to let each be subject to his neighbor (*hypotassesthō hekastos tō plēsion autou*) according to the *charisma* appointed to him—an idea not at all the same as the common submission in 37.5, but one well suited to Clement's purpose. Examples of *charismata* then follow. At the same time, 38.2 extends the mutuality theme begun at 37.4 and carried through 37.5

---

[6] Lightfoot (*Apostolic Fathers*, 1.2, 114—15) observes that the *eparchoi, chiliarchoi*, and *hekatontarchai* of 37.3 probably correspond to praetorian prefects, tribunes, and centurions; but for *pentēkontarchoi* there is no known Roman military correlate. Jaubert (*Clément*, 80) refers to Israelite military organization (see Exod 18:21, 25; Deut 1:15; 1 Macc 3:55; each of these texts mentions also an officer who is placed over ten soldiers, but there is no such rank in *1 Clement*).

[7] *En toutois chrēsis*, "therein is utility" (Lightfoot); "herein lies the advantage" (Lake) with the Greek manuscripts. Knopf and Jaubert (in translation) take the Latin *aliud alio opus est* seeming to imply *en allēlois chrēsis*.

[8] Compare the Stoic concept of the harmonious working of the cosmic organism, e.g., M. Aurel. 7.9 (partially quoted by Dibelius, *Der Hirt*, 553).

[9] All indications point to the conflict in the Corinthian community as one between lesser and greater officers and/or between older and younger leadership. It cannot be assumed from this brief treatment in a paraenetic context that the actual situation was polarized between social classes. For a general discussion of the purpose and the situation of the letter, see Lightfoot, *Apostolic Fathers* 1.1.

with the image of the body: let the strong take care of[10] the weak and let the weak show respect for the strong (*ho ischyros tēmeleitō ton asthenē, ho de asthenēs entrepesthō ton ischyron*), again reminiscent of a Pauline theme though the language and the context are different.[11] The rich are to help the poor, and the poor are to render thanks to God for the help.[12] The wise must show wisdom not in words but in deeds. The humble-minded must leave it to the other to bear witness to his virtue. The one who is pure in the flesh[13] must be mindful that his gift of continence is not from himself. Here the list of spiritual gifts ends; 38.3 is a brief meditation on creation and human dependence on God, terminating in a simple doxology in 38.4.

The saying about rich and poor in *1 Clem.* 38.2 has in common with *Sim.* 2.5c–d, 6 the presentation of complementary roles between the two groups and use of the word *epichorēgeō* for the duty of the rich to the poor as well as in one case *eucharistein tō theō* (v. 6) for the response of the poor one—who is, however, a *ptōchos* in *1 Clement* and a *penēs* in *Sim.* 2. In these passages, both poverty and wealth can be construed as spiritual gifts or important elements in the community—in *1 Clem.* 38.2 on the basis of the exegesis developed above regarding the *charismata* of 38.1 and in *Sim.* 2 because one of the major points of the parable is that both social groups have an important role to play in the community vis-à-vis one another. There the similarity stops, however, and some important differences must be pointed out. The brief saying in *1 Clement* occurs in a paraenetic passage in which exhortations are addressed to several categories of people, presumably in the community. *Sim.* 2, on the other hand, is an entire chapter devoted to the roles of rich and poor regarding each other. This produces a notable difference of emphasis.

The most important difference between the two passages is the way in which the complementarity is worked out. In *1 Clem.* 37.4–5 the correlations

---

[10] *Tēmeleitō* (Knopf and Jaubert); or *mē atēmeleitō* (Lightfoot), "not neglect," which could be the original reading, confused through haplography (see Lightfoot, *Apostolic Fathers* 1.2, 116).

[11] See Rom 14:1–2 (*asthenōn*); 1 Cor 8:9 (*exousia—asthenēs*); 9:22 (*asthenēs*); Rom 15:1 (*asthenēs—dynatos*); but cf. 1 Cor 1:27 (*asthenēs—ischyros*). All these contexts except the last seem to refer to food laws, a problem not treated here in *1 Clement*. It is either coincidentally or deliberately ironic, however, that *1 Clement* is presumably from one church in which Paul used the weak—strong image to another in which he employed the same image.

[12] Here ends the sense of parallelism and mutual benefit begun at 37.4: great—small, head—feet (37.5), strong—weak, rich—poor (38.2). The *sophos* of the next phrase could possibly be parallel to the *ischyros* above, but hardly to the *plousios* in between. Nor could the *tapeinophrōn* who follows be complementary to the *sophos*. *Tapeinophrosynē* is opposed to *hybris* (Prov 29:23), *megalorēmosynē* (Ign. *Eph.* 10.2), or *hypsēlophrosynē* (*Barn.* 9.3) and therefore is more to be identified with than opposed to *sophia*.

great—small and head—feet clearly develop the idea that *both* sides are necessary, that one cannot exist and function normally without the other; and 38.1 exhorts *each* to submit to the neighbor according to the role given. But the examples in 38.2 fall short of these ideals. While the strong have a definite contribution to make in caring for the weak, the weak can only show deference to (*entrepeō*[14]) the strong; while the rich have the important role of materially helping the poor, the poor can only thank God that the help comes.[15] The weak and the poor are left in a position of subservience and cannot really do anything to be *useful* to their benefactors.

Sim. 2 is explicit at several points that the effectiveness is mutual. Instead of being able to respond only with gratitude, the poor recipient of charity has the reciprocal power of *enteuxis*, intercessory prayer, in which he is rich and in which the rich are weak and poor: ὁ μὲν πλούσιος ἔχει χρήματα, τὰ δὲ πρὸς τὸν κύριον πτωχεύει (v. 5a) . . . ὁ πένης πλούσιός ἐστιν ἐν τῇ ἐντεύξει καὶ ἐν τῇ ἐξομολογήσει καὶ δύναμιν μεγάλην ἔχει παρὰ τῷ θεῷ ἡ ἔντευξις αὐτοῦ (v. 5c) . . . ὅτι ἡ τοῦ πένητος ἔντευξις προσδεκτή ἐστιν καὶ πλουσία πρὸς κύριον (v. 6). Moreover, twice in *Sim.* 2 the view is explicitly set forth that *together* both groups complete a joint spiritual effort: ἀμφότεροι οὖν τὸ ἔργον τελοῦσιν (v. 7a); γίνονται οὖν ἀμφότεροι κοινωνοὶ τοῦ ἔργου τοῦ δικαίου (v. 9a). The process is envisioned as a mutual fulfilling of or complementing (*plērophorein*) what is lacking on either side: οὕτως καὶ οἱ πένητες ὑπὲρ τῶν πλουσίων ἐντυγχάνοντες πρὸς τὸν κύριον πληροφοροῦσι τὸ πλοῦτος αὐτῶν (i.e., the wealth of the rich), καὶ πάλιν οἱ πλούσιοι χορηγοῦντες τοῖς πένησι τὰ δέοντα πληροφοροῦσι τὰς εὐχὰς[16] αὐτῶν (i.e., the prayers of the poor) (v. 8b).

Although *1 Clem.* 37.4, 5 presents a similar but weaker picture of mutual helpfulness, 38.2 does not continue and develop the theme. If it is true, as Dibelius remarks, that Hermas has more feeling than has Clement for the neediness of the rich,[17] it is equally true that he has far greater feeling for the spiritual power of the poor.

---

[13] Probably a reference to sexual abstinence, identified at the end of the sentence with *enkrateia* (cf. Ign. *Pol.* 5).

[14] With gen. pers. "turn towards, give heed or regard to, respect, reverence" (LSJ s.v., second meaning).

[15] Jaubert (*Clément*, 162-63) notes a possible alternative translation of *hoti edōken autǭ di' hou anaplērōthē autou to hysterēma*: "d'avoir donné au riche de quoi combler son indigence." This is grammatically possible but not likely, both because the most immediately obvious antecedent of *autǭ* is *ho ptōchos* and because the strong one of the preceding statement has no need posited of him.

[16] In spite of the better textual evidence for *psychas*, followed by Whittaker, Lake's reconstruction *euchas* makes better sense in context.

[17] *Der Hirt*, 555. In the light of the above analysis, however, Dibelius is simply uncritical

Summary

One short sentence in *1 Clem.* 38.2 bears an interesting similarity of language and idea to the second *Similitude* of *Hermas*, both in the use of *epichorēgeō* for the action of the rich toward the poor and in the corresponding action of the poor in giving thanks to God (*Sim.* 2.5c-d, 6). The brevity of the passage in *1 Clement* in contrast to the full development of the theme in *Sim.* 2 provides a sharp difference in emphasis. The greatest contrast is the absence in *1 Clem.* 38.2 of the strong sense of mutual usefulness that is dominant in *Herm. Sim.* 2 and produces a notably different theology of community there. The similarities suggest that Clement may be drawing on a parallel tradition and possibly even that *1 Clem.* 38.2, undoubtedly known in the Roman Church, may have influenced the social theology of the author of the second *Similitude* of *Hermas*.

The Perspective of *Sim.* 2

Terminology

In *Sim.* 2 the rich are called *hoi plousioi* except in the macarism at the end of the chapter (v. 10). There they are *hoi echontes*, as in *Vis.* 3.9.4. The word *plousios* occurs elsewhere in *Hermas* only in *Sim.* 9.20.1-2, but *ploutos* and *plouteō* appear several times.[18] Although *plousios* is used infrequently in *Hermas*, its clear reference to a member of the community in *Sim.* 2 indicates that in the whole *Shepherd* as it now stands there is no attempt to avoid using the term to refer to a Christian, as there is in Luke.[19]

The ordinary words for the poor, *ptōchos* and *penēs*, do not occur in *Hermas* outside *Sim.* 2.[20] Elsewhere the poor are *hysteroumenoi* and less frequently *endeeis* and *peinōntes*. Within *Sim.* 2 *ptōchos* appears only in v. 4d, where the exact application of the parable is first set forth: *hautē oun hē parabolē eis tous doulous tou theou keitai, eis ptōchon kai plousion*.[21]

(ibid.) when he says "In ähnlicher Weise (i.e., similar to *Sim.* 2) ist die gegenseitige Ergänzung auch *1 Clem.* 38.2 gefordert." It is precisely the lack of *Gegenseitigkeit* that is the point.

[18] *Ploutos* in *Vis.* 1.1.8; 3.6.5-6; 3.9.6; *Man.* 10.1.4; *Sim.* 1.8; *plouteō* in *Vis.* 3.6.7; *Sim.* 1.9; 8.9.1.

[19] See above, pp. 29-31.

[20] See above, pp. 40-41.

[21] On the juxtaposition of opposites in Hellenistic literature, see H. Riesenfeld, "Accouplements de termes contradictoires dans le N.T.," *ConNT* 9 (Lund: Gleerup, 1944) 1-21; esp. Plato *Theaet.* 24 (175A); Rev 13:16 (*plousios—ptōchos*); Dio Chrys. 25.1 (*plousios—penēs*); see also BAG s.vv.; Tatian *Orat.* 11.1, 2; 32.1.

This is the sole appearance of the common word *ptōchos* in *Hermas*.[22] In *Sim.* 2.5b the verb *ptōcheuō* is used figuratively to describe the rich who are poor in prayer and confession, while the poor are rich in these qualities (v. 5c; cf. Jas 2:5). After v. 4d the word consistently used for the poor in *Sim.* 2 is *penēs*, which occurs in v. 5c (three times); 5d; 6a (three times); 7a, b, c; 8b (twice)—a total of twelve times—but nowhere else in *Hermas*. On this evidence alone an independent source for the application of the parable seems likely.[23] The often cited distinction made by Aristophanes between *ptōchos* and *penēs* is clearly not applicable here.[24] *Ptōchos* and *penēs* seem to be interchangeable.

Theology

In order to explore the distinctive theology and paraenesis of rich and poor in the second *Similitude*, the same four questions that were asked in the discussion of Luke, James, and the other material in *Hermas* will be examined with regard to *Sim.* 2.

Who are the poor and who are the rich in the eyes of God?

In contrast to other passages discussed (e.g., *Vis.* 1.1.8–9; 3.9.2–6), the rich are not here objects of condemnation for their activity or of a call to repentance. Similarly, the poor are not merely objects of the neglect or dutiful charity of the rich (e.g., *Sim.* 1.8; 5.3.7). Here the two groups are clearly defined and different, but both are explicitly valuable. If the rich one is poor regarding the Lord (v. 5b), he has nevertheless received his wealth from the Lord (v. 7b) and with it accomplishes a great and acceptable work (v. 7c). However, the traditional bias in favor of the poor remains. If the rich person is poor in the things of God (v. 5b), the poor one is rich in intercession and thanksgiving (v. 5c), and that prayer is powerful before God (*dyna-*

---

[22] *Vis.* 3.12.2 couples *ptōchotēs* with *astheneia* to describe old age; it is more likely that lack of physical vigor is intended here, even though the subject goes on to receive an inheritance. This is the only use of the uncommon word *ptōchotēs* in the literature indexed by BAG.

[23] On the other hand, the unusual word *adistaktōs*, "without doubting, without hesitating," occurs twice in *Sim.* 2 (vv. 5d, 7b) and also in *Man.* 9.2, 4, 6; *Sim.* 8.10.3; 9.24.2; 9.29.2, but nowhere else in earlier Christian literature (see BAG s.v.). Its use in the discourse on *dipsychia* in *Man.* 9 suggests that the attitude and behavior it represents may be for the author the opposite of *dipsychia*.

[24] *Plutus* 552–64. For the *ptōchos* life means having nothing; for the *penēs* life means working hard and having neither abundance of anything nor lack of what is necessary. The distinction was already blurred in the LXX, where the two terms are often combined, e.g., Ps 108 (109):16, 22 (see above, chapter II, n. 5). See further Finley, *Ancient Economy*, 41; Dupont, *Béatitudes* 2.19–34.

min megalēn echei para tǫ theǫ hē enteuxis autou, v. 5c; cf. v. 6).[25] It is the latter statement especially that recalls the whole theology of the "pious poor" and their oppressors e.g., Deut 24:15; Sir 4:6; 35:12–17; Jas 5:4; *Vis.* 3.9.6) but in a positive way—to bring help to their benefactors.

How should rich and poor relate to one another?

The obvious answer is: in mutual dependence. The whole point of the story is that each group has an important role to play for the other and both together accomplish the task (*amphoteroi oun to ergon telousin,* v. 7a; *ginontai oun amphoteroi koinōnoi tou ergou tou dikaiou,* v. 9a). This is the position developed throughout the explanation of the parable in vv. 5–9. It stands in contrast to the expectation expressed elsewhere in *Hermas* and in the whole previous literature of the "pious poor" that it is only the rich who have an obligation toward the poor and that the poor have no complementary responsibility.

A related question centers on the correlates of the two symbolic elements in the parable: which is the elm and which is the vine? The correlation is nowhere explicit. One way of reading the text can suggest that the poor are the elm, which supports the vine—the rich—by their prayer and intercession. The order of elm and vine in v. 1 matches the order of poor and rich in v. 4d. The vine cannot bear good fruit unless it is cast upon the elm (vv. 3a, b, 4c), and when this does happen the elm bears more fruit, not less, than the vine (v. 4a). Even so, the rich have no power before God without the support of the intercession of the poor (v. 5b), but with this intercession they and their wealth become fruitful (v. 5c). This last mentioned verse, 5c, is especially open to the present interpretation: *hotan oun epanapaę̄*[26]*epi ton penēta ho plousios,* taking the first meaning of *epanapauomai,* i.e., "rest upon."[27] In this case the meaning is that when the rich person (the vine) rests upon (the spiritual strength of) the poor (the elm) and supplies what he needs, namely, material support, then the rich one believes that what is done to the poor will find its reward with God—the reward, that is, of being supported before God by the intercession of the poor.

---

[25] *Enteuxis* can mean "petition," "prayer," or specifically, "prayer of intercession." Because in *Sim.* 2 the focus of the *enteuxis* of the poor is on its benefit to the rich, "intercession" seems to be the most suitable translation. *Exomologēsis* occurs only here in early Christian literature indexed by BAG (though the verb is common; see the participial combination with *entugchanō* in *Man.* 10.3.2) and should be rendered in the sense of "prayer of thanksgiving" (BAG s.v. and Dibelius, *Der Hirt,* on *Man.* 10.3.2, p. 535).

[26] This is the preferred reading from POxy. For the textual problem, see Appendix A, n. 3.; Dibelius, *Der Hirt,* 555. The second aorist passive form *-paēn* is also attested in *Did.* 4.2 as well as the future passive *-paēsomai* in Luke 10:6 and Rev 14:13. See BAG s.v. *epanapauomai.*

[27] LSJ and BAG s.v.

This interpretation, however, meets with some difficulties. The image of bearing fruit is already a firmly established Christian metaphor for spiritual growth and productivity.[28] The fruitfulness of the vine in *Sim.* 2 is more likely a symbol of prayer than one of material abundance, making the vine correspond to the poor. Likewise the activity of the rich, to supply what is lacking (vv. 5c, 8b; cf. 5d, 6, 7a), corresponds more easily to the elm, which furnishes the necessary support for the growth and fruitfulness of the vine. Moreover, the epilogue of the parable (v. 8a), which adds the detail of the elm supplying continuous water to the vine in time of drought, does not make sense if the elm is the poor and the vine, the rich. In that case the poor would be providing continuous intercession in difficult times in order[29] to keep the wealthy wealthy so that they can supply double fruit, i.e., material support not only for themselves but also for the poor. Such a description is theologically feasible but not at all to the point of *Sim.* 2. Similarly, because the elm is thought to bear no fruit of its own (vv. 3a, 8a), it is difficult to see how the poor could be intended since the whole perspective of the parable is spiritual effectiveness, not material, and the spiritual power of the poor is never questioned. The unusual word *adialeiptos,* "increasing," "constant," "lacking nothing"[30] is used twice in *Sim.* 2, first to apply to the life of the poor because of the ministrations of the rich (v. 6), second to describe the water supplied to the vine by the elm (v. 8a), suggesting that the two relationships are parallel. Finally, the difficult phrase *hotan oun epanapaȩ epi ton penēta ho plousios* (v. 5c) can be taken in another sense. *Epanapauomai,* besides meaning "rest upon," is also attested in Hellenistic usage meaning "rely upon."[31] This meaning fits well the context of *Sim.* 2.5: when the rich person relies upon the poor (for intercession) and supplies what he needs, he believes that what is done to the poor will find its reward before God.

The parable reads more easily, then, if the elm is understood to be the rich and the vine, the poor. This was undoubtedly the author's intention. The fact that the correspondences are neither immediately apparent nor explicitly stated, gives rise to three observations: (1) that we have here more truly a parable form than the allegory typical of the rest of the *Similitudes*; (2) that interdependence is the point stressed, not correlation of symbols; (3) that the mutual dependence of rich and poor envisioned by the author is enhanced by the very ambiguity of the text.

---

[28] See esp. Matt 3:8, 10 par. Luke 3:8, 9; Mark 4:7-8 and pars.; Rom 6:21-22; 7:4-5; Heb 12:11; Jas 3:17-18; cf. *Sim.* 4.3.5, 8; 9.19.2.

[29] V. 8a is to be understood as a parataxis.

[30] BAG s.v.

What are the ethical/theological implications of wealth, considered apart from the question of responsibility to the poor?

There is no condemnation of the wealthy for their conduct, nor are they expected to divest themselves of their wealth except by using it in the right way. In *Sim.* 1, spiritual wealth is preferred (1.8-11), and the way to acquire it is spelled out in v. 8—spending one's wealth and investments on "afflicted souls" such as widows and orphans. This is indeed the reason why God has given material wealth to some (v. 9), and its proper use is the means for acquiring the superior kind of wealth, that which is spiritual (vv. 10-11; cf. *misthos* in 2.5c).

Sim. 2 expands the same line of thought by paradoxically juxtaposing the wealth of the poor and the poverty of the wealthy. The spiritual wealth of the poor is a familiar theme;[32] the motif of the spiritual poverty of the wealthy *as redeemable* is less common. V. 5b describes the wealthy one as poor in the things of God because he is distracted about his wealth (*perispōmenos peri ton plouton heautou*).[33] His intercession and thanksgiving are therefore weak, small, and ineffective (*blēchran kai mikran kai megalēn*[34] *mē echousan dynamin*). He is no less favored by God, however, for he has an essential role to play in the common effort of the community. Both the poor who pray well and the rich who share their wealth will receive the promise of blessing: they shall not be abandoned by God but rather recorded in the books of the living (v. 9b; cf. *Vis.* 1.3.2). Though the poor have some spiritual advantage from the beginning, the rich have an equal chance to be saved.[35]

To whom is the parable addressed?

Throughout the chapter both rich and poor are described in the third person. While the poor have the spiritual advantage from the beginning, both they and the rich are given equal attention. The decisive point comes in

---

[31] Epict. *Disc.* 1.9.9; Mic 3:11; Rom 2:17; see BAG, LSJ, *LPGL* s.v.

[32] See esp. *T. Gad* 7.6 (*ho gar penēs . . . hyper pantas ploutei, hoti ouk echei ton perispasmon tōn mataiōn anthrōpōn*); Jas 2:5; perhaps Rev 2:9.

[33] Cf. *Sim.* 4.5. *Perispasthai* is a frequent term for distraction toward worldly matters (Epict. *Disc.* 4.1.159; M. Aurel. 2.7.1; 4.3.3; 6.22; 8.1; *T. Gad* 7.6; Dibelius, *Der Hirt*, 554-55).

[34] See the reasons for this suggested emendation in Appendix A, n. 2.

[35] The data of *Sim.* 1 and 2 could be interpreted so as to put the rich in an ethical dilemma: material wealth should be spent on charitable works (1.8) and this is according to divine plan (1.9); it should not be sought after (1.10); it is the reason why the prayer of the rich is ineffectual (2.5); yet it is the actual means by which the wealthy work out their salvation (2.5c, 7c, 10), i.e., wealth is not to be sought but is eminently useful when possessed. Perfect logical consistency cannot be asked of paraenetic material of this type.

the last verse, which unexpectedly breaks out into a macarism of the wealthy
who understand that their wealth comes from the Lord (*makarioi hoi echontes kai synientes, hoti para tou kypiou ploutizontai*), for the one who understands this will be able to perform some good service (*ho gar syniōn touto
dynēsetai kai diakonēsai ti agathon*,[36] v. 10). A blessing pronounced in favor
of the rich is unknown in Christian tradition before Hermas.[37] The blessing
is conditional, to be sure, and depends on right understanding and a will to
act correctly by spending one's wealth in the service of those who need it.
The author refrains, perhaps deliberately, from saying plainly *makarioi hoi
plousioi*, which would perhaps have been too blatant, too much a break with
tradition; but the constant use of *plousioi* in the passage makes clear that
that is what he means. The introduction of a prophetic promise in v. 9b
breaks with the narrative form that began in v. 5a. This promise and the
blessing of v. 10 are extraneous to the movement of the parable and may
have been added by the final redactor. V. 10 makes clear the purpose of the
whole parable as intended by the redactor: it is addressed to the rich and
contains implicitly the admonition to understand the meaning and reason
for their wealth.

The second *Similitude* represents one of the best efforts at creative
theology in the *Shepherd*. The traditional preference for the poor, with
which the author shows a definitive sympathy, is confronted by the conviction that being wealthy is not evil but provides an important way of serving
God. The theological tension between the value of being rich and the value
of being poor is at its strongest here, and it is resolved by a compromise
which, instead of combining the weaknesses of both sides, emphasizes the
strengths of both. Yet the evidence remains from 2.10 that it is primarily the
rich and not the poor who are being reassured that they do indeed have an
important part in the whole community.

Summary

The term used for the rich in *Sim.* 2 is the familiar *plousioi* except in
v. 10. The words used for the poor, *ptōchos* and *penēs*, are used in the
Shepherd only in *Sim.* 2. The rich person is considered poor in the eyes of
God, yet is not condemned for being wealthy; he has received his wealth

---

[36] Dibelius (*Der Hirt*, 557) here chooses the shorter form *diakonēsai ti* without *agathon*,
following the Berlin Papyrus and Vulgate Latin manuscripts against POxy. and the Palatine
Latin and Ethiopic translations, on the basis of the absolute use of *diakonian telein* in *Man.* 2.6;
Sim. 1.9 and 2.7c (where the same ministry of generosity to the needy is envisioned).

[37] It is natural to see Clement of Alexandria's treatise *Quis Dives Salvetur* as the next step
in this development (Dibelius, *Der Hirt*, 555–56; Dibelius/Greeven, *James*, 45; Hengel, *Property and Riches*, 58).

from the Lord for a purpose. The poor retain their traditional favored status with God as in the theology of the "pious poor." Rich and poor are to relate to one another in mutual dependence, each supplying what the other lacks, the rich supplying material support of the poor and the poor supplying effective intercession before God for the rich. Though it is not specifically stated, the parable and the explanation fit together more smoothly when the elm is understood to be the rich and the vine, the poor, rather than vice versa. The wealth of the poor and the poverty of the rich are paradoxically juxtaposed in such a way that both groups are essential to the common work and to one another. Even if the poor have an advantage in the spiritual realm, both have equal access to salvation through the sharing of their strength. Here the theological creativity of the author is most manifest. Unexpectedly the last verse of the chapter contains a blessing for the wealthy on the condition that they understand the true reason for their wealth. This theological shift and the change of terminology for the wealthy suggest that vv. 9b–10 may have been added by the redactor. These concluding lines make it clear that the parable as it stands is addressed to the rich and is intended for their exhortation and consolation.

Conclusion

In order to understand the significance of the second *Similitude* for Hermas' theology of rich and poor, we have investigated the literary and theological relationship of the parable to a short passage with similar language in *1 Clement*. The investigation has yielded the following results.

The brief passage in *1 Clem.* 38.2 resembles the language and thought of *Sim.* 2 regarding the contribution of the rich, but it fails to develop the reciprocal contribution of the poor to the rich and consequently falls short of the model of mutual service proposed in the second *Similitude*.

Outside *Sim.* 2 the material about the rich focuses on the dangers of wealth for the Christian and its adverse effects on the community. *Sim.* 1 and 2, on the contrary, focus on the positive aspect of wealth and its advantages for the community. *Sim.* 1 develops a Christian theology of wealth that goes beyond mistrust of riches and the superior quality of spiritual wealth to posit a divine plan behind the presence of wealthy members in the community. *Sim.* 2 carries this position forward and weaves it into a symmetrical design, interlacing need and fulfillment of need between rich and poor. The treatment of wealth outside *Sim.* 2 does not contradict this position; it simply looks at the reality from the other side. The only exception is the thrice articulated theme of the uselessness of the wealthy with their wealth, but even within these texts a compromise with the tone of the rest of the book is reached.

The variety of theological perspectives and the variety of literary genres within which the problem of wealth is treated in *Hermas* indicate not only a strong preoccupation on the part of the author but also a complex real situation with which he is creatively struggling. The mutual dependence of rich and poor and the blessing pronounced on those with possessions in *Sim.* 2.10 represent new directions in the early Church's search for a viable existence within its own social context.

RICH AND POOR IN SECOND-CENTURY ROME

The conclusions that have been reached in the preceding chapters provide the bases for the discussion of this chapter. They may be repeated briefly.

First, the possession and proper use of wealth are of great concern to the author or editor of *Hermas*. After the major themes of repentance and doublemindedness, wealth remains one of the most frequently discussed issues throughout the book in a variety of literary genres and contexts.

Second, though the author attempts to retain and speak from a theology of the "pious poor," the credibility of that theological framework is being stretched by the presence of wealthy members in the community. Therefore, "poor" and "rich" must refer primarily to economic realities. In contrast to the Gospel of Luke and the Epistle of James, these terms in *Hermas* are used in such a way that they cannot be understood as theological terms for believers versus outsiders. The wealthy described by Hermas are clearly insiders.

Third, there is sufficient evidence to conclude that the problem of wealth is associated in the mind of the author with preoccupation with business and worldly concerns. This wealth is therefore largely acquired through commercial transactions.

Fourth, the treatment of wealth is not limited to stern conventional warnings about the difficulties for individuals who expect to have both riches and salvation. The author also raises concerns about how preoccupation with wealth and business on the part of some affects the general quality of Christian life in the community.

Fifth, the poor are spoken of only in the context of their relationship with the rich, and usually only from the perspective of the responsibility of those who are in a position either to help or to oppress them. The poor as such are never spoken of alone, nor are they directly addressed, as are the rich on several occasions.

Who Are the Rich?

When speaking of "social classes" in imperial Rome, one should keep in

mind the three social classifications distinguished by M. I. Finley.[1] The first
and most obvious group for Rome is the *ordo* or estate, understood as "a
juridically defined group within a population, possessing formalized privileges and disabilities . . . and *standing in a hierarchical relation to other
orders.*" Though in theory both freeborn plebeians and freedmen constituted
ordines, in reality the term referred only to the senatorial and equestrian
categories, those properly referred to as "aristocrats" along with the elite
families of the provinces who through the conferral of citizenship and privilege became part of the same system. "Class" is more difficult to define; it
suggests "persistent uncertainty" about boundaries, membership, and criteria, yet it is a "safe but vague" means of classification.[2] It is in that general
sense that the term "lower classes" appears below to designate all those not
belonging to the *ordines*. It is not a satisfactory expression, for it includes a
freeborn plebeian sunk in poverty, a well-fed house slave, or a ridiculously
wealthy freedman like Narcissus, Pallas, or Petronius's Trimalchio. To com-
pensate for the overly broad word "class," Finley suggests a third distinction,
"status"—"an admirably vague word with a considerable psychological element." It designates those ordered relationships with no legal basis which
nevertheless structure social behavior inevitably into a variety of "pecking
orders": the self-designated "nobility" of consular families within the senatorial *ordo*; the reason a Pompeiian could refer to himself as *princeps liber-
tinorum*, first among freedmen;[3] the reason for shifts in lifestyle and values
among those who considered themselves upwardly mobile.

Evidence for Aristocrats

Commentators have recognized that there were people in Hermas' community with considerable possessions and property.[4] The first possibility is
that aristocratic Christians, i.e., of the senatorial and equestrian classes, are intended.

Pomponia Graecina

Pomponia Graecina, wife of Aulus Plautius,[5] was accused in 57 or 58 C.E.
of *superstitio externa*, tried by her husband in the presence of the whole

---

[1] *Ancient Economy*, 46-51. See too the remarks on this topic in J. Gagé, *Les classes
sociales dans l'Empire romain* (Paris: Payot, 1964) 37-42.

[2] Gagé (*Classes sociales*, 41-42) offers as examples of nonformalized classes that developed during the empire the municipal bourgeoisie, the military, and freedmen.

[3] *CIL* 4.117.

[4] E.g., Dibelius, *Der Hirt*, 528; Joly, *Pasteur*, 36.

[5] *Consul suffectus* of 29 C.E., governor of Pannonia in 43, commander of Claudius's
British expedition; Dio Cass. 60.19-21. Cf. *PIR*[1] P344 Aulus Plautius; P579 Pomponia Graecina.

familia, according to the ancient custom, and acquitted.[6] There is nothing unusual about the report; the popularity of foreign cults among the upper classes is well known for the period beginning just after this.[7]

In the catacomb of Callistus on the Via Appia the name *POMPONIOS GRĒKEINOS* was reconstructed from two fragments of a Greek inscription. On the basis of this single piece of evidence, several modern historians and archaeologists, including G. B. de Rossi, have concluded that the *superstitio* of which Pomponia Graecina was accused was indeed Christianity and that the inscription was of a descendant of hers. But no ancient Church writer speaks of such a tradition, and a Greek inscription from a senatorial family in Rome in the second or third century is most unlikely. The case for the Christianity of Pomponia Graecina can be dismissed.[8]

T. Flavius Clemens, Flavia Domitilla, M. Acilius Glabrio

Thirty-eight years after the trial of Pomponia Graecina, Domitian ordered the execution of the consul Titus Flavius Clemens and Manlius Acilius Glabrio, who had been consul with Trajan in 91 C.E. At the same time, Clemens's wife, Flavia Domitilla, who was also Domitian's niece, was exiled to the island of Pandateria.[9] The charges were atheism and Jewish customs according to the account of Dio Cassius.[10] Eusebius repeats part of the story

---

[6] Tac. *Ann.* 13.32. Pliny (*Ep.* 10.96.8-9) calls Christianity *superstitio*, but the term is common for "unreasonable religious belief" in contrast to *religio*, sensible religion. See Lewis and Short, *Latin Dictionary*, s.v. See too Min. Felix, *Octavius* 1.5, where the terms are reversed by a Christian: paganism becomes *superstitio*, Christianity *religio*.

[7] One thinks immediately of the scandalous incident involving the matron Paulina and the equestrian Decius Mundus under Tiberius (Tac. *Ann.* 2.85; cf. Suet. *Tib.* 36; Jos. *Ant.* 18.3.4 §§65-80) several years earlier. See J. Beaujeu, *La religion romaine à l'apogée de l'Empire*. Vol. I: *La politique religieuse des Antonins* (Paris: Belles Lettres, 1955) 67-75. A. D. Nock ("Religious Developments from the Close of the Republic to the Death of Nero," *CAH* 10.503) conjectures that the real charge may have been adultery, but as he himself points out, neither Paulina (in whose case the offense was clearly sexual) nor Fulvia (Jos. *Ant.* 18.3.5 §§81-85) was accused.

[8] For discussions of the material, see H. Leclerq, "Aristocratiques (Classes)," *DACL* 1.2 (1924) 2847-48; G. B. de Rossi, *Roma Sotterranea Cristiana* (Rome: Pontificio Istituto di Archeologia Cristiana, 1867) 362-65. Reproductions of the inscription can be found in Leclerq (ibid.) and de Rossi (pl. 49-50, n. 27). For the inscription, see also *ICUR* 4.10669; Diehl *ILCV* 3958; O. Marucchi, *Le Catacombe Romane* (Rome: Desclée, Lefebvre, 1903) 192. It is true that in the same area burials of other branches of the Pomponius family were discovered, but the connection with Pomponia Graecina is not thereby significantly strengthened.

[9] Dio Cass. 67.14; Suet. *Dom.* 10, 15, 17; cf. F. Clemens, *PIR*[2] F240; F. Domitilla F418. Suetonius connects the incident with the later execution of Domitian by Domitilla's steward, Stephanus. For more information on the family, see Gavin Townend, "Some Flavian Connections," *JRS* 51 (1961) 54-62, esp. 55-56, 58 n. 15.

[10] I.e., *es ta tōn Ioudaiōn ēthē exokelontes.* For further discussion of what the expression may have meant to a pagan writer vis-à-vis Christianity, see below, pp. 115-119.

but with several significant changes: only the exile of Domitilla is mentioned; she is sent to the island of Pontia; she is Flavius Clemens's niece instead of his wife; she is exiled because of her profession of Christianity.[11] The accounts do not agree, but of the three Suetonius and Dio Cassius are to be preferred, and only Dio Cassius mentions the charge of Judaizing.[12] Eusebius's identification of this Domitilla as Clemens's niece could have resulted from confusion about her relationship to Domitian. On the basis of the literary evidence no connection with Christianity need be posited, in spite of Eusebius's assertion of over two hundred years later.

Archaeological discoveries of the last hundred years have strengthened the argument in this case. The catacomb on the Via Ardeatina that later came to be known under the name of Domitilla produced good evidence that one of its earliest burial regions, dating at least from the second century, was a hypogeum of a Flavian family, owned by a Flavia Domitilla.[13] A second area belonging to the Flavii Aurelii dates from the beginning of the second century, and there is a third contiguous burial area from at least the beginning of the third century. From these three adjoining funerary regions the complex Christian catacomb developed. The possibility cannot be entirely ruled out that the first region of this catacomb already belonged to the Flavia Domitilla of Domitian's reign, whose Christianity continued to be passed on to her descendants and extended family; in this case the reason given by Eusebius for her exile would be substantially correct. But the lack of continuous evidence from the late first century, makes this interpretation tenuous. Other possibilities are that Christianity came into the same family at a later date, perhaps through Jewish ties established earlier, or that the property passed into the hands of Christian slaves and freedmen of the family and that the name of Domitilla thus became associated with the cemetery.[14]

---

[11] Eusebius, *Hist. eccl.* 3.18.4; *Chronicon* ad ann. Abraham 2110. The variation in the name of the island is of little consequence, since both islands are off the coast of Campania in the Tyrrhenian Sea. Jerome (*Ep.* 108.7) echoes Eusebius. By the time of Jerome the island had become a place of pilgrimage because of its connection with Domitilla.

[12] According to Suet. *Dom.* 10, Acilius Glabrio was accused of conspiracy, with two others, but he was already in exile on another charge (atheism and Judaizing?) when he was executed. According to Dio Cassius one charge against him was that he fought animals as a gladiator (cf. Juv. *Sat.* 4.95-103; Fronto to Marcus Aurelius 5.22-23), an activity not easy to reconcile with Christianity or Judaism.

[13] The evidence includes a funerary grant from a woman of that name to P. Calvisius (*CIL* 6.16246) and another inscription of a daughter of Flavia Domitilla, of the same name (*CIL* 6.948).

[14] For a presentation of the evidence that favors Christianity, see H. Leclerq, "Aristocratiques (Classes)," 2850-54; O. Marucchi, *Le Catacombe Romane* 2d ed. (Rome: Libreria dello

The catacomb of Priscilla on the Via Salaria Nova is universally recognized as one of the oldest Christian burial places in Rome. Though later legends incorporated into the apocryphal *Acts of Pastor and Timothy* and the *Liber Pontificalis* asociate it with the preaching of Peter in Rome, archaeological evidence of Christian use, and with it the name Priscilla, can be pushed back only to the second century. One of the earliest regions of the cemetery was originally a water cistern, later turned into a burial crypt for several branches of the Acilii family, among them the Acilii Glabriones. This crypt was not connected with the nearby area associated with the name Priscilla until a later date, but at some point the several regions of the catacomb were joined to create a vast system for Christian use. Again, three explanations of origin that were offered for the catacomb of Domitilla are possible here: perhaps already in the first century the family of Manlius Acilius Glabrio was Christian; perhaps at a later time they became Christian; perhaps it was their slaves and freedmen who acquired the property and opened it to the Christian community.[15]

Justin, *Apology* 2

From the middle of the second century there is the account in Justin's second *Apology* of a Roman woman denounced by her husband as a Christian. Charges against her are eventually dropped, but her teacher Ptolemaeus and a bystander named Lucius are prosecuted. Harnack's description of her as a "prominent Roman lady" may be overstated since Justin calls her merely *gynē tis*. Her husband traveled and had military contacts. Yet the questions remain, why such a commotion should have been made of the affair, and why she was acquitted when those responsible were not, if she were not of considerable social position and influence.[16]

Stato, 1933) 135-78; for a more conservative interpretation, see P. Styger, "L'origine del Cimitero di Domitilla sull' Ardeatina," *Rend. Pont.* 5 (1926-27) 89-144; H. J. Leon, *The Jews of Ancient Rome* (Philadelphia: Jewish Publication Society, 1960) 33-35.

[15] For discussion of the material on the catacomb of Priscilla, see Marucchi, *Catacombe Romane*, 461-90; G. B. de Rossi, "Gli Acilii sepolti nel cimitero di Priscilla," *Bull. di Arch. Crist.* 6 (1888-89) 37-49, esp. 42-45; Leclerq, "Aristocratiques (Classes)," 2854-60. De Rossi traces the Acilius Glabrio family through several centuries, past the time when apparently the area was in use by Christians, thus excluding the possibility that the property was taken over by someone unconnected with the family unless they abandoned the crypt, which is not likely. His suggestion that Priscilla and Aquila, the companions of Paul, may have been *liberti* of these two families (assuming Aquila could have been a corruption of Acilius) is ingenious but must remain in the area of conjecture ("Aquila e Prisca e gli Acilii Glabrioni," *Bull. di Arch. Christ.* 6 (1888-89) 128-33).

[16] Justin, *Apol.* 2.2. Harnack discusses the incident in a section on the spread of Christianity among the wealthy and well born (*The Mission and Expansion of Christianity in the*

Eusebius, *Hist. eccl. 5.21.1.*

By the end of the second century the pattern is growing stronger. Eusebius's testimony that during the reign of Commodus many Romans distinguished by wealth and high birth became Christians with their households and families[17] may have a basis in fact, for it is at this point that the Church in Rome begins to acquire property of its own, particularly cemeteries that were originally private plots. The best evidence for this is the burial region now known as the catacomb of Callistus, of which one of the earliest nuclei was the hypogeum of the Caecilius family. The use of the area as a private crypt may extend back as far as the middle of the second century, and there were probably Christian burials in it before the property was acquired and administered by the Church.[18]

Summary

The middle of the second century presents only slim evidence concerning Christians in the Roman aristocracy: a few dubious literary texts, combined in three cases (i.e., Pomponia Graecina, Flavia Domitilla, and Acilius Glabrio) with later archaeological associations of the same names with Christianity and much later literary evidence of a tradition tying the first-century names to Christianity. Did Eusebius and his sources leap at coincidences in the same way the archaeologists did, or did he know more than we know? In the case of Domitilla and Acilius Glabrio the connections may be pure coincidence. The meager evidence for aristocratic Christians in the early and mid-second century does not leave much upon which to build.

First Three Centuries [2d ed; New York: Putnam, 1908] 2.33-42). He takes Pomponia Graecina, T. Flavius Clemens, and Domitilla as "evidently Christians" and Acilius Glabrio "perhaps." He also makes the common mistake of confusing wealth with rank and assuming that belonging to the imperial household means membership in the upper classes (e.g., pp. 38-39). From elsewhere in the empire, there is the letter of Pliny regarding investigation of Christians of every age and rank and both sexes (*omnis aetatis, omnis ordinis, utriusque sexus, Ep.* 10.96.9), but from the rest of the letter it must surely be concluded that he is using the word *ordo* loosely, not to refer to the aristocracy as such. However, some of those arrested were Roman citizens (96.4). A. N. Sherwin-White (*The Letters of Pliny: A Historical and Social Commentary* [Oxford: Clarendon, 1966] 709), is silent on this point.

[17] *Hist. eccl.* 5.21.1: *tōn epi Rhōmēs eu mala ploutō kai genei diaphanōn pleious epi tēn sphōn homose chōrein panoikei te kai pangenei sōterian.* For similar claims from the same period in North Africa, see Tertullian, *Ad Nat.* 1.1; *Apol.* 1.7; *Ad. Scap.* 2, but rhetorical intent must also be taken into consideration here. The parallel passages in *Ad Nat.* and *Apol.* are worth comparing for terminology to Pliny's *Ep.* 10.96.9 (see n. 16 above).

[18] The material is well summarized by George LaPiana ("The Roman Church at the End of the Second Century," *HTR* 18 [1925] 259-69); see also Marucchi, *Catacombe Romane*, 167; de Rossi, *Roma Sotterranea* 2.137-47.

Evidence for Lower Classes

Several allusions to Christians from the middle and the last third of the second century offer a different picture—a group composed mainly of the uneducated lower classes. It cannot be assumed that ignorance and "lower class" are synonymous; many of the best-educated leaders of the Church give no evidence of having been aristocrats or exceptionally wealthy (i.e., Justin, Tatian, Valentinus, Tertullian). Yet the association of lack of education and lower class is for the most part based on reality.

Justin, 2 Apol.; Tatian, Orat. 32

In his second *Apology* Justin states that not only philosophers and the well-educated have renounced glory and scorned fear and death for Christ but also craftsmen and the completely unskilled (*kai cheirotechnai, kai pantelōs idiōtai, Apol.* 2.10.8). Similarly, Tatian, Justin's disciple, says that not only the rich follow this philosophy (i.e., Christianity) but also the poor freely profit from the teaching (*philosophousi te ou monon hoi ploutountes, alla kai hoi penētes, Orat.* 32).[19] Both of these statements would seem to argue that the average Christian was well educated (Justin) and/or rich (Tatian). In the apologetic context, however, the point is that Christianity is a true philosophy and therefore will naturally appeal to the educated and the leisure classes. They are at pains to emphasize its respectability. But also by way of showing its universality, its appeal to all kinds of people, they acknowledge that the poor (Tatian), the craftsmen and the uneducated (Justin) are attracted by it. Regarding the educated, the apologists have a point to prove. Within the apologetic objective there is less of a point to prove regarding the uneducated, and so the information can be assumed to be reliable.

---

[19] Tatian was a Syrian (*Orat.* 42) who studied with Justin in Rome (Iren. *Adv. Haer.* 1.28.1; Hipp. *Ref.* 8.16) and left there after his teacher's death (*Orat.* 19). He produced the *Oratio ad Graecos* sometime later (*Orat.* 35), possibly in the 170s or 180s (see A. Puech, *Recherches sur le Discours aux Grecs de Tatian* [Paris: Félix Alcan, 1903] 6-10; R. M. Grant, "The Date for Tatian's Oration," *HTR* 46 [1953] 99-101; M. Elze, *Tatian und seine Theologie* [Göttingen: Vandenhoeck and Ruprecht, 1960] 16-19). Reference to Christianity as a philosophy (i.e., a way of life informed by a unified set of teachings) in response to popular use of the term was an apologetic commonplace (Justin, *Dial.* 8.1, 3; Melito, *Apology* quoted in Eus. *Hist. eccl.* 4.26.7; Miltiades, quoted in Eus. 5.17.5). Justin considered himself a philosopher (*Dial.* 1.8; 8.2; see R. Walzer, *Galen on Christians and Jews* [London: Oxford, 1949] 44). The fact that Tatian uses the conventional terminology *plousios—penēs* and goes on to stress that Christianity is also for all ages, including old women and youths, raises the suspicion that he is engaging in the same kind of universalizing rhetorical device as Pliny (*Ep.* 10.96.9) and especially Tertullian, *omnen sexum, aetatem, condicionem, etiam dignitatem* (*Apol.* 1.7; cf. *Ad Nat.* 1.1).

Minucius Felix, *Octavius 8.3-4; 31.6*

Toward the end of the second century another Christian apologist, Marcus Minucius Felix, set his dialectic exposition of the Christian faith within the imagined framework of a conversation between a friend and his pagan acquaintance, who is converted at the end of the discussion in a rather abrupt and unconvincing way. Though the author was probably a North African, the setting of the story is an autumn vacation in Ostia away from the law courts of Rome.[20] Among many charges of undesirable traits, the antagonist, Quintus Caecilius Natalis, levels against Octavius the complaint that Christian leaders pull together the least desirable segments of the population, including gullible women, and so organize a horde of godless conspirators who engage in indecent rites and dishonorable conduct (*homines . . . deploratae, inlicitae ac desperatae factionis grassari in deos . . . Qui de ultima faece collectis imperitioribus et mulieribus credulis sexus sui facilitate labentibus plebem profanae coniurationis instuunt, Octavius* 8.3-4; cf. 12.7; 16.5). Though Octavius is eloquent in refuting the charges of immorality (chaps. 28-31), he responds quite lamely to the charge of predominantly lower-class membership, saying only that Christians are not comprised of the lowest level of society, even if they reject official dignities and rank (*nec de ultima statim plebe consistimus, si honores vestros et purpuras recusamus,* 31.6). The second part of the statement is puzzling. Does it mean that Christians decline to serve in public office or high positions when they are offered to them? If so, Octavius must have in mind Christians eligible for such office. The context and the brevity with which the author treats the issue suggest that what he really means is that the majority of Christians are not from the "dregs of society" with the negative moral connotations carried by the expression. But neither do they have large numbers of people in a position to assume magistracies and other public offices, so that they are free to spurn any importance that might be attached to such positions.

Celsus

A similar witness, though unfortunately not restrictable to Rome, is the antagonist of Origen's *Contra Celsum.*[21] Probably writing at about the same

---

[20] *Octavius* 2.1, 3. Manuscript and literary connections with Tertullian, Arnobius, and Lactantius link *Octavius* to North Africa. It is also possible that the work comes from the early third century, after the writing of Tertullian's *Apology.* See G. H. Rendall, *Minucius Felix* (LCL; Cambridge, MA: Harvard University, 1966) 304-13.

[21] Of the several persons named Celsus of whom we know, the most likely referent of this work—and the Celsus Origen assumed it was—is Lucian's Epicurean friend to whom the satirist dedicated *Alexander the False Prophet,* a man who was probably also in correspondence with

time as the author of *Octavius*, Celsus claims that among the Christians there are more uneducated and unrefined (*idiōtai kai agroikoteroi*) than cultured people because Christianity is characterized by lower-class appeal (*to idiōtikon*). Origen replies that the variety of Christians is simply in proportion to the rest of the population, i.e., he does not deny the claim (*Contra Celsum* 1.27). Christians are accused of deliberately seeking out the stupid (*anoētoi*), the uneducated (*apaideutoi*), and the servile (*andrapodōseis*), children and women, while excluding the wise (3.18; cf. 3.50, 55, 74). Celsus satirically claims that Christians cry out that no one educated, wise, or sensible should come to their celebration—for such persons would be considered undesirable—but rather anyone who is unlearned, ignorant, uneducated, or a mere child should come with confidence (*ei tis amathēs, ei tis anoētos, ei tis apaideutos, ei tis nēpios, tharrōn hēketo*).[22] Thus, he claims, Christians show that they can and want to convince only the silly, the low-born, the tasteless, the servile, women, and children (*Contra Celsum* 3.44). Origen responds to this charge by admitting that some who are supposed to be Christians are such extremists but that it is somewhat of an exaggeration so stated. He then goes on to describe ways in which Christians seek after divine wisdom. Again, he does not deny the substance of the statement, only the extremity of it. In a cynical paraphrasing of the Gospel beatitudes, Celsus berates Christians for not bothering to require purificatory rites, as do the other mysteries, but instead allowing any sinner, ignoramus, child, or simply anyone who is unfortunate (*hamartōlos, . . . asynetos, . . . nēpios, kai hōs*

---

the noted physician Galen (see below). The major problem with this identification is that, though Celsus was branded an Epicurean by Origen, the excerpts from his work, *The True Word* (*Ho Alēthēs Logos*), quoted in *Contra Celsum* seem rather to indicate a Middle Platonist. His extensive knowledge of Gnostic sects and teachers (including Marcellina who according to Irenaeus was active in Rome at the time of Anicetus, in the 160s, *Adv. Haer.* 1.25.6) and his acquaintance with Neo-Pythagoreanism suggest a date near either 180 in Rome or Alexandria (see H. Chadwick, ed., *Contra Celsum* [Cambridge: Cambridge University, 1953] xxiv-xxix; M. Borret, ed., *Contre Celse* [SC 132; Paris: Editions du Cerf, 1967] 4 vols.). Chadwick's reason for preferring to place the work in Alexandria rather than Rome is superficial; with an appeal to W. Bauer (*Orthodoxy and Heresy in Earliest Christianity* [rev. G. Strecker; ed. R. Kraft and G. Krodel; trans. P. J. Achtemeier et al.; Philadelphia: Fortress, 1971] he assumes that in Rome the dividing line between orthodoxy and heresy was more sharply drawn and that therefore Celsus's confusion between the two could more easily have happened in Alexandria (p. xxix)!

[22] The formula is in imitation of the introductory proclamation preceding mystery rites, as at Eleusis (see G. Mylonas, *Eleusis and the Eleusianian Mysteries* [Princeton: Princeton University, 1961] 247, esp. refs. in n. 116; Lucian, *Alexander* 38, where the charlatan hero of Abonouteichos warns away Christians and Epicureans from his rites; *Ap. Const.* 8.12.2, an introductory proclamation by a deacon before the oblation, excluding catechumens, auditors, infidels, heretics, unrestrained children, quarrelers, and hypocrites).

haplōs eipein hostis kakodaimōn) to come in, for this kind the kingdom of God will receive (3.59; cf. Matt 5:3, 10; Luke 6:20).

The most interesting passage for the present study is the one that specifies by occupation those people who are targets for Christians. In their own houses Christians instruct wool workers, cobblers, laundry workers, and the most uneducated and rustic types of people, who would not dare to speak before their elders or the learned, teaching them disobedience to their fathers and teachers. Because Christians think they alone know the right way, they go to the area of the wool workers, to the cobbler's shop, and to the fuller's shop (*hē gynaikōnitis*,[23] *to skyteion, to knapheion*) (*Contra Celsum* 3.55). These people are to Celsus synonymous with the unlearned of the lower classes, and his criticism constructs a picture of Christian activity among them which Origen is only effectively able to answer in terms of pursuit of a deeper spiritual wisdom that is open to all. He cannot deny the social reality at which Celsus, from a different perspective, scoffs.

In view of the evidence for a tradition of anti-Christian polemic, of which Celsus's *Ho Alēthēs Logos* and the antagonistic material in Minucius Felix's *Octavius* are examples,[24] it can be concluded with reasonable certainty that by the end of the second century a literary tradition *Contra Christianos* had developed. The tradition incorporated a certain amount of conventional material that was indiscriminately repeated and can be compared with the development of the *Adversus Judaeos* literature within Christianity and anti-pagan polemic, of which Origen's *Contra Celsum* is a good example.[25] The supposed existence of such traditional material raises some question about the reliability and applicability of its information in any given circumstance. However, the claim of a predominantly lower-class and uneducated Christian membership is never successfully refuted by Christian authors, whereas the scandalous charges of immorality are vehemently denied. From the Christian perspective of salvation for all who accept faith in Christ regardless of social standing, there is little need to apologize for

---

[23] Most obviously indicating "women's quarters," but see Chadwick, *Contra Celsum*, 166 n. 1, and W. den Boer, "Gynaeconitis, a Centre of Christian Propaganda," *VC* 4 (1950) 61-64. Den Boer links this phrase with several passages in Clement and with Vitruvius *De archit.* 6.7.2, *haec pars aedificii (sc. in quibus matres familiarum cum lanificio habent sessionem) gynaeconitis vocatur,* as well as with several legal texts in which the related words *gynaikeion* and *gynaik(e)iarios* mean a weaving establishment and a worker or manager in such a shop. This interpretation also preserves the parallelism in the two lists of terms.

[24] The defamatory arguments in *Octavius* apparently came from a lost treatise by M. Cornelius Fronto, born at Cirta in Numidia, a famous rhetor in Rome and tutor of Marcus Aurelius (*Octavius* 9.6; 31.2).

[25] For further discussion, see P. de Labriolle, *La Réaction païenne: Etude sur la polémique antichrétienne du Ier au VIe siècle* (Paris: L'Artisan du livre, 1934).

Christianity's lower-class profile. Yet, if people like Minucius Felix and Origen could have boasted of prominent and noble members within the Christian ranks, it would have been to their advantage to do so.

Galen and the Christian Schools

For this study, the final witness concerning the social status of Christians in Rome during the middle years of the second century is Galen, the great physician, who lived most of his adult life in the capital.[26] His passing references to "the followers of Moses and Christ" show at least a second-hand knowledge of Christian and Jewish lifestyle and manner of religious instruction. Three times in his preserved writings he alludes to their requiring pupils to accept what they say on faith rather than on demonstrated proofs, a practice abhorrent to Galen but one he considered common to the philosophical schools, all of which he criticized as inimical to free critical thinking: Θᾶττον γὰρ ἄν τις τοὺς ἀπὸ Μωσοῦ καὶ Χριστοῦ μεταδιδάξειν ἤ τοὺς αἱρέσεσι προστετηκότας ἰατρούς τε καὶ φιλοσόφους ("one might more easily teach novelties to the followers of Moses and Christ than to the physicians and philosophers who cling fast to their schools").[27] Or again: . . . ἵνα μή τις εὐθὺς κατ' ἀρχάς, ὡς εἰς Μωσοῦ καὶ Χριστοῦ διατριβὴν ἀφιγμένος, νόμων ἀναποδείκτων ἀκούῃ, καὶ ταῦτα ἐν οἷς ἥκιστα χρή (". . . in order that one should not at the very beginning, as if one had come into the school of Moses and Christ, hear talk of undemonstrated laws, and that where it is least appropriate").[28] Another work preserved only in Arabic reads, "If I had in mind people who taught their pupils in the same way as the followers of Moses and Christ teach theirs—for they order them to accept everything on faith—I should not have given you a definition."[29]

Galen did admit, however, that a system of inculcating faith through imaginary examples rather than proofs could produce good results: "just as now we see the people called Christians drawing their faith from parables (and miracles) and yet sometimes acting in the same way (as those who

[26] Born at Pergamon in 129 C.E., Galen came to Rome at the age of thirty-three and lived there for the rest of his life except for a three-year visit to his home city when the plague invaded Italy in 166. He had extensive philosophical training before beginning his medical studies and was a friend of Marcus Aurelius, who appointed him official physician for the child Commodus. See Walzer, *Galen*, 6-10; G. Bowersock, *Greek Sophists in the Roman Empire* (Oxford: Clarendon, 1969) 60-66.

[27] *De pulsuum differentiis* 3.3 (Walzer's translation, *Galen*, 14; text in Greek and Arabic, pp. 38-39).

[28] *De pulsuum differentiis* 2.4 (Walzer, *Galen*, 14, 46). The context of the passage is in regard to the uncritical methods of the physician Archigenes, of the previous generation.

[29] Walzer, *Galen*, 15, 48-49.

philosophize)."[30] "For their contempt of death (and of its sequel) is patent to us every day, and likewise their restraint in cohabitation. For they include not only men but also women who refrain from cohabiting all through their lives; and they also number individuals who in self-discipline and self-control (in matters of food and drink) and in their keen pursuit of justice have attained a pitch not inferior to that of genuine philosophers."[31]

One of the most significant aspects of Galen's remarks about Christians is that he seems to consider them similar to a philosophical school. He is the first pagan author to do so. Their methods are not always those of true philosophers, but some of the results are the same, and for Galen this has a certain importance. According to Walzer, Galen holds that philosophy as it should be practiced is possible only for a chosen few, while myth and poetry are the means of education to virtue for the masses. Without having the highest kind of education or nobility of birth, Christians are nevertheless exemplary in the demonstration of the specifically philosophical virtues of courage, temperance, and justice.[32]

The presence of various Christian "schools" in Rome is known from other sources, though it is not clear whether they were chiefly for the purpose of catechetical instruction, in which case they would have been more tightly under the control of church authorities, or for advanced theological training, similar to the centers conducted later by Clement in Alexandria and Origen in Caesarea. Justin instructed students at his own lodgings (*Acts of Justin* 3); Tatian began his own school in Rome after the death of Justin (Iren. *Adv. Haer.* 1.28.1, quoted in Eus. *Hist. eccl.* 4.29.3); Marcion established his *didascaleion* there (Iren *Adv. Haer.* 1.27.2); in a story narrated by Justin, a certain Ptolemy instructed in the faith a woman accused of Christianity by her husband (*Apol.* 2.2); Marcellina, who came to Rome in the middle of the century, was a successful teacher of the Carpocratian school (Iren. *Adv. Haer.* 1.25.6; Epiph. *Pan.* 27.6).[33]

---

[30] The quotation is preserved in Arabic from a summary of Plato's *Republic* (Walzer, *Galen*, 15, 16, 57). The words in parentheses here and in the next quotation are textual variants in the Arabic version or versions.

[31] This quotation too is preserved in Arabic in the summary of the *Republic* (Walzer, *Galen*, 15-16, 65). Does Galen know this at first hand, or has he read Justin, *Apol.* 1.15, 29? Two other similar remarks are made of Moses and his teachings, one in *De usu partium* 11.14 (Walzer, *Galen*, 11–13) and the other from a work on Hippocratic anatomy preserved only in Arabic (Walzer, *Galen*, 10-11).

[32] See further Walzer, *Galen*, 42-43, 65-69.

[33] Though rival groups often called each other "schools," they may have considered themselves separate "churches." See the remarks of P. Carrington (*The Early Christian Church* [Cambridge: Cambridge University, 1957] 2.86-87) and the imaginative reconstruction of G. Bardy ("Les écoles romaines au second siècle," *RHE* 28 [1932] 501-32).

While according to one perspective these Christian schools may have provided intellectual leadership, Galen did not view them thus. In his opinion they lacked critical reflection, demanding belief without sufficient proof; they were for the general populace. This is similar to the views expressed by Caecilius in *Octavius* and by Celsus, though Galen agrees with the Christian apologists that the Christian way produces remarkable virtue. Galen's disdain for the intellectual quality of "the followers of Christ" indicates his judgment that they are not well educated.

Another significant point in Galen's comments is the close association he makes between Christianity and Judaism, which will be discussed below in the section entitled "Jewish Connections."

The evidence from Justin, Tatian, Minucius Felix, and Celsus has shown that there was in the course of the second century a general impression, especially on the part of opponents of Christianity, that the majority of Christians were craftsmen and other lower-class groups and that the evangelizing efforts of Christian teachers were aimed largely at these kinds of people. The remarks of Galen, while indicating nothing directly about social standing, support that impression by adding his criticism of the lack of any serious intellectual content in their religious instruction, a quality that would have been more emphasized in those leisure classes and social circles which had behind them a strong tradition of vigorous intellectual training.[34]

Nomenclature

Some limited information can be gained by examining the names of Christians that occur in literary documents connected with Roman Christianity in the early and middle parts of the second century and comparing them with what we know about the association of names and social standing at that time. Though the sample is too small to yield definite conclusions, the evidence should not be overlooked. From *1 Clement*,[35] *Hermas*, *Acts of*

---

[34] The conflict between heresy and orthodoxy, which goes back into the first century, may well have been immensely complicated in the mid-second century by such social factors. Valentinus and many other Gnostic teachers, as well as Hippolytus and Novatian in later years, appear to have been more intellectually sophisticated than their orthodox antagonists, and the doctrinal conflicts were no doubt aggravated by social differences as well. See J. G. Gager, *Kingdom and Community: The Social World of Early Christianity* (Englewood Cliffs, NJ: Prentice Hall, 1975) 76-88.

[35] Though *1 Clement* probably was written in the last decade of the first century, the persons named in it would presumably have survived into the second, and there may be a chronological overlap with the earliest part of *Hermas* (i.e., the Clement of *Vis.* 2.4.3 may be the author of *1 Clement*.

Justin,[36] and Eusebius's list of Roman bishops drawn from Hegesippus,[37] the following list has been compiled and arranged alphabetically according to Latin spelling:

Alexandros, bishop from about the twelfth year of Trajan (110) to the third year of Hadrian (120) (Eus. *Hist. eccl.* 4.1, 3)

Anikētos, bishop succeeding Bishop Pius after the latter's fifteenth year (159?) until about the eighth year of Marcus Aurelius (168?) (Eus. *Hist. eccl.* 4.11.7; 19.1)

Charitō, woman martyr with Justin (*Acts of Justin*)

Charitōn, male martyr with Justin (*Acts of Justin*)

Claudius *Ephēbos*, messenger from the Roman Church to the Corinthian Church (*1 Clem.* 65.1)

Clemens, official of the Roman Church in *Herm. Vis.* 2.4.3; he may be the one mentioned as bishop from the twelfth year of Domitian (93) to the third year of Trajan (101) (Eus. *Hist. eccl.* 3.15, 34); he is traditionally identified as the author of *1 Clement*.

Eleutheros, bishop from the seventeenth year of Marcus Aurelius (178) to the tenth year of Commodus (190) (Eus. *Hist. eccl.* 5.1.1; 22.1)

Euaristos, bishop from the third (101) to about the twelfth year (109?) of Trajan (Eus. *Hist. eccl.* 3.34; 4.1)

Euelpistos, from Cappadocia; martyr with Justin (*Acts of Justin* 4.7)[38]

Fortunatus, messenger from the Roman Church to the Corinthian Church (*1 Clem.* 65.1)

Graptē, instructor of widows and orphans (*Herm. Vis.* 2.4.3)

---

[36] *Acts of Justin*, extant in three recensions, covers the trial of Justin and six companions before the urban prefect Q. Junius Rusticus between the years 163 and 168. The text is generally accepted as being based on authentic material, and recension A is preferred as perhaps the original, e.g., by T. D. Barnes ("Pre-Decian Acta Martyrum," *JTS* 19 [1968] 515-16). But G. Lazzati ("Gli Atti di San Giustino Martire," *Aevum* 27 [1953] 473-97) argues that none of the three is dependent on any other but all go back to an earlier common form. For further bibliography, see H. Musurillo, *The Acts of the Christian Martyrs* (Oxford: Clarendon, 1972) introduction, pp. xvii-xx; texts and translations, pp. 42-61.

[37] Eus. *Hist. eccl.* 4.22.3. Hegesippus's list agrees with that of Irenaeus (*Adv. Haer.* 3.3.3 = *Hist. eccl.* 5.6.4), but later lists have variants (see L. Duchesne, ed., *Liber Pontificalis* [Paris: Cyrille Vogel, 1866] vol. 1, introduction and passim). The existence of this list as early as the middle of the second century need not be construed as evidence for the monarchical episcopate in Rome at that early date, but rather as Hegesippus's desire to create an orthodox succession (*diadochē*) all the way back to Peter and Paul (see G. LaPiana, *Le Successione episcopale in Roma e gli albori del primato* [Roma: Libreria di Cultura, 1922] 10–15).

[38] In the *Acts*, *Euelpistos* says he is from Cappadocia (4.7) and Hierax from Iconium (4.8); Hierax even says he was dragged away (rec. A *apespasthēn*; rec. B. *apospastheis*), yet in the text their legal status is not questioned by the prefect. But this may have been excised by the Christian editor.

Hermas, traditional author of *The Shepherd*

Hierax, from Iconium in Phrygia; martyr with Justin (*Acts of Justin* 4.8, recension B)[39]

Hyginos, bishop from the first year of Antoninus Pius (139) for four or fourteen years (Eus. *Hist. eccl.* 4.10; 11.6)[40]

Justinus, from Flavia Neapolis in Samaria; Christian teacher; author of the *Dialogue with Trypho* and two *Apologies*; martyred under the prefect Q. Junius Rusticus between the years 163 and 168 (*Acts of Justin*)

Liberianus, martyr with Justin (*Acts of Justin*)

Lucius, martyr at the time of Justin (*Apol.* 2.2)

Maximus, apostate (?) in the Roman Church at the time of Hermas (*Vis.* 2.3.4)

Paiōn, martyr with Justin (*Acts of Justin*)

Pius, bishop from ca. 144 to 159 (Eus. *Hist. eccl.* 4.11.6, 7)

Ptolemaios, Christian teacher; martyr at the time of Justin (*Apol.* 2.2)

Rhodē, former owner of Hermas (*Vis.* 1.1)

Sixtus, bishop from the third to the twelfth year of Hadrian (120 to 129 or 130) (Eus. *Hist. eccl.* 4.4; 4.5.5)

Sōtēr, bishop from about the eighth year of Marcus Aurelius (168–177?) (Eus. *Hist. eccl.* 4.19; 5.1.1)

Telesphoros, bishop from the twelfth year of Hadrian (129 or 130) to the first year of Antoninus Pius (139) (Eus. *Hist. eccl.* 4.5.5; 4.10); martyr (Eus. 4.10; 5.6.4 = Iren. *Adv. Haer.* 3.3.3)

Valerius Vito, messenger from the Roman Church to the Corinthian Church (*1 Clem.* 65.1)

Victor,[41] bishop from the tenth year of Commodus (190) to the ninth year of Alexander Severus (200) (Eus. *Hist. eccl.* 5.22; 28.7)

Though the sample is not large enough to be significant, most of the names on the list are single names and seventeen out of the twenty-seven are

---

[39] See above, n. 38.

[40] Eus. 4.11.6 has four years; his *Chronicon* has fourteen, which fits the rest of the chronology of both.

[41] With Victor's successor, Zephyrinus, begin the stories of Hippolytus, Church owner-ship of the catacomb of Callistus, and new theological controversies that mark the beginning of another era. The above list could be expanded to include other known teachers who visited Rome during the same period: Marcion, Valentinus, Cerdo, Marcellina, Polycarp, Hegesippus, and Tatian. All of them, however, are known to have come from elsewhere. So, of course, is Justin, but his martyrdom is the occasion of a Christian document of Roman provenance, and on this basis he is included.

of Greek provenance, leaving only ten of Latin origin.[42] The important question is whether anything can be detected about social status from the names themselves.

Much study has been devoted to the social interpretation of the funerary inscriptions of imperial Rome, but the results lack clarity largely because of the haphazard selection of what has survived and the fact that the inscriptions do not always answer the questions raised by modern scholars. Most of our information about the lower classes comes from the epitaphs of freedmen because they, more than slaves or the freeborn, had an improved social status which they wished to make explicit.[43]

While Greek names are not of themselves proof either of foreign provenance or of servile status, there was a tendency, which was noted by Frank, for families in Rome bearing Greek names to change to Latin names within the first two generations.[44] On the other hand, the number of Greek names used by members of senatorial families increased gradually but decisively from Vespasian to Caracalla. This tendency, however, does not indicate a change in nomenclature customs but rather that increasing numbers of Greek-speaking families from the East and families with servile origins were entering the ranks of the senatorial *ordo*. Solin concluded that among the "per-

---

[42] This is counting Claudius *Ephēbos* as Greek, since the second name is probably his personal name, now a *cognomen* with the addition of his patron's *gentilicium*.

[43] For important studies of slave and freedmen epitaphs, see M. Bang, "Die Herkunft der römischen Sklaven," *Römische Mitteilungen* 25 (1910) 223-251 (on geographical provenance of slaves); T. Frank, "Race Mixture in the Early Roman Empire," *American Historical Review* 21 (1916) 689-708, reprinted in *Problems of European Civilization*, ed. D. Kagan (Boston: Heath, 1968) 44-56 (with the conclusion that 80 to 90 percent of the urban-born population in the early empire was of slave stock); M. L. Gordon, "Nationality of Slaves under the Early Roman Empire," *JRS* 14 (1924) 93-111, reproduced in *Slavery and Classical Antiquity*, ed. M. I. Finley (Cambridge: Cambridge University, 1970) 171-89 (in reaction to Frank); also M. L. Gordon, "The Freedman's Son in Municipal Life," *JRS* 21 (1931) 65-77; L. R. Taylor, "Freedmen and Freeborn in the Epitaphs of Imperial Rome" *AJP* 82 (1961) 113-32 (in agreement with Frank's findings); I. Kajanto, *The Latin Cognomina* (Commentationes Humanarum Litterarum 26.2; Helsinki: Societas Scientarum Fennica, 1965) and "The Significance of Non-Latin Cognomina," *Latomus* 27 (1968) 517-34; P. R. C. Weaver, "Cognomina Ingenua," *CQ* 14 (1964) 311-15, and *Familia Caesaris: A Social Study of the Emperor's Freedmen and Slaves* (Cambridge: Cambridge University, 1972); H. Solin, *Beiträge zur Kenntnis der griechischen Personennamen in Rom* (Commentationes Humanarum Litterarum 48; Helsinki: Societas Scientarum Fennica, 1971). For further references, see the bibliography in Weaver, *Familia Caesaris*, 313-18.

[44] "Race Mixture," 693. Moreover, a freedman upon obtaining equestrian status might drop his Greek name and take on a Latin one with an aristocratic tone. Witness the case of the freedman Icelus, who either adopted or was given the name Marcianus along with his gold ring (Tac. *Hist.* 1.13; Plutarch, *Galba* 7; Suet. *Galba* 14), even though Claudius had earlier forbidden name changing as a means of social climbing (Suet. *Claud.* 25.1); see Weaver, *Familia Caesaris*, 87-88, for these and other examples.

manent" population of Rome, a Greek name in the first century and a half of the empire meant membership either in the slave-freedman social class or in the relatively small group of *peregrini*—freeborn tradesmen and craftsmen of foreign extraction living in the city. Since masters named slaves without regard for ethnic origins,[45] Solin concluded that for that period the presence of a Greek name is highly likely to establish legal status but not ethnic origin. In the later decades of the second century, however, this pattern begins to break down, and by the end of the century Greek names have lost their social function.[46]

During most of the period from which the present selection of Christian names comes, it is to be supposed that a Greek name stands a much better chance of indicating slave or freedman (or perhaps *peregrinus*) status than freeborn. An exception should probably be made for *Alexandros*, a name widely used in the East, attested but not common among aristocrats without known Eastern connections before the third century.[47] Thus the names *Charitō, Charitōn, Euaristos, Euelpistos, Graptē, Paiōn, Rhodē*, and *Sōtēr* do not appear in *PIR* at all. *Anikētos* is the name of a *libertus* of Nero, his tutor, *praefectus classis*, assistant in intrigue, and victim (*PIR²* A589); and of a *librarius* of Marcus Aurelius (A591). Claudius *Ephēbos* may be a freedman of a branch of the Claudian family in the late first century, perhaps still an imperial freedman of Nero or the descendant of one.[48] The name *Eleutheros* is borne by Aurelius Num. Eleuther, possibly an equestrian, of the time of Commodus.[49] The name *Hermas* does not occur with final -*s* in *PIR*, but a Laelius Herma is referred to in the life of one of the famous grammarians mentioned by Suetonius, and he is a freedman; there is also a T. Claudius Herma.[50] *Hierax* occurs only as the name of a member of the provincial aristocracy, a rhetor and Asiarch from Ephesus.[51] *Hyginos* occurs in the

---

[45] M. L. Gordon ("Nationality," 99) gives a good example: Caecilia Graecula, natione Hispana (*CIL* 6.13820).

[46] Solin, *Beiträge*, 159, 137-44. In spite of his conservative method, Solin concluded that 70 percent of the inscriptions of imperial Rome are of people of servile origins, a figure surprisingly close to the much-assailed findings of T. Frank.

[47] E.g., I 140 Fl. Iulius A. Capito, a late second-century equestrian. Alexander was a popular name among Roman Jews (*CII* 84, 85, 92, 140, 210, 370, 501; and the feminine form in 8 and 501).

[48] Weaver (*Familia Caesaris*, 97-100) discovered from the limited data available that a high number of imperial slaves were manumitted in their early thirties. In the last decade of the century, a Neronian freedman could still be active. The single name Claudius occurs in one Jewish inscription (*CII 37*).

[49] *PIR²* E1563a (add. p. xviii).

[50] Laelius Herma *PIR²* L54, and Suet. *Gramm.* 10.

[51] T. Fl. Lucius Hierax, third century, *PIR²* F308.

derivative form ". . . sius Hyginianus" for a member of the senatorial *ordo*, but not until the early third century; before that it appears as the name of two writers and a *medicus* in Rome.[52] *Ptolemaios*, a name common in the East, has twelve entries in *PIR*, none of them Roman.[53] *Telesphoros* occurs at the time of Martial in the person of one Faenius Telesphorus who has built a funerary monument to his daughter, Antulla.[54] He is most probably a freedman of the Faenius family. Thus, seventeen Greek names on the list accord with what is known about Greek names in Rome: most are of no aristocratic prominence and the few that are (*Eleutheros*, *Hierax*, *Hyginos*) are either from the third century, when there was no longer a social distinction made regarding them, or are of the provincial Greek-speaking aristocracy (*Heriax*). One (*Alexandros*) is an exception by virtue of the name itself. The double names (Claudius *Ephēbos*; other names combined with *Hermas* or *Telesphoros*) are best explained as names of freedmen.

The case for Latin names is somewhat more complex. A. M. Duff formulated a sample list of forty names, of which twenty were considered "servile" and twenty "ingenuous."[55] The criterion for the second list was that all were *cognomina* from prominent families of the republic "who would have been the last to be suspected of servile descent." Duff has often been criticized for oversimplification,[56] and perhaps rightly so, yet his own remarks show that he was aware of the tenuousness of such divisions.[57] He was not entirely wrong: eight of his twenty "servile" names do not appear at all in

---

[52] Hyginianus *PIR²* H237, *quaestor pro praetore prov. Siliciae* under Caracalla. The others are H238, 239, and 1357. By the second century equestrian procurators began using *cognomina* ending in -ianus, and slowly so too did senators (see Weaver, *Familia Caesaris*, 89-90). The name in H237, however, could be an *agnomen*. *Agnomina*, names added informally to officially given names, were commonly of the -ianus variety.

[53] There is an *epistrategus* in the Thebaid in 17 B.C.E. (*PIR¹* P763).

[54] *PIR¹* F75; Martial 1.114, 116.

[55] *Freedmen in the Early Roman Empire* (Oxford: Clarendon, 1928) 110-11. "Servile" names: Agilis, Amandus, Auctus, Communis, Donatus, Faustus, Felix, Fortunatus, Ianuarius, Lascivus, Marinus, Possessor, Primigenius, Primio, Restitutus, Rufio, Salvius, Successus, Vitalis, Vividus. "Ingenuous" names: Aquila, Bassus, Capito, Carus, Celer, Crescens, Crispinus, Fortis, Fronto, Frugi, Gratus, Iustus, Lucanus, Marcellus, Maximus, Princeps, Probus, Romanus, Saturninus, Secundus.

[56] E.g., by Weaver in "Cognomina Ingenua."

[57] ". . . often it has been necessary to follow impression. . . . From these lists it will be seen how unsafe it is to draw hard and fast conclusions. . . . Almost every one of the names in the second list somewhere can be found belonging to a freedman . . ." (*Freedmen*, 100-111). Many names on his "servile" list can also be found sparingly among equestrians and senators, e.g., Amandus (*PIR²* A554); Faustus (*PIR²* F137, a consul suff. in 121 C.E.); Felix (*PIR²* C44, consul legatus of the early third century); Vitalis (*PIR²* A277 and A1635, two equestrians of the late third century).

PIR,[58] while those that do are not frequent among the *ordines*. And he admits that nearly all of his "ingenuous" names can be found on freedmen, but not with regularity. What Duff chiefly failed to take into account was chronological development: while Greek names became more common among the freeborn population of Rome in the second and third centuries, so too did some Latin names arise with "ingenuous" connotations, for which very reason freedmen wanted them,[59] so that by the second century the distinctions were beginning to disappear, just as other social distinctions between freedmen and equestrian families were becoming blurred.

Of the Latin names on the list given above of second-century Roman Christians, there are only two about which nothing appears in *PIR*: Liberianus and Valerius Vito. Liberianus follows a tendency common in the second century, that of adding -ianus to a *cognomen*.[60] Valerius is a common aristocratic *gentilicium*, but Vito does not occur in *PIR*; this is most likely the name of a freedman of the Valerian *gens* whose personal name is Vito. Four of the Christian names are very common among senatorial, equestrian, and other groups: Clemens, Maximus, Pius, and Victor. Clemens is a popular *cognomen* with thirty-eight entries in *PIR²*, mostly senatorial and equestrian, but the first entry is C1134, a slave of Agrippa Postumus (first century). There are over one hundred entries in *PIR¹* under the name of Maximus, including many of senatorial rank, but noteworthy is M312, a *libertus* and procurator of Trajan working in Bithynia during Pliny's term of office there.[61] There are twenty-one entries for Pius, a *cognomen* or *agnomen* in use before the conferral of the title on the emperor Antoninus by the senate as well as later. (It is to be noted, however, that according to Eusebius's reckoning the Christian Pius was bishop during the reign of Antoninus Pius.) Victor is a popular *cognomen* used at all levels of society, represented by twenty-one entries in *PIR*.[62]

Three names that would be expected to be commonly used are not: Justinus, Lucius, and Sixtus. For this study there is only one Justinus of

---

[58] Agilis, Communis, Lascivus, Possessor, Primigenius, Primio, Rufio, Vividus.

[59] Weaver ("Cognomina Ingenua") found that nearly all "ingenuous" names used by the slave-freedman group are later than the first century.

[60] But the practice most often involved aristocratic names (see Weaver, *Familia Caesaris*, 87-90, though see also the case of Fortunatianus, below, n. 64).

[61] Pliny, *Ep.* 10.27, 28, 85. Maximus is one of the names classified by Duff as "ingenuous." It appears on the epitaphs of four Roman Jews: *CII* 371, 377, 485, and the recently discovered inscription of *Maximos Thabrakenos*, i.e., from Thabraca in Numidia (see U. Fasola. "Le due catacombe ebraiche di Villa Torlonia," *Riv. di Arch. Crist.* 52 [1976] 22-23). Feminine forms appear in *CII* 70, 473.

[62] It was also popular among Roman Jews: *CII* 98, 102, 312, 313 (#312 may be a woman).

importance, M. Ceccius Justinus, an early second-century consul.[63] Lucius was of course ubiquitous as long as the *tria nomina* system lasted.[64] For Sixtus there are no entries in *PIR*, though Sextius is a common *gentilicium*, and for the alternate form Sextus there are five listings, all probably from the first or the second century, including one of consular rank.[65]

Fortunatus has often been considered a typical servile name, and this may have been true at first.[66] But like most servile names, which were used increasingly by the upper classes in the second and third centuries, the name Fortunatus rose in status with its bearers. Of eight entries in *PIR*, three are *liberti* and they are all of the first century.[67] Three are senatorial; two of these are not dated,[68] and the third, L. Fabius Fortunatus Victorinus, is of the third century.[69] Finally, there is one equestrian, M. Aurelius Fortunatus, and he too is of the late third century.[70]

Of the ten Latin names on the list of second-century Christians, therefore, several are known to be popular aristocratic names, yet most are attested by the second century for freedmen as well, while at least three (Fortunatus, Liberianus, Valerius Vito) are more likely slaves or freedmen. There is admittedly less certainty than in the case of the seventeen Greek names, because Latin names are simply more abundant in the data considered by *PIR*. The very rarity of the Greek names in the categories selected by *PIR* is indicative of their generally lower-class use. Of the twenty-seven names at least twenty

---

[63] *PIR*[2] C593. The other two entries are the Christian Justin, who appears on the Christian list above (I871), and another later (and probably fictitious) Christian martyr (I870). The name Justus is included in Duff's list of "ingenuous" names. Both Justus and Justinus are undoubtedly good Latin names, though Justin Martyr came from Palestine. Perhaps his good philosophical education (*Dial.* 2-8) and his Latin name are indications that his family was at least prosperous if not in line for the privileges of the local municipal aristocracy. Justus appears to have been a very popular Jewish name, at least in Rome (*CII* 3, 13, 125, 224, 245, 252, 358, 359, 502; see also Fasola, "Due Catacombe," 25, the son of a Catanian). Feminine forms appear in *CII* 240, 244, and Just-? in 469.

[64] One Lucius occurs among the Jewish inscriptions (*CII* 155).

[65] F33 -inius Sextus Florentinus is probably from the late second century; see also S489, a jurist possibly from the time of Hadrian or later.

[66] It is the only name on Duff's list of "servile" names to appear on the list of second-century Roman Christians above; Maximus is the only one of Duff's "ingenuous" names included.

[67] *PIR*[2] 479, 480, 481.

[68] C660 M. Centullius F.; *PIR*[1] 023 Q. Octavius F.

[69] F34.

[70] A1508. One wonders if his grandfather had been an imperial freedman of a century before. Of the derivative name Fortunatianus there is already an equestrian in the early second century, as well as another and two of senatorial rank that are undated (*PIR*[1] 1320; undated: 1319; F403; *PIR*[1] M413a). There is one Jewish Fortunatus (*CII* 418) and one Fortunatianus (*CII* 240).

are more likely to indicate slave or freedman status (the seventeen Greek names plus Fortunatus, Liberianus, and Valerius Vito). For the remaining seven there is no decisive evidence concerning social class.

Summary

Justin, Tatian, and Minucius Felix give the impression from inside Christianity that people of every social stratum are welcome and that the uneducated and members of the lower classes abound in Christian communities. They see this as a credit to the universality of the Christian message. Celsus and Galen confirm the same picture from the outside and see in it an occasion for scorn and contempt. The little evidence available from Christian names in use in Rome in the late first and the early and middle second century, both Greek and Latin, is best viewed in the social context of the lower classes, particularly people of recent foreign extraction, slaves, and freedmen.

Jewish Connections

The early history of Christianity in Rome is closely connected with that of the Jewish community there.[71] For this reason it will be helpful to summarize the data from the first and second centuries that shed light on the social status of Roman Jews at the time, particularly in relation to Christianity.[72]

---

[71] For more complete studies of the origins of Roman Christianity and its bonds with Judaism, see G. LaPiana, *Successione episcopale*, esp. 17-23; E. A. Judge and G. S. R. Thomas, "The Origin of the Church at Rome: A New Solution?" *Reformed Theological Review* 25 (1966) 81-94 (Paul was originally and primarily responsible for creating an identity of Roman Christians separate from Judaism); W. Wiefel, "Die jüdische Gemeinschaft im antiken Rom und die Anfänge des römischen Christentums," *Judaica* 26 (1970) 65-88. Studies specifically on the relationship of Paul's letter to the Romans and the community there include G. LaPiana, "La primitiva communità di Roma e l'epistola ai Romani," *Ricerche Religiose* 3-4 (1925) 209-26, 306-26; Karl P. Donfried, "A Short Note on Romans 16," *JBL* 89 (1970) 441-49, "False Presuppositions in the Study of Romans," *CBQ* 36 (1974) 332-58; R. J. Karris, "Rom 14:1-15:13 and the Occasion of Romans," *CBQ* 35 (1973) 155-78, "The Occasion of Romans: A Response to Professor Donfried," *CBQ* 36 (1974) 356-58. The articles by Wiefel (in English), Donfried, and Karris are also available in *The Romans Debate* (ed. K. P. Donfried; Minneapolis: Augsburg, 1977).

[72] Only incidents especially relevant to social standing and the development of Christianity are discussed here. See further J. Juster, *Les Juifs dans l'Empire Romain: leur condition juridique, économique et sociale* (2 vols.; Paris; Paul Geuthner, 1914); E. Schürer, *The History of the Jewish People in the Age of Jesus Christ* (now Eng. version rev. and ed. G. Vermes and F. Millar; Edinburgh: T. and T. Clark, 1973) vol. 1; Leon, *Jews of Ancient Rome*, 1-45.

Important Events of the First Century

From early in the first century there is evidence of important Jewish influence in high places in Roman society and government.[73] Under Tiberius four Jewish confidence men swindled Fulvia, the proselyte wife of the senator Saturninus, out of a large gift of money and expensive materials on the pretext that they were to be sent to Jerusalem for use in the temple. When notified of the successful plot by Fulvia's husband, Tiberius ordered a general retaliation upon the whole Jewish community. Resisters were expelled, drafted into the military, executed, or reduced to slavery.[74] Though the purported reason for the overreaction of widespread persecution was the scandal involving a woman of high birth, Dio Cassius says that the real reason for the expulsion of Jews (including proselytes, according to Suetonius) was the fear of the growing success of Jewish proselytism.[75] It is odd that no punishment is mentioned for the four Jewish charlatans.[76] While those who were freedmen or sons of freedmen were conscripted (Tacitus), those with the lower status of *peregrini* were probably expelled.[77]

[73] Even earlier, in the last years of the republic, a numerous Jewish community in Rome was already considered a power to be reckoned with in popular politics, as is shown by Cicero's remarks during the trial of Flaccus (*Pro Flacco* 66-69). Herod's family had extensive contact with the court and some aristocratic families. Several of his sons were educated in Rome, but it is uncertain how much contact they had with local Jews (see Leon, *Jews of Ancient Rome*, 5-8, 14-15; Schürer, *History*, 1.442-45).

[74] Jos. *Ant.* 18.3.5 §§ 81-84. According to Josephus, four thousand Jews were impressed into the army and sent to Sardinia; the consuls "punished" (*ekolasan*) those who resisted the draft for religious reasons. Josephus's report that Tiberius ordered *all* Jews to leave Rome (*keleuei pan to Ioudaikon tēs Rhōmēs apelthein*) can hardly be correct. The account of the incident has become garbled with that of the Isis scandal (see above, n. 7), which Josephus narrates just before (*Ant.* 18.3.4 §§ 65-80) perhaps because the names of both husbands are the same. Tacitus (*Ann.* 2.85) and Suetonius (*Tib.* 36) also connect the two incidents; Tacitus reports that those who were sent to Sardinia were "of the freedman class," *libertini generis*. See L. Feldman, *Jewish Antiquities* (LCL; Cambridge, MA: Harvard University, 1969) 9.50-61; Leon, *Jews of Ancient Rome*, 17-19. E. M. Smallwood (*The Jews under Roman Rule* [Leiden: Brill, 1976] 202-10) examines the conflicting reports closely and chooses as the most reliable Dio's statement that "the majority" were forced out (*tous pleionas exēlasen*, 57.17.5a) through conscription as auxiliaries (which meant temporarily revoking Augustus's guarantee of exemption from military duty for the Jews) and expulsion (see also Smallwood, "Some Notes on the Jews under Tiberius," *Latomus* 15 [1956] 314-29).

[75] Dio Cass. 57.17.5a; Suet. *Tib.* 36. For further references to expanding Jewish proselytism in first-century Rome, see Smallwood, *Jews under Roman Rule*, 205 n. 13.

[76] The priests of Isis and Decius Mundus's freedwoman Ida were crucified according to Jos. *Ant.* 18.3.4 §80. Mundus was only exiled, not because—as Josephus suggests—his was merely a crime of passion rather than deceit, but because he was the only conspirator of the equestrian *ordo*.

[77] As Smallwood points out (*Jews under Roman Rule*, 207), citizens or even *Latini Iuniani* (freedmen of citizens not manumitted in the full legal way) could not be expelled without a trial, and freedmen were likely to belong to either group.

Another report of expulsion of Jews from Rome comes from the reign of Claudius, the well-known but brief statement of Suetonius that Claudius expelled the Jews from Rome because of their continuous disturbance instigated by "Chrestus" (*Iudaeos impulsore Chresto assidue tumultuantis Roma expulit, Claudius* 25.4). This event, whatever it was in actuality, probably occurred in the first year of Claudius's reign. We have Dio Cassius's seemingly contradictory statement, placed in the same period, that Claudius did not expel the Jews because they were too numerous (though by implication he would have liked to), but rather he forbade them, while continuing in their accustomed way of life, to assemble (60.6.6). Several questions arise in regard to the two reports. Who is correct, Suetonius or Dio Cassius? Or could each be speaking of a different phase of the same sequence of events? If there was an expulsion, did it include a large group of Jews at random or only those involved in the disturbances?[78] And, a question of particular interest to the present investigation, was Chrestus a contemporary Roman Jewish troublemaker, or did Suetonius's source pick up a name connected with the disturbances without realizing that Chrestus was actually a Galilean crucified some ten years earlier whose followers were causing disruption in the synagogues by proclaiming him the Messiah, *ho Christos*?

Various attempts have been made to reconcile the accounts of Suetonius and Dio Cassius. Suetonius may mean that only the rioters were expelled and Dio fails to mention that detail;[79] or an exile did take place and Dio has picked up the first mitigation of the edict, allowing Jews to return but not to assemble;[80] or Dio's report refers to an edict of prohibition of assembly early in Claudius's reign, while Suetonius refers to a later edict of expulsion.[81] The additional evidence of Acts 18:2 complicates the story even more. At Corinth Paul meets the Jewish couple Aquila and Priscilla, who have recently come from Italy because Claudius ordered *all* Jews to leave Rome (*dia to diatetachenai Klaudion chōrizesthai pantas tous Ioudaious apo tēs Rhōmēs*). These two are the only people known to have left Rome in connection with the incident—provided Acts is reliable here, and there is no reason to doubt its reliability in this instance. This is the first mention in Acts of Aquila and

---

[78] As with the earlier account of expulsions under Tiberius (n. 74 above), the idea of the entire Jewish community leaving Rome all at once with so little effect on history (especially on Josephus, who is silent about such an incident under Claudius) is implausible, notwithstanding Acts 18:2 (see below, n. 82).

[79] Leon, *Jews of Ancient Rome*, 24.

[80] Wiefel, "Jüdische Gemeinschaft," 77-78.

[81] Smallwood, *Jews under Roman Rule*, 212-16. This explanation would solve the discrepancy between Dio's dating of 41 c.e. and Orosius's date of 49. On the problem of dating, see also Leon, *Jews of Ancient Rome*, 24-25.

Priscilla, who were to become coworkers and fellow travelers with Paul.[82] Their Christianity is already taken for granted; Paul does not convert them. It is therefore likely that they came from Rome already as Christians.[83] This supposition lends weight to the possibility that only those Jews held responsible for the riots were expelled, namely, those who were Christians. It is even possible that by "all Jews" in Acts 18:2, Luke understands all Jews who are followers of the Way, i.e., all Christian Jews, which would make sense if the trouble had been caused because of the preaching of Christ by some of them in the synagogue.[84] Moreover, a trial before expulsion would have been feasible for such a limited number of people. Though opinion is divided on the interpretation of the Chrestus incident, it is likely that it is a reference to Christianity.[85]

Josephus reports that Poppaea Sabina, successively mistress and wife of Nero, helped on two occasions to obtain a successful outcome for Jewish embassies to the imperial court. The term "God-fearer" (*theosebēs*), by which he refers to her, may indicate not only sympathy with Jewish causes, as Josephus had opportunity to experience personally from her, but also conformity to some of the beliefs and practices of Judaism.[86] The possible connection between Poppaea's influence over Nero in favor of the Jews and Nero's persecution of Christians was proposed long ago, but the lack of evidence relegates this suggestion to the level of conjecture.[87]

---

[82] Cf. Acts 18:18, 26; Rom 16:3; 1 Cor 16:19; 2 Tim 4:19. The Pontic origin of Aquila and the aristocratic Roman names of both suggest either that they came from the provincial aristocracy or, more likely, that they were freedman and freedwoman of Roman families and therefore probably Roman citizens.

[83] See the remarks of E. Haenchen, in *The Acts of the Apostles: A Commentary* (trans. R. McL. Wilson et al.; Philadelphia: Westminster, 1971) 533 n. 4.

[84] Though the meaning of *Ioudaios* in Acts is usually Jews as opposed to Christians or among whom Christians preach (e.g., 2:5; 11:19; 12:3; 13:45, 50; etc.), Peter speaks of himself as a Jew (21:39; 22:3); Aquila (18:2) and Apollos (18:24) are both called Jews even though they are already Christians; James and the Jerusalem presbyters refer to observant Jewish Christians (21:20, 21).

[85] Among those accepting allusion to Christians in Suetonius's passage are Donfried ("Short Note," 444), Leon (*Jews of Ancient Rome*, 25), Wiefel ("Jüdische Gemeinschaft," 76), W. Marxsen (*(Introduction to the New Testament* [trans. G. Buswell; Philadelphia: Fortress, 1964] 98-99), and Smallwood (*Jews under Roman Rule*, 210-11), who calls it "the only reasonable interpretation."

[86] Jos. *Ant.* 20.8.11 §195 and *Life* 3 §16. The designation *sebomenos* is applied in Acts to Gentile converts to Christianity who had been associated with the synagogue (Acts 13:43, 50; 17:4, 17; less certainly, 16:14; 18:7), but it may be an expression indicating general piety as well, since it can also be applied to pious Jews (see Leon, *Jews of Ancient Rome*, 253; L. Feldman, "Jewish 'Sympathizers' in Classical Literature and Inscriptions," *TAPA* 81 [1950] 200-208).

[87] See Smallwood, *Jews Under Roman Rule*, 217-19; unfortunately the idea became a ploy in modern politics and was used by Paul Styger in prewar Germany. See the documenta-

Under Vespasian, Titus, and Domitian, the Jew Josephus lived comfortably in Rome, basking in the enjoyment of imperial favor. Agrippa II and his sister Berenice also enjoyed life at the court during their visits, and Berenice's liaison with Titus drew considerable attention before its unhappy ending in 79.[88] But as in the earlier case of Herod the Great and his sons,[89] whether their presence had any impact on the life of the Roman Jewish community is doubtful.

The case of Flavia Domitilla, her husband Flavius Clemens, and Manlius Acilius Glabrio should be reexamined in this context. They were accused of atheism and probably of following Jewish customs (presumably food laws and circumcision). The epitome of Dio Cass. 67.14 reads regarding Clemens and Domitilla: ἐπηνέχθη δὲ ἀμφοῖν ἔγκλημα ἀθεότητος, ὑφ' ἧς καὶ ἄλλοι ἐς τὰ τῶν Ἰουδαίων ἤθη ἐξοκέλλοντες πολλοὶ κατεδικάσθησαν ("the charge brought against them both was that of atheism, a charge on which many others who drifted into Jewish ways were condemned").[90] After saying that many were killed, that others had their property confiscated, and that Domitilla was "only" (*monon*) banished to Pandateria, he says of Glabrio that he was put to death, accused of the other things like the others, besides the charges of fighting animals as a gladiator.

It is possible to understand the text to mean that Clemens and Domitilla were prosecuted *only* for atheism because of following Jewish customs, i.e., that for Clemens and Domitilla the specifics were not connected with Judaism. However, the text reads more easily if *kai alloi* is understood as inclusive of the two names: the charge of atheism was leveled against Clemens and Domitilla and others as well who followed Jewish customs. The charges against Glabrio are vaguer, and Suetonius (*Dom.* 10.15, 17) is no help. "The same crimes as most of the others" may or may not link Glabrio to Judaism. For Clemens and Domitilla the connection may safely be established and is of course presumed by those who would make them Christians. The text thus provides another piece of evidence for the influence and popularity of Jews among aristocratic and highly placed Romans in the first century.[91] It

---

tion and defensive reaction by Leon, *Jews of Ancient Rome*, 28 n. 2. A. Momigliano's colorful depiction of Poppaea's personality with "its mixture of sensuality, love of luxury and vague spiritual aspirations" is intriguing but fanciful ("Nero," *CAH* 10.715-16).

[88] Jos. *Life* 76 §§ 422-29. Suet. *Titus* 7; Schürer, *History*, 1.471-72, 76-83; Leon, *Jews of Ancient Rome*, 31-33.

[89] See above, n. 73.

[90] The text and translation are from E. Cary, *Dio's Roman History* (LCL; Cambridge, MA: Harvard University; London: Wm. Heinemann, 1968) 8.348-51.

[91] In this connection, the midrashic legend of the circumcised senator is intriguing. *Midr. Deut* on 2:24 relates that at the time R. Eliezer, Joshua, and Gamaliel visited Rome (under

cannot be forgotten, however, that there must have been a large Jewish community in Rome on a continuing basis and that the majority of its members were not distinguished by influential positions.

The Second Century

The incident of Flavius Clemens and Flavia Domitilla in the last decade of the first century raises a question that becomes more sharpened in the early decades of the second: At what point were government officials, historians, and the general populace able to distinguish Christians from Jews? It is not impossible to see in the charge of atheism and the following of Jewish customs a reference to Christianity, assuming that Domitian did not know the difference between Judaism and Christianity; this is what later Christian tradition accepted. Nor is it impossible to interpret Domitian's rigorous enforcement of the *fiscus Iudaicus* even against those who lived the Jewish way of life without professing to be Jews (*qui improfessi Iudaicam viverent vitam*, Suet. *Dom.* 12.2) as a confusion on his part between Jewish "God-fearers" and Jewish Christians. Such a situation could then be the basis for later vague traditions of a persecution of Christians by Domitian which are based on very little evidence.[93]

To accept the interpretation that Domitian was really persecuting Christians instead of Jews and their associates who were guilty of tax evasion necessitates the assumption that even in the early second century the Christian profile was so closely tied to that of Judaism that an author like Suetonius could not tell the difference, even though he is speaking of events which happened in his own lifetime. In his account of the earlier Chrestus incident (*Claud.* 25.4) he seems to be speaking only of Jews, and if Christians are involved there, he apparently does not distinguish them; but he names Christians as victims of Nero (*Nero.* 16.2) with no mention of Judaism. Moreover,

---

Domitian), the senate decreed that no Jews could live in Rome. Because no decree of the senate could be promulgated if one of the senators participating in the decision died within thirty days, a certain senator who was a "God-fearer" committed suicide at the bidding of his wife so that the decree could not take effect. When the three rabbis came to offer condolences to the widow, they expressed their regret that the senator had not belonged fully to the community by circumcision, whereupon the wife produced a box containing bloody rags and the foreskin to show that he had indeed secretly been circumcised.

[92] The noteworthy events of the second century that affected Jews in the Roman Empire (i.e., the revolt of 132-35, Hadrian's prohibition of circumcision and Antoninus Pius's mitigation of the law) have no recorded repercussions specifically on Roman Jews and their relationship with Christians, and so they are discussed here only in passing (see Leon, *Jews of Ancient Rome*, 36-38; E. M. Smallwood, "The Legislation of Hadrian and Antoninus Pius Against Circumcision," *Latomus* 18 [1959] 334-47; Schürer, *History*, 1.537-40 and passim).

[93] See Eus. *Hist. eccl.* 3.18-20.

Suetonius's contemporaries and colleagues, Pliny the Younger and Tacitus, clearly knew the difference. Neither Pliny's well-known correspondence with Trajan over the procedure to follow in investigating Christians' activities and legality (*Ep.* 10.96) nor Tacitus's account of Nero's persecution (*Ann.* 15.44. 2-8) suggests any confusion between Christians and Jews. Indeed Tacitus seems especially well informed about Christianity's Palestinian origins: *Auctor nominis eius Christus Tiberio imperitante per procuratorem Pontium Pilatum supplicio adfectus erat; repressaque in praesens exitiabilis superstitio rursum erumpebat, non modo per Iudaeam, originem eius mali, sed per urbem etiam* ("Christ, the source of the name, had suffered the death penalty under Tiberius by sentence of the procurator Pontius Pilate; the destructive superstition, temporarily restrained, broke out again not only in Judaea, origin of the disease, but even in Rome").

Lest it be assumed, however, that by the early second century Roman Christianity had lost all external resemblance to Judaism, we have the contrary testimony of Justin Martyr several decades later in the *Dialogue with Trypho.*[94] In chapter 47 Justin singles out several categories of Christians involved in Jewish practice: (1) Jewish-born Christians who keep the Law but do not compel Gentile Christians to do so (v. 1); (2) Jewish Christians who do try to impose the Law on Gentile believers and refuse to eat with them otherwise, or with the Jewish Christians of v. 1 (v. 3); (3) Gentile Christians who keep the Law (v. 4); (4) Jews who were once Christians but have returned to Moses (v. 4).[95] In reaction, there are even some (Jew or Gentile?) who refuse to share fellowship or table with those who do keep the Law (v. 2; *Apol.* 1.14.4 may be referring to the reverse, where they do share together, which seems to have been more common). Justin grudgingly accepts Gentile observance of the Law by those who wish (*sōthēsesthai isōs hypolambanō*, "they will be saved too, I suppose," v. 4). He disapproves of those who would pressure Jewish Christians into abandoning the Law but thinks rather that they should be allowed full membership in the community as

---

[94] The *Dialogue* was written after 150 C.E. and probably in Rome even though it is dramatically set in Ephesus twenty years earlier (see B. Altaner, *Patrology* [trans. H. Graef; 2d ed.; New York: Herder and Herder, 1961] 122-23; L. W. Barnard, "Justin Martyr in Recent Study," *SJT* 22 [1969] 152-64; R. M. Grant, "The Chronology of the Greek Apologists," *VC* 9 [1955] 25-34). Intended readers included Jews and Christians but probably not pagans (see T. Stylianopoulos, *Justin Martyr and the Mosaic Law* [SBLDS 20; Missoula, MT: SBL/Scholars Press, 1975] 8-20, 40-41, 169-95). For an opposing view, see J. Nilson, "To Whom Is Justin's *Dialogue with Trypho* Addressed?" *TS* 38 (1977) 538-46. It is unlikely that in portraying actual community situations Justin would be thinking of a fictitious setting two decades earlier halfway across the empire rather than the situation with which he and his readers were familiar in Rome.

[95] Groups (1), (2), and (4) need not refer only to converts from Judaism. They can just as well be persons born into Jewish Christian families of similar observance.

brothers and sisters in unity (v. 2).[96] In addition, he refers to Jewish-born Christians who do not keep the ceremonial law but only the moral law of the Jewish scriptures (*Dial.* 23.3) and proselytes and "God-fearers" of pagan background who were attracted to Christianity through Judaism and consequently face the dilemma of acceptance of the Law by circumcision versus acceptance of Christianity alone by baptism (*Dial.* 10.4; 122.2). Justin is also aware that there are Jews anathematizing Christians in their synagogues (*Dial.* 38.1; 47.4).[97]

In short, the picture provided by Justin suggests an exceedingly complex relationship between Jewish and Gentile observance and even between Jewish and Christian communities, with every conceivable variety of position represented. Despite the clear identification of Christianity by Suetonius, Pliny, and Tacitus, Justin's remarks seem to portray a "still quite Jewish and Jewish-Christian milieu of the community of faith out of which Justin writes."[98] Distinction between Jews and some Christians on the basis of way of life or external form may still not have been obvious to a Roman outsider in the middle of the second century, and while Gentile Christians had for some time seen themselves as separate from Judaism it is not at all certain that all of the groups of Jewish Christians described by Justin would have unhesitatingly called themselves Christians rather than Jews.

Later in the century Galen's remarks, discussed above, show both the association of Jews and Christians and the ability to distinguish them one from the other. Three times he refers together to the followers (or school) of Moses and Christ;[99] twice to the teachings of Moses only;[100] and twice to Christians.[101] Perhaps the evidence from Galen reflects what would have been the prevailing understanding of pagans through most of the second century: that Christianity had its roots in Judaism and shared with it a common theological base; that there were still points of close contact but also points of broad divergence; and that like most parent-child relation-

---

[96] Indeed, he may have been more favorable to Judaizers than to Marcionites or Valentinians; compare *Dial.* 47.2 with 35.5.

[97] See further G. H. Williams, "Baptismal Theology and Practice in Rome as Reflected in Justin Martyr," in *The Ecumenical World of Orthodox Civilization: Russia and Orthodoxy. Essays in Honor of Georges Florovsky,* ed. A. Blane and T. Bird (The Hague: Mouton, 1974) 3.27-30; idem, "Justin Glimpsed as Martyr Among His Roman Contemporaries," in *The Context of Contemporary Theology: Essays in Honor of Paul Lehmann,* ed. A. McKelway and E. Willis (Atlanta: John Knox, 1974) 104-6.

[98] Williams, "Baptismal Theology," 11. In view of this evidence it should not be surprising that deep traces of Jewish literary and paraenetic tradition are everywhere present in *Hermas.*

[99] See above, nn. 27-29.

[100] See above, n. 31.

[101] See above, nn. 30-31.

ships, the struggle for independence on the part of the child and for control on the part of the parent left a history of conflict and tension behind.

The Social Composition of the Jewish Community

The close connections between Judaism and Christianity in Rome in the late first and the early second century diminished as the second century progressed. The apparent lack of centralized religious government among Roman Jews has long been noted.[102] The comparison of this decentralized form of Jewish community organization with what we know of Christian life in Rome in the first and second centuries is provocative. As G. LaPiana and others have seen, the first stage of the Quartodeciman controversy in the middle of the second century shows not only the absence of a strong central authority in the Christian community but also the presence of many Greek-speaking Christians in Rome with ethnic origins in the East.[103] By comparison, an analysis of the Jewish funerary inscriptions reveals that 76 percent of them are written in Greek, 23 percent in Latin, and 1 percent in Hebrew, Aramaic, or bilingual wording.[104] The scant evidence we have of Roman Christian nomenclature in the second century indicates a predominately lower-class amalgam.[105] The nomenclature of the Jewish inscriptions offers some surprises. Though three-fourths of the inscriptions are in Greek, Latin names outnumber both Greek and Semitic names combined, probably reflecting the tendency of foreigners to give their children Latin names.[106] Dating is

[102] See Schürer, History (1891 ed.) 2.243-52; J.-B. Frey, "Les communautés juives à Rome aux premiers temps de l'Eglise," RSR 20 (1930) 267-91; 21 (1931) 129-68; Leon, Jews of Ancient Rome, 167-71; Wiefel, "Jüdische Gemeinschaft," 73-75. Others (e.g., Juster, Juifs, 1.420-21; G. LaPiana, "Foreign Groups in Rome during the First Centuries of the Empire," HTR 20 [1927] 361-63) posited at least a central gerousia or city council, though not a supreme officer. There is no new evidence since these studies except for one new inscription from excavations at the Villa Torlonia catacomb in 1973-74: that of one ANASTASIOUS ARCHIGEROUSIARCHĒS UIOS AN(as)TASIOU OI-, probably datable from its location to the third or fourth century (Fasola, "Due catacombe," 36-37). This is the only known example of the office of archigerousiarchēs, an apparently redundant title.

[103] LaPiana, "Roman Church," 208-19. LaPiana does, however, assume the existence of the office of bishop in the mid-second century without monarchical authority, which differs from what we know of the Jewish community. A true episcopal office at this time need not be assumed.

[104] Leon, Jews of Ancient Rome, 76-77. The dating of the inscriptions is difficult to control. The best evidence seems to point to the third and fourth centuries. Fasola ("Due catacombe") established in the recent excavations that the Villa Torlonia catacomb was originally two separate catacombs begun at different times, the lower in the late second or early third century, the upper in the mid-third (pp. 61-62).

[105] See above, pp. 103-111.

[106] See the extensive tables in Leon, Jews of Ancient Rome, 95-112; see also n. 44 above.

also a factor. Since most of the Jewish inscriptions are later than the second century, the degree of Latinization in names is probably meaningless.[107] There is a great variety in the types of Latin names that occur. Both "servile" and "ingenuous" names are amply represented among the 254 examples. Again, since most represent third- and fourth-century persons, the distinctions are ultimately meaningless.

Still the question remains why the language of the majority of the inscriptions should be Greek if the preponderance of Latin names witnesses against the hypothesis of vast numbers of Jewish latecomers to the capital. There is no basis for assuming that Jews clung more tenaciously to their Greek because it was the common language of their social milieu. A study of the patterns of grammar, spelling, and pronunciation of both the Greek and Latin inscriptions indicates that they are representative of the common "less educated" language of the day and do not constitute any kind of special Jewish dialect.[108]

The decorative art of the Jewish catacombs included several beautifully painted tomb chambers and sculptured sarcophagi from the Via Appia and Via Nomentana (Villa Torlonia) catacombs. Many of the inscriptions on the *loculi* also contain decorative figures, some executed with more skill than others.[109] Yet most of the inscriptions contain either very simple and conventional iconography or no decorative attempts at all. While this archaeological evidence suggests the presence of some prosperous members and families in the Jewish communities, it also indicates that those who could afford expensive and artfully executed funerary monuments were in the minority. Even in the period from which most of the catacomb material comes, i.e., the third and fourth centuries, most of the Roman Jews whose memorials have survived seem to represent the common and ordinary people who made up the lower echelons of society in the capital.[110]

---

[107] Brick-stamp dating indicates that the Monteverde catacomb was used from the late republican period to Diocletian, but the heaviest use was under Hadrian and Septimius Severus, which Smallwood plausibly connects with the aftermath of the Jewish wars of 71 and 135. Fifty to seventy years later, the children and grandchildren of slaves are *libertini* buried in Jewish catacombs (*Jews under Roman Rule*, 519-20).

[108] Leon, *Jews of Ancient Rome*, 78-92.

[109] See the illustrations of Leon, *Jews of Ancient Rome*, figs. 12-16, 28-29, 31, 40-47.

[110] On the basis of early catacomb use at Monteverde, it can be established that the earliest Jewish settlement was in Trastevere; later residential districts to receive Jewish settlements were the Campus Martius (synagogue of the Campesians) and the Subura (synagogue of the Siburesians). None of these areas was noted for the prosperity of its inhabitants. Perhaps there was a settlement of poor Jews at the Porta Capena (see Juv. *Sat.* 3.11-14). See the summary of times and places of Jewish residence in Smallwood, *Jews under Roman Rule*, 519-25.

Summary

This examination of the literary, historical, and archaeological evidence of the Roman Jewish community of the first centuries of the empire compared with the evidence about the Christian community yields the conclusion that there is more information placing Jews in influential positions, at the court and among aristocratic families. The interconnections among local Jews and visiting dignitaries like the Herodian dynasty or Josephus are obscure. But Judaism, because of its long history and its recognition as a traditional religion, held a certain prestige and even attraction among some members of the Roman upper classes, as is shown, for example, by the incidents involving Fulvia and Flavia Domitilla.

The interconnection between Roman Judaism and Christian origins in Rome is equally obscure, and the testimony from outside sources regarding distinctions between Christians and Jews is conflicting. Still in the middle of the second century Justin shows that Jewish influence on Christian praxis is very strong. The organization of the Jewish community into local units grouped around a synagogue may have been the model for local Christian communities in Rome meeting in house churches, independent of a centralized episcopal authority.

Finally, even though both literary and archaeological evidence shows that some Roman Jews possessed a certain amount of prestige and wealth, the same sources indicate that the majority of Jews, like the majority of Christians, were of the ordinary people who constituted the lower classes of Rome, with no more and no less a foreign element than was present in the general population.

Hermas on Social Climbing and Pagan Friendships

We can now turn to several passages in *Hermas* where the author is concerned not only with the management of wealth on the part of some members of his community but also with problems of changed lifestyle and behavior as a result of wealth.

Adhering to the Servants of God

The verb *kollan, kollasthai*, "stick," "adhere," "cleave," "attach oneself" occurs fairly frequently in biblical literature, used both of inanimate objects or abstractions[111] and of people.[112] In *Hermas* the word is used inanimately of bitterness (*Man.* 10.2.3) and of punishment and torture (*Sim.* 6.5.3) adhering to a person as well as of stones joined to stones in the construction of the tower (*Vis.* 3.2.6). However, in view of the fact that in the subsequent allegory the stones symbolize various categories of Christians, the meaning of this last passage is not exhausted by classifying it as a reference to inanimate objects. Elsewhere in *Hermas* those who are strong in the faith of the Lord do not *adhere* to evil spirits but keep away from them (*Man.* 11.4), and the tenth *Mandate* closes with the exhortation to *adhere* to the Lord in order to understand and know everything (*Man.* 10.6; cf. Sir 2:3).

Six other passages in *Hermas* use the word *kollasthai* in a way that is important for the present study—in order to single out those who do not associate with the community as fully as the author thinks they should.

Vis. 3.6.2 describes some of the stones that do not fit into the tower. Those which were thrown far away were wicked and hypocrites (v. 1). But those which lie on the ground rotting are they who have known the truth but did not remain in it nor continue to *adhere* to the saints; they are therefore useless.[113] It is not specified in what way this group does not adhere to "the saints." Three verses later the white round stones which do not fit into the building are those whose faith weakens into denial in the time of persecution (*thlipsis*) because of their wealth and business concerns (v. 5). Then follows some discussion about whether or not those with wealth can be useful at all; in this case the answer is negative.[114]

Vis. 3.6.2 is a simple statement of a theme that is further elaborated in later passages in *Hermas* and explicitly connected with the problem of wealth and business. Before examining the others, it will be helpful to consider a

---

[111] E.g., of disease (Deut 28:60; 2 Kgs 5:27); dirt (Job 38:38; Luke 10:11); one part of the body to another (Job 29:10; Ps 21[22]:15; 43[44]:25; 62[63]:8; 101[102]:5; 118[119]:25; 136[137]:6; Lam 4:4); of a crocodile (Job 41:7[8], 14[15]); curses (Deut 29:20[19]; Bar 1:20; 3:4); sins (Rev 18:5); virtue (Ps 24[25]:21; Rom 12:9). The LXX most frequently uses it to translate *dābaq* from the MT.

[112] To God (Deut 6:13; 10:20; 2 Kgs 18:6; Jer 13:11; Sir 2:3 [sing.]; 1 Cor 6:17); to his testimonies (Ps 118[119]:31); to other people (2 Sam 2:20; Ruth 2:8, 21; 1 Macc 3:2; 6:21; Luke 15:15; Acts 5:13; 8:29; 9:26; 10:28; 17:34); of sexual union (Gen 2:24; Sir 19:2; 1 Cor 6:16). 1 Kgs 11:2, although about Solomon and his wives, probably refers more to cultic conformity than to sexual union.

[113] The last eight words of the passage are missing from the Sinaiticus, Palatine, and Ethiopic manuscripts. Lake (LCL 2.40) rejects the reading, but Whittaker (*Der Hirt*, 12), Dibelius (*Der Hirt*, 468), and Joly (*Pasteur*, 114) accept it. One indication of authenticity is its use of the *euchrēstos/achrēstos* theme, which recurs periodically in the chapter (vv. 1, 6, 7).

[114] For a discussion of this theme, see above, pp. 51–52.

similar expression in *1 Clem.* 46.2 and related passages. The use of *kollasthai* to describe imitation of and association with those who give good example occurs several times in *1 Clement*: 15.1 and 30.3 are exhortations to *adhere* to the virtuous; 31.1 exhorts the readers to *adhere* directly to the blessing of God by walking in the ways of blessing, and the following lines specify Abraham, Isaac, and Jacob as the models of how to do it (31.2-4). Chapter 45 again invokes biblical examples of the just, and chapter 46 opens with the exhortation that "we too must *adhere* to such examples, brethren, for it is written, '*Adhere* to the saints, for those who *adhere* to them shall be sanctified'" (46.1, 2). This otherwise unknown apocryphal saying may underlie the *kollasthai* usage in *Hermas* as well, especially that of *kollasthai tois hagiois* in *Vis.* 3.6.2 and *Sim.* 8.8.1[115] *1 Clem.* 46.4 develops the theme by exhorting the readers this time to *adhere* to the innocent and the just, for they are the elect of God. As contrasted with *Hermas*, the literary form in *1 Clement* is exhortation or paraenesis rather than description or prophetic pronouncement against those who are not measuring up, though in meaning a critique of the actual situation is surely implied (cf. *1 Clem.* 36.5-9). *1 Clement* establishes that the use of *kollasthai* for communal adhesion was familiar in Roman Christian literature but does not connect the expression with the problems of wealth.

Sim. 8.8.1 repeats the expression *mē kollōmenoi tois hagiois*, which first appeared in *Hermas* in *Vis.* 3.6.2. Here in the parable of the willow sticks, those who gave up their sticks half-green and half-dry are those who are embroiled in their business concerns and therefore (understanding the second phrase as a parataxis) do not adhere to the saints; because of this they are half-alive and half-dead. Many of them are double-minded (*edipsychēsan*), uncertain whether or not they wish to repent and change their ways (v. 3).

Similarly, *Sim.* 8.9.1 depicts those who surrendered their sticks two-thirds dry and one-third green (in slightly more desperate condition than those in *Sim.* 8.8.1) along the same lines but in more detail:[116]

οὗτοί εἰσιν πιστοὶ μὲν γεγονότες, πλουτήσαντες δὲ καὶ γενόμενοι ἐνδοξότεροι παρὰ τοῖς ἔθνεσιν· ὑπερηφανίαν μεγάλην ἐνεδύσατο καὶ ὑ-
ψηλόφρονες ἐγένοντο καὶ κατέλιπον τὴν ἀλήθειαν, καὶ οὐκ ἐκολλ-
ήθησαν τοῖς δικαίοις, ἀλλὰ μετὰ τῶν ἐθνῶν συνέζησαν, καὶ αὕτη ἡ

---

[115] Suggested by Dibelius, *Der Hirt*, 468. His interpretation of the simple statement in *Vis.* 3.6.2 as meaning that such believers are practicing a syncretistic Christianity that they use as a stepping stone to mystery cults is conjecture. Lightfoot (*Apostolic Fathers*, 1.2, 138-40) names Sir 6:34 as the closest canonical saying to the apocryphal source of *1 Clem.* 46.2.

[116] For a discussion of the parallel structures in *Sim.* 8.8.1-3 and 8.9.1-4, see above p. 50.

ὁδὸς αὐτοῖς ἡδυτέρα ἐγένετο. ἀπὸ δὲ τοῦ θεοῦ οὐκ ἀπέστησαν, ἀλλ'
ἐνέμειναν τῇ πίστει, μὴ ἐργαζόμενοι δὲ τὰ ἔργα τῆς πίστεως.

These are they who became believers but were rich and became much honored
among the unbelievers. They put on great arrogance and became haughty and
gave up the truth, and did not adhere to the righteous, but lived with the
unbelievers, and this way was more pleasurable to them. But they did not
apostatize from God, but remained in the faith, though not doing the works of
the faith.

Here those who are already believers, i.e. Christians,[117] have become
rich and therefore in better social standing among the unbelievers (*ethnē*).[118]
Pride has therefore taken over, and they have "given up the truth," which
must be a relative rather than an absolute judgment in view of the later
explicit statement that they have not become apostates. What they have
given up is the way of life suitable to a believer, requiring them to change
their social status and circle of acquaintances, so that they can no longer
continue to associate with their former (Christian) friends but must enter
into a lifestyle suitable to the unbelievers. Such people have not formally
renounced their Christian faith, but their actions and way of life are at odds
with it in the estimation of the author. The text continues that many living
this deviant way of life repented (v. 2), but those who did not change their
way of life eventually became apostates (v. 3), while others hesitated in their
uncertainty and *dipsychia* (v. 4). Finally, *Sim.* 8.9, like its companion piece,
8.8, ends with a call to repentance, which necessitates that they no longer
remain in the pleasures (*tais hēdonais*) of a pagan lifestyle.

Sim. 9.20 is the allegory of thorns and thistles from the third mountain.[119] The rich and those who are involved in their business affairs[120] do not

---

[117] The more technical meaning, "(Christian) believers," rather than the broader "those
who are faithful" is to be preferred here, since the author obviously does not consider them to be
exercising the virtue of fidelity. This designation for Christians is already established in the NT,
e.g., 1 Cor 7:12-15; 2 Cor 6:15; 1 Tim 5:16; Acts 10:45 (see BAG s.v. *pistos*). The loose usage of
the verb *ginesthai* to mean anything from "happen" to a substitute for *einai* makes it impossible
to judge whether it is here a case of Christians by birth or conversion. Nor does the perfect tense
of one of the participles clarify the meaning, since the perfect may be used with an aorist sense in
Hellenistic Greek (see BDF, #343). The translation "became" for *ginesthai* above is arbitrary in
both cases, except that in the second use, what is described seems to be part of a change that has
taken place in the group of people under discussion.

[118] *Ethnē* meaning Gentiles as opposed to Jews is of course common biblical language in
both OT and NT; with the meaning "pagan" as opposed to Christian, as here, it is already found
in Ign. *Trall.* 8.2 and frequently elsewhere in Hermas, e.g., *Vis.* 1.4.2; 2.2.5; *Man.* 4.1.9; *Sim.* 1.10
(see BAG s.v.).

[119] For a discussion of the structure and literary relationships of this passage, see above,
pp. 48-49.

[120] The two groups are distinguished only for literary effect and are to be understood as

adhere to the servants of God (*ou kollōntai tois doulois tou theou*) but rather, out of avarice and disdain, they shun the society of their would-be companions because they fear being asked to give of their resources or to perform some service for them (*hoi de plousioi dyskolōs kollōntai tois doulois tou theou, phoboumenoi mē ti aitisthōsin hyp' autōn*, v. 2). For all of this sort, repentance is held out as a possibility, provided they now turn to the doing of good (*ean . . . agathon ti poiēsōsin*), i.e., spending their money for the relief of the needy in the community (cf. *Sim.* 2.10).

Sim. 9.26.3 is the allegory of the ninth mountain. Here in v. 2 church officials who misappropriate funds intended for the needy have hope of repentance if they change their ways. A different group seems to be intended in vv. 3–6, namely, those who have denied and not turned to their Lord, not associating with the servants of God but remaining alone—they are destroying themselves (*mē kollōmenoi tois doulois tou theou, alla monazontes apollyousi tas heautōn phychas*, v. 3; cf. John 12:24-5). They are compared to a vine that is neglected and becomes useless (v. 4). There is still hope of repentance for them, only if they have not denied from the heart (v. 5). In this passage there is no mention of wealth or business, only of denial of God in connection with alienation from the community. There is, however, a definite relationship with the others through *Vis.* 3.6.5 and *Sim.* 8.8.2, where it is precisely *because* of their wealth and business that some deny their Lord in the time of persecution or trial (*thlipsis*). In *Vis.* 3.6.5 the emphasis is on the causes of denial related to money and luxury; in *Sim.* 9.26.3 the emphasis is on the factor of isolation from the community. While it would be reading too much into the text to suggest that the two types of Christians referred to in the two passages are coextensive and identical, it can at least be assumed that there is extensive overlap, i.e., that wealth, business affairs, and the enhanced lifestyle and social status that accompany them are major causes of lapses from the faith at different times.

Consequences of a Compromised Lifestyle

Man. 10.1.4, though it occurs in *Hermas* before the four passages from the *Similitudes* discussed above, is here placed last because it unites the most important strands that have appeared in the previous passages: pursuit of truth, business, wealth, and assimilation to the way of life of unbelievers. The context is a paraenetic passage in which Hermas is exhorted by the Shepherd to keep from himself the spirit of grief (*lypē*), which is a sister to *dipsychia* and *oxycholia* (10.1.1). Those who make no effort to learn about

the same (see above, chapter III, n. 21).

truth and theology[121] but simply believe and at the same time are mixed up in business ventures and wealth, friendships with unbelievers,[122] and many other worldly undertakings do not understand divine parables (i.e., such as the Shepherd reveals), for they are darkened, corrupted, and dried up by their deeds:

οἱ μηδέποτε ἐρευνήσαντες περὶ τῆς ἀληθείας μηδὲ ἐπιζητήσαντες περὶ τῆς θεότητος, πιστεύσαντες δὲ μόνον, ἐμπεφυρμένοι δὲ πραγματείαις καὶ πλούτῳ καὶ φιλίαις ἐθνικαῖς καὶ ἄλλαις πολλαῖς πραγματείαις τοῦ αἰῶνος τούτου· ὅσοι οὖν τούτοις πρόσκεινται, οὐ νοοῦσι τὰς παραβολὰς τῆς θεότητος· ἐπισκοτοῦνται γὰρ ὑπὸ τούτων τῶν πράξεων καὶ καταφθείρονται καὶ γίνονται κεχερσωμένοι.

Here those who have made business and wealth their principal concern do not make the effort to search for truth and understanding, and so their faith remains superficial (cf. *Vis.* 3.6.2; *Sim.* 8.9.1). They are simply believers who do nothing to increase and strengthen their faith. Moreover, they form friendships and social relationships with unbelievers. These associations lead them into the "other affairs of this world" which are part of their downfall. The passage continues with the analogy of a good vineyard that falls into neglect;[123] so too those whose attention is taken up with many *praxeis* cannot understand talk about righteousness (*dikaiosynē*, v. 5). Like those spoken of in *Sim.* 8.9.1, their deeds do not match their profession of faith. Though the expression *kollasthai tois hagiois* (*dikaiois, doulois tou theou*) is not used, the passage closes by quoting Sir 2:3: *kollēthēti oun tō kyriō* ("cling therefore to the Lord").

---

[121] *Peri tēs theotētos*, literally, "about the Godhead." When the doctrinal conflicts of the second-century Roman Church are seen as a struggle between an educated, intellectual minority and an organizationally oriented majority of "common people" (e.g., La Piana, "Roman Church," 204, 221; Gager, *Kingdom and Community*, 80-83; H. Langerbeck, "Zur Auseinandersetzung von Theologie und Gemeindeglauben in der römischen Gemeinde in den Jahren 135-65," *Aufsätze zur Gnosis* [ed. H. Dörries; Abhandlungen der Akademie der Wissenschaften in Göttingen, Philologisch-historisch Klasse, 3e Folge, Nr. 69; Göttingen: Vandenhoeck and Ruprecht, 1967] 167-79), Hermas is usually assigned to the ordinary, less well-educated folk (e.g., Dibelius, *Der Hirt*, 424-25; Joly, *Pasteur*, 55-57). The author does usually stand in opposition to dissenters (*Sim.* 8.8.5; 8.9.4) and teachers of new doctrines (*Sim.* 5.7; 8.6.5; 9.22), but here in *Man.* 10.1.4 he seems to be saying the opposite: it is those who do not pursue an understanding of faith with inquiring minds who come under his criticism.

[122] Note the inclusion of friendship among causes of distraction and *oxycholia* in *Man.* 5.2.2 (pointed out by Dibelius, *Der Hirt*, 533).

[123] Compare the analogy of the vine in *Sim.* 9.26.4.

Summary

The six passages discussed above, *Vis.* 3.6.2, 5; *Sim.* 8.8.1-2; 8.9.1-3; 9.20.2; 9.26.3; *Man.* 10.1.4, all reveal a specific concern—the neglect of social relationships and responsibilities within the Christian community—which is connected with the more general concern about the effects of wealth and business involvements. The author makes use of a familiar paraenetic expression, possibly drawing it from the same apocryphal source as did *1 Clem.* 46.2, and three times out of five (*Sim.* 8.8.1; 8.9.1; 9.20.2) he connects it explicitly with wealth and business as factors that draw Christians away from association with the community. From *Vis.* 3.6 the relationship can likewise be inferred, as it can at least partially from *Sim.* 9.26. *Man.* 10.1.4 does not use the expression *kollasthai tois doulois tou theou* or the equivalent but specifies, as does *Sim.* 8.9.1-3, that what is at stake is social ambition and a greater participation in the "good life" as lived by the upwardly mobile residents of Rome. Who these social-climbing Christians probably were will be discussed below.

The majority of these passages are found in allegorical contexts. There are a number of extended allegories in *Hermas*, especially the building of the tower in the *Vis.* and *Sim.* 9, the willow tree in *Sim.* 8, and the twelve mountains in *Sim.* 9. It need not be supposed that the whole range of possible responses to all issues raised in the allegories was actually known to the author. However, there are real concerns being raised about real issues affecting the life of the community for which the text was written.

Freedmen and *Hermas*

Freedmen in Business

It has already been established on the basis of the existing evidence for the social composition of Roman Christianity in the second century that those involved in business and social climbing to whom Hermas devotes his attention are not likely to be aristocrats and members of the *ordines*. However, it would be congruent with what we know of Roman Christians at the time for them to belong to the craftsmen and tradesmen, who were the backbone of the city's commercial life. Some of these people in the late republic and the early empire were lower-class native freeborn, or *ingenui*, and foreign freeborn noncitizens, or *peregrini*. The inscriptional and scant literary evidence suggests, though, that the majority of enterprising small business people engaged in trade and manufacture of products were freedmen and women and that indeed freedmen as a social class were known for their involvement in business affairs.[124]

Freedmen and Social Climbing

Another characteristic for which freedmen were known was their desire to "get ahead" both materially and socially. A few became extremely wealthy, usually through successful patronage or inheritance. Caecilius Isidorus, who died in 8 B.C.E. with 4,116 slaves, 3,600 yoke of oxen, and 257,000 head of other stock, probably inherited his fortune from a childless member of the Caecilii Metelli.[125] The wealthy Calvisius Sabinus, snobbishly satirized by Seneca for trying to appear more learned than he was by having educated slaves tutor him, was described as having both the inheritance and the natural limitations of a freedman (*et patrimonium habebat libertini et ingenium*, *Ep. Mor.* 27.5-8).[126] Of the largest known private fortunes in the early empire, at least five were in the hands of freedmen.[127] There are the well-known cases of successful imperial freedmen like Pallas or Narcissus,[128] and the literary type Trimalchio, who inherited his patron's fortune and invested it immediately in large-scale business ventures.[129] Some were even promoted to equestrian status, particularly, but not exclusively, imperial freedmen.[130]

---

[124] E.g., Duff, *Freedmen*, 202 and passim; P. Veyne, "Vie de Trimalchio," *Annales. Economies. Sociétés. Civilisations* 16 (1961) 227-31; S. Treggiari, *Roman Freedmen during the Late Republic* (Oxford: Clarendon, 1969) 33, 36, 91-106, 172. The information is largely retrievable through their leadership roles in occupational *collegia*. Though the material discussed by Treggiari is mostly of the late first century B.C.E., it represents the beginnings of social and economic tendencies that seem not to have changed substantially during the next two centuries.

[125] Pliny *NH* 33.134-35; Treggiari, *Roman Freedmen*, 109, 239 (other examples are cited in Treggiari, pp. 239-40).

[126] The scene as described by Seneca is evocative of Molière's *Burgeois Gentilhomme*. This Calvisius Sabinus is otherwise unknown (cf. *PIR*² C351; *PW* 11), and it is not certain that he was actually a freedman. But would Seneca have compared a senator, however foolish he appeared, to a freedman?

[127] See the list in Duncan-Jones, *Economy*, 343-44.

[128] For detailed evidence of the network of possessions and investments by known imperial freedmen and of honors given to them, see G. Boulvert, *Les esclaves et les affranchis impériaux sous le Haut-Empire romain* (Dissertation; Aix-en-Provence: Université d'Aix-Marseille, 1964) 2.663-68; see also idem *Domestique et fonctionnaire sous le Haut-Empire romain: la condition de l'affranchi et de l'esclave du prince* (Centre de Recherches d'Histoire Ancienne 9; Paris: Belles Lettres, 1974).

[129] Pet. *Satyr.* 76. On the significance of Trimalchio as a reflection of social developments, see Finley, *Ancient Economy*, 36; Veyne, "Vie de Trimalchio." For an attempt to place Trimalchio historically, see K. F. C. Rose, "Time and Place in the Satyricon," *TAPA* 93 (1962) 402-9.

[130] Weaver (*Familia Caesaris*, 282-85) cites the granting of the *anulus aureus* to *liberti* once under Augustus, probably three times under Claudius (including Pallas, who was voted the

Others tried apparently to usurp its rank and privileges without official sanction (Suet. *Claud.* 25.1).

Those freedmen and women who were able to amass huge fortunes are well enough documented, and yet they must be considered the small minority of a group most of whom did not fare so well. The relatively few extremely wealthy examples that we know of are not sufficient to have caused the amount of aristocratic resentment and general contempt that was manifested against them for their materialistic outlook and attempts to outdo the upper classes in pomp, ostentation, and advantageous connections. Typical of the contempt against them for these characteristics are Juvenal's remarks that a freedman can get anything he wants with his money, including social preference, because money is the goddess most worshipped.[131] Epictetus laments from his philosophical perspective that all slaves want is to be set free, then to make money by whatever means possible, then to enter the equestrian *ordo*, then to command in the military and eventually gain access to the senate, only to find themselves there in the worse slavery of all (*Disc.* 4.1.33-40).

Upper-class resentment against the ostentatious wealth of freedmen is typified by Seneca's snide comment that freedmen's baths are more luxurious than the ones he frequents,[132] or by Pliny's bitter reaction to the promotion of Pallas to the senatorial purple and Pallas's "magnanimous" refusal of the monetary fringe benefit offered with it (*Ep.* 7.29; 8.6; see also Tac. *Ann.* 12.53.3).

Though it is doubtful that freedmen and women as a class were the only ones in Roman society who were outstanding for materialistic values and the unscrupulous pursuit of social advantage, they probably had the most to gain.[133] While excluded from most public offices and subject to some definite

ornamenta praetoria by the senate in 52), once under Galba, once under Vitellius, twice under Vespasian, but only three times during the second century and possibly four during the third century. Both Weaver (pp. 267-82) and Duff (*Freedmen*, 214-20) argue that though the act was a recognition of their wealth and influence, such parvenu equestrians remained in an inferior position politically and socially to legitimate members of the *ordo*.

[131] Juv. *Sat.* 1.102-14. One of Juvenal's favorite targets was a freedman-become-equestrian named Crispinus (*Sat.* 1.26-29; 4.1 and passim, 108).

[132] *Ep.* 86.7. The ultimate in ostentation seems to be that the freedmen's baths are replete with columns built not to support anything, but just for decoration and the spending of money!

[133] Treggiari (*Roman Freedmen*, 238-41), rejecting the suggestion of M. L. Gordon ("Freedman's Son," 77) that the notable materialism and crassness of freedmen was a reaction to the deprivation they experienced as slaves, rightly concludes that they simply absorbed the values of the environment in which they had served. Horace (*Ep.* 1.1.53-54) neatly summarizes an unwritten principle of popular philosophy by saying that money is the first thing to be sought, and virtue comes after cash (*quaerenda pecunia primum est: virtus post nummos*).

social restrictions,[134] they could acquire through money a significant share in the "good life" of Roman society and thus prepare the way for their sons and grandsons, who would be able to make their mark politically as well by gaining access to those public positions closed to their fathers.[135] In a society in which prestige and social power theoretically depended on birth and civil status but often realistically were tied to wealth and personal influence, it is understandable that freedmen as a class constituted a major threat to the aristocracy. As long as individual freedmen and women remained within the bounds of their inferior social status, conflict was kept to a minimum, but prejudice, protests, and resentment broke out when they displayed arrogance or obvious affluence and were taken seriously for it, when "old aristocrats found themselves less well-off, influential, and eye-catching on the *Via Appia* than an ex-slave who had until recently been at the beck and call of a master."[136]

The majority of freedmen in Rome were not in a position to compete with the aristocracy. They were the small shopkeepers, craftsmen, and traders of the city. On the lower level of a mobile social scale, however, the temptation and the pressure to do ever better financially in order to advance socially are usually just as insistent as they are nearer to the top.

Hermas a Freedman

Within the context of what has been said about the social position of freedmen, it is important to recall that the author of the *Visions* must have been a freedman himself. The opening line says that the one who raised

---

[134] See R. MacMullen, *Roman Social Relations, 50 B.C. to A.D. 284* (New Haven: Yale University, 1974) 105, 191-92; P. R. C. Weaver, "Social Mobility in the Early Roman Empire: The Evidence of the Imperial Freedmen and Slaves," *Past and Present* 37 (1967) 3-20; Boulvert, *Esclaves*, 2.668-75, 692-93.

[135] See Duff, *Freedmen*, 50-53; Gordon, "Freedman's Son."

[136] Treggiari, *Roman Freedmen*, 226-27. By the second century many of the "old aristocrats" had been replaced by people who were only a few generations away from slavery themselves. But the social dynamic of resentment by those who had reached the top against those on the way up does not seem to have changed. Further documentation on upper-class prejudice against those below can be found in A. N. Sherwin-White, *Racial Prejudice in Imperial Rome* (Cambridge: Cambridge University, 1967) 84-86, and abundantly in MacMullen, *Roman Social Relations*, 192-99. The involvement of freedmen in trade and business, which has been stressed here, does not suggest that freedmen constituted a great "capitalist class" who were content to remain that way. Both Boulvert (*Esclaves*, 2.659-62) and Veyne ("Vie de Trimalchio," 213, 230-31) make the point that the goal at the top of the social scale was to identify with the traditional landed aristocracy and become country gentlemen. Not many made it that far, but there must have been enough; otherwise that aspect of the satire on Trimalchio would have been pointless.

Hermas sold him to a certain Rhoda at Rome (*Ho threpsas me pepraken me Rhodē tini eis Rhōmēn*, *Vis.* 1.1.1).[137] Though a *threptos* could be a foster child, the term usually referred to a child exposed by its parents and raised as a slave but with a special relationship to the adoptive family. It therefore expressed as much a familial as a legal relationship, and the Latin equivalent was closer to *alumnus*[138] than to *verna*.[139] If the term did not here include the legal condition of slavery, Hermas could hardly have been sold as a child or an adolescent, as the second part of the statement indicates. At some point before the opening of the narrative Hermas must have acquired his manumission, though not necessarily from Rhoda. The interval before the river scene (*meta polla etē*; *meta chronon tina*) would present difficulties if theirs was a normal client-patron relationship in which regular exchanges were expected. His freedom of movement in the *Visions* (the trips to Cumae in *Vis.* 1.1.3 and 2.1.1; into the country on the Via Campana in *Vis.* 4.1.1) and financial reversal (*Vis.* 3.6.7) would not have been impossible for a freedman. The peculiar reference to the field where he was engaged in some kind of agricultural activity (*elthe eis ton agron, hopou chondrizeis, Vis.* 3.1.2) does not necessarily make him a farmer.[140] The references to his wife and children (e.g., *Vis.* 1.3.1; 2.2.2-3; 2.3.1), whether intended symbolically or not, do not exclude the possibility that Hermas was a slave even though marriage and the legitimacy of children were not legally recognized.[141] However, the reference

---

[137] Though the reliability of the personal details in the *Visions* is disputed (see above, pp. 8–10), this opening statement serves no literary function in the ensuing narrative; it is doubtful that the author would have introduced a servile past if it were not true.

[138] "A nursling, a pupil, foster-son" (Lewis and Short s.v.).

[139] See Pliny, *Ep.* 10.65 and 66 on the question of whether exposed children automatically become slaves when taken in and therefore cannot later claim freedom (Trajan replies that they can); also A. Cameron, "*THREPTOS* and Related Terms in the Inscriptions of Asia Minor," *Anatolian Studies Presented to William H. Buckler* (Manchester: Manchester University, 1939) 27-62; remarks and references in Dibelius (*Der Hirt*, 425-26) with references to two first-century *threptoi* named Hermas. For further inscriptional evidence on this common Greek name, see J. Moulton and G. Milligan, *The Vocabulary of the Greek New Testament* (London: Hodder and Stoughton, 1930) s.v.; J. Rouffiac, *Recherches sur les caractères du grec dans le Nouveau Testament d'après les inscriptions de Priène* (Paris: Ernest Leroux, 1911) 91.

[140] *Chondrizō*, a *hapax legomenon*, seems to be a variant of *chondreuō*, which really means to make groats, or coarse grain, by crushing the grain in an apparatus designed for the purpose (see LSJ, BAG s.vv.). But it is unlikely that Hermas worked at such a machine, as BAG suggests (as a slave, at least), and still had the mobility he seems to have had. Against BAG, most translators have understood it as a reference to farming, e.g., Dibelius ("so gehe auf den Acker, auf dem du Dinkel baust," *Der Hirt*, 454), Joly ("viens dans le champ où tu cultives de l'épeautre," *Pasteur*, 99), Snyder ("go to the field where you raise grain," *Shepherd*, 40), Lake ("Come into the country, where you are farming," LCL 2.27).

[141] See, for example, the discussions of *contubernium* in Treggiari (*Roman Freedmen*, 209-10) and Weaver (*Familia Caesaris*, 170-71).

to his wife as *symbios* (*Vis.* 2.2.3) and especially the reference to his "household" (*ho oikos sou, Vis.* 1.3.1) are not likely to reflect the status of a slave. The information that we are given about Hermas' life and activity is more consonant with the status of freedman than that of slave or *ingenuus*.[142]

If Christianity was for an extended period successful among members of the freedman class and their descendants, it may be more than coincidental that the earliest epigraphical and historical evidence for Christians in the imperial household, half a century later, is of freedmen: Prosenes,[143] Carpophorus,[144] Callistus,[145] and perhaps Hyacinth and Marcia.[146]

Summary

The evidence indicates that the majority of small tradesmen and craftsmen in first- and second-century Rome were freedmen and women. Moreover, freedmen as a class had a reputation at the time for social and financial ambition and their growing fortune, success, and influence caused resentment and hostility on the part of the aristocracy. Hermas himself seems to have been a freedman, which would make him especially sympathetic to the needs and problems of that social group. When all these factors are then taken into account, the concern in the *Shepherd* about wealth and social climbing is best situated as addressed predominantly to a large and influential freedman group in Hermas' community.

---

[142] Joly (*Pasteur*, 36) makes the interesting observation that there is no paraenesis in *Hermas* addressed to slaves. It could be countered that there is no paraenesis addressed to masters either. But if the present analysis of the situation regarding wealth is correct, there is in fact paraenesis addressed to masters, not as such, but as *owners*—another confirmation that *Hermas* does not represent the perspective of the "have-nots."

[143] The sarcophagus of M. Aur. Augg. lib. Prosenes, an imperial procurator, contains an addition in another hand on the upper right side: "Prosenes receptus ad deum . . . scripsit Ampelius lib." with the consular date of 217 (*ICUR* 6.17246; *CIL* 6.8498 add. p. 3459; Dessau *ILS* 1738; Diehl *ILCV* 2.3332 a and b). According to A. Ferrua, this is the earliest known Christian inscription from Rome.

[144] Callistus's master in Hipp. *Ref.* 9.12, *anēr pistos . . . ek tēs Kaisaros oikias*, perhaps to be identified with a M. Aur. Lib. of the same time and place (*CIL* 6.13040).

[145] A slave and subsequently a freedman of Carpophorus, *oiketēs . . . Karpophorou* (Hipp. *Ref.* 9.12).

[146] Marcia, a freedwoman and a concubine of Commodus (*PW* 118) and Hyacinth, the eunuch who carries out her wishes by freeing the Christians in the Sardinian mines (Hipp. *Ref.* 9.12). Though neither is called a Christian, their activities indicate at least a strong sympathy with Christians (Marcia is called *philotheos*). Hyacinth is also at one point in the narrative the self-styled *threpsas . . . Markias*, which could indicate another familial master-slave relationship (see above, n. 139) or perhaps could mean that Hyacinth was a sort of head eunuch in the palace (see the interpretation of Dibelius, *Der Hirt*, 425). See the comments about this text in Beaujeu, *Politique religieuse*, 393-94.

Who Are the Poor?

It is obvious by now that there is far more to say about the identity of the rich in *Hermas* than about the identity of the poor. In chapter III it was shown that there are fewer references to the poor in *Hermas* than to the rich and that outside *Sim.* 2 the poor are treated only as a foil for consideration of the rich, that is, in relation to the question of how the wealthy should rightly use their money. It was observed that the traditional words for the poor in both Hellenistic and Greek Jewish use, *ptōchos* and *penēs*, are not even used except in *Sim.* 2. Concern is directed toward the poor only insofar as the rich neglect their pious duty toward them.

The one exception to this pattern is the second *Similitude*, where the poor have an integral part to play in the religious economy of the Christian community. Yet even here only the wealthy are said to accomplish correctly a ministry of service (*diakonia*, 2.7), and the final focus is on the blessedness of the wealthy who understand the right way to use the gifts God has given them (2.10).

There seems to be no large group of Christian "poor" about whom the author is genuinely concerned. Perhaps the community in which Hermas writes is characterized by relative economic homogeneity and those who best fit the category "poor" are simply those who are less prosperous than most or the economically dependent who could benefit from a common community fund because of a temporary financial setback, widowhood, etc. It could almost be said that the poor in *Hermas* appear chiefly for a literary purpose. A Jewish or Christian paraenesis for the rich would be unthinkable without stressing the obligation of the rich toward the poor. Even in the second *Similitude* the essential insight of mutual complementarity that is developed necessitates the involvement of the poor, even if the real focus does not rest on them. But to say that the poor are nothing but a literary creation to serve the author's purpose would be to deny the reality of the social situation in imperial Rome. Even if the impoverished and the needy did not constitute a significant part of Hermas' community, they were always present in the world around it. However, economic poverty and the plight of the poor were not major concerns of Hermas.

Conclusion

Who are the rich in Hermas' community likely to be? In answer to this question, a majority of aristocrats or members of the *ordines* must be eliminated on the basis of lack of evidence. Most of the little evidence there is about aristocratic Christians in Rome comes from the first century. The case for Pomponia Graecina cannot be sufficiently established; those for Flavia Domitilla, Titus Flavius Clemens, and Manlius Acilius Glabrio are slightly stronger but still tenuous. Justin's story of a Christian woman narrated in his second *Apology* does not show that she is of noble birth, contrary to some opinions. It is only at the end of the second century that adequate evidence begins to appear that significant numbers of the upper classes in Rome began joining Christian communities. On the other hand, the indications of predominantly lower-class membership are stronger. Random remarks made by Justin, Tatian, and Minucius Felix confirm this judgment from within Christianity, while pagan writers like Celsus and Galen use the same idea to attempt to discredit Christianity as a movement for the lower classes and the uneducated.

An examination of the small sampling of names of Roman Christians from the late first through the middle of the second century, shows that most of them, both Greek and Latin, best fit people of the lower classes, especially slaves, freedmen, and persons of recent foreign extraction.

The origins of Roman Christianity in Judaism and the continuing Jewish influence in Christian theology and praxis are indicated by the evidence but not well documented. The Jewish community was established in Rome long before the arrival of Christianity, and at times it exercised a certain power both politically through important connections and religiously through the appeal of its ethos and rituals. During the second century the relationship between the two groups was complex. Though some Roman Jews were always distinguished for prestige and wealth, literary and archaeological evidence indicates that the majority of the Jewish residents were the same kind of ordinary people as the Christians of the city.

Specific concerns raised by Hermas about wealth and business involvements point to the abandonment of social relationships and responsibility in the Christian community in favor of a more luxurious way of life, one more in keeping with the surrounding culture, and the seeking of pagan friendships and social advancement. There is one emergent social group in imperial Rome that fits the qualifications of being part of the lower classes and at the same time of having been known for its interest in acquiring prestige, wealth, and social preference—freedmen. They made up the larger portion of the craftsmen, tradesmen, and small business people of the city, and they caused hostility and resentment on the part of the upper classes for their ambition and ability to succeed socially. Added to all of this is the probability that Hermas himself was a freedman, a fact that would make him highly sensitive to the situation of the freedman group in his community. Thus, it seems most likely that the "rich" addressed and spoken of in the *Shepherd* are predominantly a large and influential group of freedmen and women in the Christian community.

The poor do not occupy an important place in *Hermas*. They are spoken of only in the context of the traditional duty of the rich to share their goods with those in need. There seems to be no large group of Christian poor; perhaps those who best fit the category are those less prosperous than most or suffering from temporary disabilities, widowhood, etc. But to say that the poor are nothing more than a literary device in *Hermas* would be too strong, even though they do serve that purpose.

CONCLUSIONS

Though the proclamation of a second repentance in a context of eschatological urgency is usually taken to be the primary purpose of the *Shepherd of Hermas*, questions about possessions and the use of wealth also emerge as a strong concern. In contrast to the theological perspective of Luke and James, Hermas attempts to address the experience of the rich. For Luke and James "poor" is not so much an economic category as a theological designation, with deep biblical roots, identifying those who rely completely on God and who are susceptible to abuse and persecution by the rich and powerful. The "rich," on the other hand, are precisely those who abuse the believers. Luke examines with greater intricacy than James the question of the danger of possessions. When Luke considers whether rich people can become followers of Jesus, he nearly always decides in the negative. As a result, the categories of rich and poor function more in a symbolic than a literal way.

Hermas' theological roots come from the same tradition. He too is at home with a theology of the poor, in which the poor and humble are those preferred and protected by God. Yet the reality of his community is such that this kind of theology is difficult to preach. The ideal of humility remains, but there are people in the community who are quite well established in the goods of this world and are eager for more. They are in sufficient numbers that the appeal to the ideals of humility and poverty do not always seem credible. Hermas' problem simply stated is how to proclaim a theology of the poor in a church of the rich, and if this is impossible, what alternatives to develop.

In the second *Similitude* the creative alternative appears: both rich and poor are necessary for the work of God, and they support each other with their own strength, be it economic or spiritual. The rich person who knows how to use wealth wisely in the service of God is proclaimed as blessed as the poor. The rich, however, are neither members of the aristocracy nor necessarily others with vast fortunes. The notion of wealth is relative and depends on a comparison with former companions and especially with one's own former condition. By reason of his written style and his theology, Hermas is usually situated among the uneducated populace rather than the intellectual elite. His "rich" people are members of the lower classes of Rome who have enough money to advance in the acquisition of possessions and in social standing. Those who fit that description best are the freedmen and women who made up the majority of the tradesmen, craftsmen, and small business people of the city, and Hermas himself belonged to this class. The "poor" are for Hermas predominantly those to whom the rich have a religious obligation. They therefore serve primarily a theological and literary function in the *Shepherd*, and they do not seem to have been a group with a large representation in Hermas' community.

Despite differences between given historical situations, which must always be carefully distinguished, some patterns reappear with such frequency in different contexts that they can almost be said to be constants in human society, at least within the same cultural tradition. The struggle to be faithful to the Gospel preference for the poor in a Christianity firmly established among the comfortable classes has faced countless generations of religious thinkers and is no closer to a resolution today than it was in the second century. Hermas' solution that wealth is all right for a Christian as long as it is used responsibly has been echoed many times in a variety of forms. Clement of Alexandria in *Who Is The Rich Man Who Can Be Saved?* emphasized the virtue of detachment as the key to being a true yet wealthy Christian, while for Calvin prosperity, not poverty, was a sign of blessedness. In every attempt at creative adaptation the notion of poverty is refined in an effort to join biblical faith with contemporary experience.

The data provided in the *Shepherd* cannot be considered descriptive of the entire social situation of Roman Christianity in its time any more than the later narrative of the conflict between Hippolytus and Callistus can be considered a complete description of community leadership in its time. What we learn from the discussion of rich and poor in *Hermas* faithfully reflects some of the problems of at least one Christian community in Rome in the early to the mid-second century.

APPENDIX A

Text and Translation of the Second *Similitude*[1]

1. [a] Περιπατοῦντός μου εἰς τὸν ἀγρὸν καὶ κατανοοῦντος πτελέαν καὶ ἄμπελον, καὶ διακρίνοντος περὶ αὐτῶν καὶ τῶν καρπῶν αὐτῶν, φανεροῦταί μοι ὁ ποιμὴν καὶ λέγει· Τί σὺ ἐν ἑαυτῷ ζητεῖς περὶ τῆς πτελέας καὶ τῆς ἀμπέλου; [b] Συζητῶ, φημί, (κύριε,) ὅτι εὐπρεπέστατί εἰσιν ἀλλήλαις.

2. [a] Ταῦτα τὰ δύο δένδρα, φησίν, εἰς τύπον κεῖνται τοῖς δούλοις τοῦ θεοῦ. [b] Ἤθελον, φημί, γνῶναι τὸν τύπον τῶν δένδρων τούτων ὧν λέγεις. [c] Βλέπεις, φησί, τὴν πτελέαν καὶ τὴν ἄμπελον; [d] Βλέπω, φημί, κύριε.

3. [a] Ἡ ἄμπελος, φησίν, αὕτη καρπὸν φέρει, ἡ δὲ πτελέα ξύλον ἄκαρπόν ἐστιν· ἀλλ' ἡ ἄμπελος αὕτη ἐὰν μὴ ἀναβῇ ἐπὶ τὴν πτελέαν, οὐ δύναται καρποφορῆσαι πολὺ ἐρριμένη χαμαί, καὶ ὃν φέρει καρπόν, σεσηπότα φέρει μὴ κρεμαμένη ἐπὶ τῆς πτελέας. [b] ὅταν οὖν ἐπιρριφῇ ἡ ἄμπελος ἐπὶ τὴν πτελέαν, καὶ παρ' ἑαυτῆς φέρει καρπὸν καὶ παρὰ τῆς πτελέας.

1. [a] As I was walking in the country taking notice of an elm and a vine and thinking about them and their fruits, the shepherd appeared to me and said, "What are you seeking within yourself regarding the elm and the vine?" [b] "I am thinking, sir," I said, "that they are well fitted to one another."

2. [a] "These two trees," he said, "are a symbol of the servants of God." [b] "I would like to know," I said, "the symbol of these trees of which you speak." [c] "Do you see," he said, "the elm and the vine?" [d] "I see them, sir," I said.

3. [a] "This vine," he said, "bears fruit, but the elm is a barren tree; but this vine, if it does not grow up the elm, cannot bear fruit lying on the ground, and the fruit it bears, it bears rotten when it does not hang upon the elm. [b] But when the vine is cast upon the elm, it bears fruit both from itself and from the elm.

---

[1] The text is based on that of Whittaker except where noted; the translation is that of the present author.

4. ᵃ Βλέπεις οὖν, ὅτι καὶ ἡ πτελέα πολὺν καρπὸν δίδωσιν, οὐκ ἐλάσσονα τῆς ἀμπέλου, μᾶλλον δὲ καὶ πλείονα. ᵇ (Πῶς, φημί, κύριε, πλείονα;) ᶜ Ὅτι, φησίν, ἡ ἄμπελος κρεμαμένη ἐπὶ τὴν πτελέαν τὸν καρπὸν πολὺν καὶ καλὸν δίδωσιν, ἐρριμένη δὲ χαμαὶ ὀλίγον καὶ σαπρὸν φέρει. ᵈ αὕτη οὖν ἡ παραβολὴ εἰς τοὺς δούλους τοῦ θεοῦ κεῖται, εἰς πτωχὸν καὶ πλούσιον.

5. ᵃ Πῶς, φημί, κύριε, γνώρισόν μοι. ᵇ Ἄκουε, φησίν· ὁ μὲν πλούσιος ἔχει χρήματα, τὰ δὲ πρὸς τὸν κύριον πτωχεύει, περισπώμενος περὶ τὸν πλοῦτον ἑαυτοῦ, καὶ λίαν μικρὰν ἔχει τὴν ἔντευξιν καὶ τὴν ἐξομολόγησιν πρὸς τὸν κύριον, καὶ ἣν ἔχει, βληχρὰν καὶ μικρὰν καὶ μεγάλην² μὴ ἔχουσαν δύναμιν. ᶜ ὅταν οὖν ἐπαναπαῇ³ ἐπὶ τὸν πένητα ὁ πλούσιος καὶ χορη-

4. ᵃ So you see that the elm gives much fruit, not less than the vine, but rather more." ᵇ "How, sir, is it more?" I said. ᶜ "Because," he said, "the vine hanging upon the elm gives fruit that is plentiful and good, but when it lies on the ground it bears little and rotten fruit. ᵈ So this parable is fitting for the servants of God, for poor and rich."

5. ᵃ "How, sir?" I said, "show me." ᵇ "Listen," he said. "The rich person has money, which is poor in the sight of the Lord, since he is distracted about his wealth, and his intercession and confession are very small in the sight of the Lord, and what he has is weak and small and has no great² power. ᶜ So when the rich person relies³ upon the poor and supplies to him

---

² *Megalēn* is a suggested emendation. The manuscript evidence on this word is varied and tenuous. Rendered *allēn* in the major manuscripts except Athous, which has a̅n̅o̅u̅ (*anthrōpou*), it is omitted entirely by three translations (L¹, Eth, Sdh.), possibly rendered *apud Dominum* by L² (but this could be merely a gloss from the two appearances of *pros ton kyrion* immediately above), and *a(. .)ēn* by POxy. Tischendorf conjectured *anō* after Athous; Dibelius, *hagnēn* after POxy.; and Whittaker, *archēn* (see Dibelius, p. 555, and Whittaker, p. 48 for variants). Neither the most popular reading, *allēn* (other than *what?*), nor any of the emendations really makes sense. On the other hand, reading *magalēn* enhances the parallel contrast (see C') between rich and poor. Copyists' confusion at a stage earlier than any of the surviving manuscripts could have resulted in the loss of the initial *me*, perhaps thought to be a misplaced negative. The resulting confusion would be what our manuscripts have picked up. It is to be observed that all the suggested readings except Athous's *anthrōpou* require that there be a break in thought after *mikran* and that the problematic word, whatever it be, modify *dynamin*.

³ *Epanapaē̄* is another textual problem, but the consensus of POxy., Dibelius, Whittaker, and Lake seems best. The *anaplē* of Athous and conjectures such as *anapnē̄*, *anaphthē̄* (Hilgenfeld), or *anabē̄* (Hollenberg) cause more problems than they solve. For example, the last mentioned would reverse the allegorical correspondence of rich and poor (see Dibelius, *Der Hirt*, 555). Harnack's suggestion *dapanē̄* would create a parallelism between (D) and (E) and would make sense. But POxy.'s *epanapaē̄* is quite acceptable in the sense of *vertrauen auf* (Dibelius), or "rely upon" (for *enteuxis* and *homologēsis*).

γῇ αὐτῷ τὰ δέοντα, πιστεύει ὅτι ἐὰν ἐργάσηται εἰς τὸν πένητα δυνήσεται τὸν μισθὸν εὑρεῖν παρὰ τῷ θεῷ· ὅτι ὁ πένης πλούσιός ἐστιν ἐν τῇ ἐντεύξει αὐτοῦ καὶ ἐν τῇ ἐξομολογήσει, καὶ δύναμιν μεγάλην ἔχει παρὰ τῷ θεῷ ἡ ἔντευξις αὐτοῦ. ᵈ ἐπιχορηγεῖ οὖν ὁ πλούσιος τῷ πένητι πάντα ἀδιστάκτως.

6. ὁ πένης οὖν ἐπιχορηγούμενος ὑπὸ τοῦ πλουσίου ἐντυγχάνει τῷ θεῷ εὐχαριστῶν αὐτῷ, ὑπὲρ τοῦ διδόντος αὐτῷ· κἀκεῖνος ἔτι καὶ ἔτι σπουδάζει⁴ περὶ τοῦ πένητος, ἵνα ἀδιάλειπτος γένηται ἐν τῇ ζωῇ⁵ αὐτοῦ· οἶδε γάρ, ὅτι ἡ τοῦ πένητος ἔντευξις προσδεκτή ἐστιν καὶ πλουσία πρὸς κύριον.

7. ᵃ ἀμφότεροι οὖν τὸ ἔργον τελεῦσιν· ὁ μὲν πένης ἐργάζεται τῇ ἐντεύξει, ἐν ᾗ πλουτεῖ, ἣν ἔλαβεν παρὰ τοῦ κυρίου· ταύτην ἀποδίδωσι τῷ κυρίῳ τῷ ἐπιχορηγοῦντι αὐτῷ. ᵇ καὶ ὁ πλούσιος ὡσαύτως τὸ πλοῦτος, ὃ ἔλαβεν παρὰ τοῦ κυρίου, ἀδιστάκτως παρέχεται τῷ πένητι. ᶜ καὶ τοῦτο ἔργον μέγα ἐστὶν καὶ δεκτὸν παρὰ τῷ θεῷ, ὅτι συνῆκεν ἐπὶ τῷ πλούτῳ αὐτοῦ καὶ ἠργάσατο εἰς τὸν πένητα ἐκ

what he needs, he believes that whatever he does to the poor will be able to find its reward from God; for the poor person is rich in intercession and confession, and his intercession has great power before God. ᵈ Therefore the rich person supplies everything to the poor without hesitating;

6. and the poor one, sustained by the rich, prays to God thanking him for the one who gives to him; and that one [i.e., the rich] continues to be concerned⁴ about the poor, so that he can be unceasing in his life⁵; for you know that the prayer of the poor is acceptable and rich in the sight of the Lord.

7. ᵃ So both together complete the work: the poor person works at intercession, in which he is rich, which [gift] he received from the Lord; this he returns to the Lord who sustains him. ᵇ And likewise the rich person with his wealth, which he received from the Lord, supports the poor without hesitation. ᶜ Now this work is great and right before God, because he understands about his wealth and has

---

⁴ Whittaker follows Dibelius on this emendation indicated by POxy.'s doubtful *eti kai eti epispoudazei*.

⁵ Dibelius here emends the given *zōē* to *enteuxei* (*Der Hirt*, 556) on the basis of the confusion in POxy. over the same expression in *Sim.* 2.5c and the immediate discussion of *enteuxis* in the next sentence preceded by *gar*. But he seems to argue against himself when he suggests that *adialeiptos* in the same sentence means with the Latin manuscripts "unneglected" ("*unvernachlässigt*") rather than the more grammatically justified "uninterrupted" ("*ununterbrochen*"). Either "unneglected in his living" *or* "unceasing in his prayer" makes more sense than the reverse.

τῶν δωρημάτων τοῦ κυρίου καὶ
ἐτέλεσεν τὴν διακονίαν ὀρθῶς.

used the gifts of the Lord for the poor and accomplished the ministry rightly.

8. [a] παρὰ τοῖς οὖν ἀνθρώποις ἡ πτελέα δοκεῖ καρπὸν μὴ φέρειν, καὶ οὐκ οἴδασιν οὐδὲ νοοῦσιν ὅτι, ὅταν ἀβροχία γένηται, ἡ πτελέα ἔχουσα ὕδωρ τρέφει τὴν ἄμπελον, καὶ ἡ ἄμπελος ἀδιάλειπτον ἔχουσα τὸ ὕδωρ διπλοῦν τὸν καρπὸν ἀποδίδωσιν, καὶ ὑπὲρ ἑαυτῆς καὶ ὑπὲρ τῆς πτελέας. [b] οὕτως καὶ οἱ πένητες ὑπὲρ τῶν πλουσίων ἐντυγχάνοντες πρὸς τὸν κύριον πληροφοροῦσι τὸ πλοῦτος αὐτῶν, καὶ πάλιν οἱ πλούσιοι χορηγοῦντες τοῖς πένησι τὰ δέοντα πληροφοροῦσι τὰς ψυχὰς αὐτῶν.

8. [a] Thus to human eyes the elm seems not to bear fruit, and they do not know that when drought comes the elm which has water nourishes the vine, and the vine having an uninterrupted flow of water produces double fruit, both for itself and for the elm. [b] Likewise the poor by interceding for the rich before the Lord supply what is lacking to their wealth, and again the rich by furnishing to the poor what they need supply what is wanting to their prayers.

9. [a] γίνονται οὖν ἀμφότεροι κοινωνοὶ τοῦ ἔργου τοῦ δικαίου. [b] ταῦτα οὖν ὁ ποιῶν οὐκ ἐνκαταλειφθήσεται ὑπὸ τοῦ θεοῦ, ἀλλὰ ἔσται γεγραμμένος εἰς τὰς βίβλους τῶν ζώντων.

9. [a] So both are partners in the work of justice. [b] Therefore the one who does these things will not be abandoned by God but will be enrolled in the books of the living.

10. μακάριοι οἱ ἔχοντες καὶ συνιέντες, ὅτι παρὰ τοῦ κυρίου πλουτίζονται· ὁ γὰρ συνίων τοῦτο δυνήσεται καὶ διακονῆσαί τι ἀγαθόν.

10. Blessed are those who have possessions and understand that their wealth is from the Lord; for the one who understands this will also be able to accomplish something good."

APPENDIX B

The Structure of the Second *Similitude*

A general and obvious structure of the ten verses of *Sim.* 2 is given by Dibelius: vv. 1-4 contain the parable; vv. 5-7 present the application; vv. 8-10 are an epilogue which gives the chapter the character of a commandment even without a customary formal ending to denote it as such.[1] The general shape of Dibelius's outline holds, but the actual structure is far more intricate:

v(v).	1-2	Introduction
	3-4c	Parable of the elm and the vine
	4d-7	Application
		4d-5a transition
		5b-7b body
		7c conclusion
	8a	Continuation of the parable, picked up from 4c
	8b-9a	Continuation of application (9a is a reprise of 7a)
	9b-10	Conclusion (10 is a reprise of 7c).

Within the parable itself, K. Grobel discovered an elaborate chiasm covering the whole of v. 3 and worked it out in great detail using the English text.[2] His structuring is given below using both the English and the Greek text.

---

[1] *Der Hirt*, 553.

[2] K. Grobel, "Shepherd of Hermas, Parable II," *Vanderbilt Studies in the Humanities* (Nashville: Vanderbilt, 1951) 1.50. It is strange that he did not give the Greek text at all even though he quotes Cicero in Latin without translation (and without reference!) on the next page. It was Grobel's contention (p. 51) that, though there are other examples of chiastic structure in the second Parable, "none have been detected elsewhere in the book." Partly on this basis he argued for an independent source. Though there are other linguistic arguments to support the hypothesis of a separate source for parts of *Sim.* 2, there are nevertheless other examples of chiastic structure to be found in *Hermas*, e.g., *Man.* 8.12 or 11.8. Admittedly, they do not have the polished form of *Sim.* 2.3. Grobel went on to conclude that "it is scarcely conceivable that the inartistic author of the whole work is responsible for this composition." But Dibelius used the same argument against the literary integrity of the list of virtues in *Man.* 8.3 in its context (*Der Hirt*, 526). As examples multiply, this argument can become circular, so that other criteria must be used.

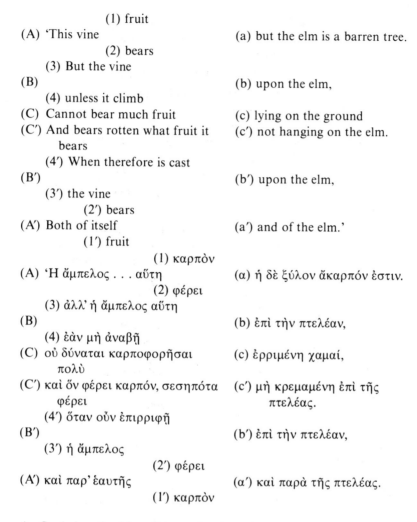

(1) fruit
(A) 'This vine   (a) but the elm is a barren tree.
     (2) bears
     (3) But the vine
(B)   (b) upon the elm,
     (4) unless it climb
(C) Cannot bear much fruit   (c) lying on the ground
(C') And bears rotten what fruit it   (c') not hanging on the elm.
     bears
     (4') When therefore is cast
(B')   (b') upon the elm,
     (3') the vine
        (2') bears
(A') Both of itself   (a') and of the elm.'
        (1') fruit
            (1) καρπὸν
(A) Ἡ ἄμπελος . . . αὕτη   (α) ἡ δὲ ξύλον ἄκαρπόν ἐστιν.
            (2) φέρει
     (3) ἀλλ' ἡ ἄμπελος αὕτη
(B)   (b) ἐπὶ τὴν πτελέαν,
     (4) ἐὰν μὴ ἀναβῇ
(C) οὐ δύναται καρποφορῆσαι   (c) ἐρριμένη χαμαί,
     πολὺ
(C') καὶ ὅν φέρει καρπόν, σεσηπότα   (c') μὴ κρεμαμένη ἐπὶ τῆς
     φέρει   πτελέας.
     (4') ὅταν οὖν ἐπιρριφῇ
(B')   (b') ἐπὶ τὴν πτελέαν,
     (3') ἡ ἄμπελος
        (2') φέρει
(A') καὶ παρ' ἑαυτῆς   (α') καὶ παρὰ τῆς πτελέας.
            (1') καρπὸν

As Grobel noticed but did not develop, there are other chiastic structures in the second *Similitude*, though none as perfectly formed as the one he pointed out. Vv. 5b-c and 5d-7b, both within the body of the first and principal application of the parable, are structured circularly.

The first of the two chiastic sections, vv. 5b-c, is actually a combination of inverted and parallel structure:

5b (A)   ὁ μὲν *πλούσιος* ἔχει χρήματα,
             τὰ δὲ πρὸς τὸν κύριον *πτωχεύει*,
             (περισπώμενος περὶ τὸν *πλοῦτον* ἑαυτοῦ,)

(B)   καὶ λίαν μικρὰν ἔχει τὴν *ἔντευξιν*
       καὶ τὴν *ἐξομολόγησιν* πρὸς τὸν κύριον,
       (καὶ ἣν ἔχει, βληχρὰν καὶ μικρὰν)
(C)   καὶ *μεγάλην*[3] μὴ ἔχουσαν *δύναμιν.*

5c (D)   ὅταν οὖν *ἐπαναπάῃ*[4] ἐπὶ τὸν πένητα ὁ πλούσιος
    (E)   καὶ *χορηγήσῃ* αὐτῷ τὰ δέοντα, πιστεύει
    (E′)   ὅτι ἐὰν *ἐργάσηται* εἰς τὸν πένητα
    (D′)   δυνηθήσεται τὸν *μισθὸν εὑρεῖν* παρὰ τῷ θεῷ.
    (A′)   ὅτι ὁ *πένης πλούσιός* ἐστιν
    (B′)   ἐν τῇ *ἐντεύξει* καὶ ἐν τῇ *ἐξομολογήσει,*
    (C′)   καὶ *δύναμιν μεγάλην* ἔχει παρὰ τῷ θεῷ ἡ *ἔντευξις* αὐτοῦ.

5b (A)   The *rich* person has *money,*
                which is *poor* in the sight of the Lord,
                (since he is distracted about his wealth,)
    (B)   and his *intercession* and *confession* are very
           small in the sight of the Lord,
           (and what he has is weak and small)
    (C)   and has no *great*[3] power.
    (D)   So when the rich person *relies*[4] upon the poor
    (E)   and *supplies* to him what he needs, he believes
    (E′)   that whatever he *does* to the poor
    (D′)   will be able to *find* its *reward* from God;
    (A′)   for the *poor* person is *rich*
    (B′)   in *intercession* and *confession,*
    (C′)   and his intercession has *great power* before God.

The second example of chiastic structure within the application unit of
vv. 5b-7b is contained in vv. 5d-7b:

5d (A)   *ἐπιχορηγεῖ* οὖν ὁ πλούσιος τῷ πένητι πάντα *ἀδιστάκτως.*
6   (B)   ὁ πένης οὖν (ἐπιχορηγούμενος ὑπὸ τοῦ πλουσίου) *ἐντυγ-
           χάνει*
                τῷ θεῷ εὐχαριστῶν αὐτῷ ὑπὲρ τοῦ διδόντος αὐτῷ·
                (κἀκεῖνος ἔτι καὶ ἔτι σπουδάζει[5] περὶ τοῦ πένητος,)
    (C)   ἵνα *ἀδιάλειπτος* γένηται
    (D)   ἐν τῇ *ἐντεύξει*[6] αὐτοῦ·
    (D′)   οἶδε γὰρ, ὅτι ἡ τοῦ πένητος *ἔντευξις*
    (C′)   *προσδεκτή* ἐστιν καὶ *πλουσία* πρὸς κύριον.

---

[3] See Appendix A, n. 2.
[4] See Appendix A, n. 3.

7a   (ἀμφότεροι οὖν τὸ ἔργον τελοῦσιν·)
(B′) ὁ μὲν πένης ἐργάζεται τῇ ἐντεύξει,
      (ἐν ᾗ πλουτεῖ, ἣν ἔλαβεν παρὰ τοῦ κυρίου·)
      ταύτην ἀποδίδωσι τῷ κυρίῳ τῷ ἐπιχορηγοῦντι αὐτῷ.
7b   (A′)   καὶ ὁ πλούσιος ὡσαύτως τὸ πλοῦτος,
      ὃ ἔλαβεν παρὰ τοῦ κυρίου,
      ἀδιστάκτως παρέχεται τῷ πένητι.

5d   (A)   Therefore the *rich* person *supplies* everything to the
             poor *without hesitating*;
6   (B)   and the *poor* one (sustained by the rich) *prays* to God
             thanking him for the one who gives to him;
             (and that one [i.e., the rich] continues to be
             concerned[5] about the poor,)
      (C)   so that he can be *unceasing*
      (D)   in his *prayer*;[6]
      (D′)   for you know that the *prayer* of the poor
      (C′)   is acceptable and *rich* in the sight of the Lord.
7a   (So both together complete the work:)
      (B′)   the *poor* person *works* at *intercession*, (in which
             he is rich, which [gift] he received from
             the Lord;)
             this he *returns* to the Lord who sustains him.
7b   (A′)   And likewise the *rich* person with his wealth,
             which he received from the Lord,
             supports the poor *without hesitation*.

[5] See Appendix A, n. 4.
[6] See Appendix A, n. 5.

APPENDIX C

THE *ARBUSTUM* METHOD OF VITICULTURE

Hermas' literary use of the vine growing upon an elm tree does not cause great surprise. His opening statement that he noticed it as he was walking in the country (*peripatountos mou eis ton agron*[1] *kai katanoountos ptelean kai ampelon . . .*) creates a realistic setting, for the cultivation of grapevines supported on trees, commonly known as an *arbustum*, was one of the most popular methods of viticulture in central Italy. Horace (*Ep.* 1.16.3; cf. 1.7.84) speaks of the land where his estate lies as rich farmland abounding in elms covered with vines (*amicta vitibus ulmo*). Quintilian (8.3.8) complains of farms which cultivate lilies, violets, anemones, and fountains instead of the more serious crops and vines, of farmers who prefer the sterile but trim plane trees and myrtles to elm vineyards and fruitful olive trees (*quam maritam ulmum et uberes oleas*).[2] Virgil refers several times in passing to the practice of joining vines to elms and pruning them (*Georg.* 1.2-3; 2.361,367; *Eclog.* 2.70).

The Latin term *arbustum*, meaning generally a grove of trees, came to have also the more specified meaning of a grove of trees supporting a vineyard, with or without grain crops sown between the trees. Cicero (*De senect.* 54) speaks of the farmer who finds delight in his *vineis et arbustis*, as does Pliny the Younger (*Ep.* 5.6.9) in his description of his villa at Tifernum. Because of the juxtaposition of *arbusta* and *vinea* in both texts, the former could mean a simple grove of trees as it clearly does in Cato (*De ag.* 1.7). However, when Pliny the Elder discusses the provenance of different quality wines (*NH* 14.65) he praises the wines of both the *vineae* and the *arbusta* of

---

[1] *Agros* can mean open countryside or cultivated land (LSJ s.v.); the expression *eis ton agron* would suggest a general rural setting with an *arbustum* nearby rather than Hermas walking *in* the *arbustum* itself, as suggested by Grobel ("Parable II," 53; cf. Dibelius, *Der Hirt*, 553-54).

[2] Horace (*Carm.* 2.15.4) likewise complains of the encroachment of luxury farming. To "marry" the vine to the elm was both the ordinary technical term for the conjunction of the two plants and the source of poetic analogies to human marriage; however, *marita ulmus* is the common agricultural description and does not of itself indicate metaphorical usage. See further below. Dibelius (*Der Hirt*, 554) speaks of the sight as *naheliegend* but cites only these two passages given above, seemingly unaware of the more substantial ones that follow here.

one place (*juncta iis praeponi solebant Calena et quae in vineis arbustisque nascuntur Fundana*), thus making it clear that they are alternate methods of producing wine, the *arbustum* method on trees, the *vinea* method on stakes or trellises or on the ground. The *arbustum* method had the advantage of more efficient use of land that was not rich enough to be profitable if it produced only wine. With proper spacing other crops could be sown and effectively harvested from between the trees.

The two major sources for detailed description and evaluation of the *arbustum* method are Pliny the Elder and Columella; Cato (*De ag.* 32) discusses it only briefly and Varro not at all. Pliny (*NH* 17.35.19ff.) indicates some controversy over the best kinds of trees to use and how to grow them, but he demonstrates the assumption that the better wine comes from higher grapes. He expresses preference for the elm, except the Gallic or "Atinian" elm as being too leafy, but he also approves of black poplar,[3] ash, fig, olive, and even the willow in Venetia. Columella (*De arboribus* 16) reports, on the other hand, that the poplar is most used, then the elm, then the ash—and that the species called *Ulmus Atinia* by the country people is best, contrary to the opinion of Pliny.[4] Though the local way in central Italy is to tie the branches together, the Gallic method is to spread vines like chains from tree to tree,[5] and along the Via Aemilia in northern Italy vines are laid over the foliage of Atinian elms (*NH* 17.35.208) instead of being placed along the branches.

Columella's instructions about planting an *arbustum* (*De arb.* 16; *De re rust.* 5.6.11-16) are as follows. In early March an elm is planted—and a poplar or ash in the same trench in case the elm fails; if both live, one is later replanted. The trees are planted at intervals of forty feet if crops are sown between them, twenty feet if they are not.[6] The sapling is allowed to grow

[3] Elsewhere (*NH* 14.10-12) he reports that vines wed to poplars in Campania attain extraordinary heights. The remark is background for a story about Cineas, ambassador of King Pyrrhus, who expressed amazement at the height of the vines at Aricia—whose altitude, contrary to the common opinion, did not seem to help the *austeriorem gustum* of their wine. Upon tasting it, he cynically joked that its mother deserved to hang on such a high cross (*merito matrem eius pendere in tam alta cruce*). See also Horace *Ep.* 2.9-10 (*ergo . . . adulta vitium propagine/altas maritat populos*).

[4] Virgil (*Georg.* 2.291-92) also recommends the oak as a supporting tree because of the strength of its deep roots.

[5] In this case (the *rumpotinum* method) lower trees are used (see Columella, *De re rust.* 5.7).

[6] Pliny (17.35.205-7) repeats basically the same procedure but specifies the distance between trees as forty feet one way and twenty feet in the other direction in the case of plowed land. Duncan-Jones's discussion (*Economy*, 57-59) includes a description of the *arbustum* as "vines planted irregularly between trees which were used as their supports"—hardly the careful plan that Columella and Pliny describe.

freely for three years, at the end of which time it is trimmed every other year to form a ladder of branches for the vine. When the tree has attained sufficient height, seven or eight feet are to be left between the ground and the first branches and at least three feet between tiers of branches. Already in the sixth year of the tree's growth, however, the vine can be wed to the tree in this way (*maritabis hoc modo*): a ten-foot vine is planted one foot from the tree[7] and carefully tied onto the branches. As much care must be given to the binding as to the pruning of the vine, for the quality of the fruit depends on it (*arbustivam vitem quam putare, tam alligare diligenter oportet. Nam in eo fructus maxime consistit*). Pliny (17.35.205-7) adds that elms used in an *arbustum* are cut off in the middle so that they broaden and never attain a height greater than twenty feet. Contrary to the image suggested by the singular *ampelos* of Hermas, Pliny states also that normally the correspondence is not one vine to one elm but as many as ten vines on a tree and a minimum of three. After the harvest, he adds pictorially (pars. 209-10), the vines should be untied and allowed to lie on the ground, which they have been contemplating during the whole growing season, like oxen or dogs who like to roll on the ground when they are untied, thus providing a relief for the tree, too, since all nature enjoys alternation.[8] Hermas' suggestion (*Sim.* 2.8) that in the time of drought the elm stores up water for the vine is not mentioned by the agriculturalists.[9]

The whole *arbustum* method seems to have been a highly labor-intensive manner of producing wine but one probably well adapted to the Italian soil and climate as well as to a slave economy. It was evidently used throughout the peninsula and in lower Gaul with a wide variety of trees, depending on

---

[7] Columella's directions (*De arb.* 16.3) to dig a furrow one foot from the tree, but four feet long, three feet deep, and two and a half feet wide are obscure. Pliny (17.35.203) states quite clearly that one foot should be the distance between tree and vine. Columella's long furrow must therefore be for several vines, though he does not say so.

[8] The actual reason for untying the vines after harvest was probably in order to retie them in the spring with allowance for new growth of both vine and tree during the year. Pliny cautioned against forcing a vine to produce before its seventh year (17.35.182). Modern grapevines begin producing in their fourth or fifth year and are at their prime between the ages of ten and twenty-five. Most varieties today keep producing for half a century, some even longer. See further T. Frank, *An Economic Survey of Ancient Rome* (5 vols.; Baltimore: Johns Hopkins, 1933-40) 5.148 n. 14; Duncan-Jones, *Economy*, 57-59; F. Olck, "Arbustum," *PW* 2.422. For labor ratios of various types of viticulture and crops, see Frank, *Economic Survey*, 5.39, 327 (taken mostly from Columella).

[9] Joly (*Pasteur*, 218) remarks: "Nous n'avons pas trouvé ailleurs l'idée bizarre selon laquelle l'ormeau ravitaillerait la vigne en eau." The idea, though not taken up by the agricultural commentators, need not be considered bizarre; that an extended root system retains moisture in the soil is common knowledge. Hermas' saying may be based on no more than that.

variations in climate. As Grobel states, there is no direct evidence of the elm *arbustum* outside central Italy, but there is much evidence of its popularity there.[10] Pliny's preference for the elm, however, was not shared by all; Columella names the poplar as the favorite, but the elm as the best. In most other wine-raising regions, the vine was apparently left to sprawl on the ground (17.35.184-86).[11] But Polybius, quoted in Athenaeus (*Deipn.* 1.31d), praises the overriding excellence of the *oinos anadendritēs* from Capua, and the "petulant wife" in Juvenal (*Sat.* 6.150) cries for the famous Falernian wine as *ulmos Falernas.*[12]

The so-called Gallic or Atinian elm caused a difference of opinion among agriculturalists. Pliny (17.35.200) considers it too leafy to allow the grapes sufficient sunlight (*prima omnium ulmus, excepta propter nimiam frondem Atinia*), but he also reports that it is used differently to the north along the Via Aemilia (17.35.208), where the vines are hung using the trees as props and spread over the outside of the foliage (*Aemiliae viae in ridicas Atiniarum ambitu, frondem earum fugiens*), in which case the thickness of the foliage would provide firmer support and thus be an advantage. Columella, however, (*De arb.* 16.1) names the species called *Ulmus Atinia* by the rural inhabitants as the best variety (*Ulmus autem quam Atiniam vocant rustici, generosissima est et laetissima, multamque frondem habet*) for an *arbustum*. In *De re rust.* 5.6.4-5 he gives his reason: though the poplar furnishes the best support for vines, its leaves are not good to feed cattle, while the luxuriant foliage of the Atinian elm is favored by them. The Atinian therefore serves a double purpose, support of vines and feed for cattle, and is thus preferable.

It is possible that the *arbustum* seen by the author of the second *Similitude* contained Atinian elms. He (or rather the Shepherd) observes in v. 3 that the vine bears fruit but the elm is sterile (*hē ampelos . . . karpon pherei, hē de ptelea xylon akarpon estin*). In his discussion in *De re rust.* 5.6.1-4, Columella adds an interesting remark that is not found elsewhere. He states

---

[10] "Parable II," 54-55. However, his insistence that the use of the elm *arbustum* was strictly confined to central Italy is weakened by Pliny's discussion of types of trees used for an *arbustum* in 17.35.200-201 where he lists several varieties including the elm for central Italy and goes on to say *Transpadana Italia praeter super dictas . . .* then names seven more, implying that the first list is not excluded for the North. The use of the elm by Hermas cannot therefore absolutely localize the piece in central Italy as Grobel claims, though the best evidence points in that direction.

[11] But see Ps 79(80):9-11; Ezek 17:6 and LSJ s.v. *anadendras*. This being the general case, however, Hermas' observations (*Sim.* 2.3) that the vine on the ground cannot bear much fruit and that whatever it bears on the ground rots must reflect the central Italian supposition, expressed by Pliny, that vines must be raised off the ground to produce quality wine.

[12] Cited by Grobel, "Parable II," 55.

that Tremellius Scrofa, a well-known agriculturalist of the previous century, and many after him, wrongly thought that the Atinian elm was sterile and did not bear *samera*, the seed of the tree.[13] It certainly does, he counters, but the seeds are sparse and hidden among the leaves; for this reason one does not grow it from seed, but rather by planting shoots (*nam rariorem sine dubio creat, et idcirco plerisque et sterilis videtur, seminibus inter frondem, quam prima germinatione edit, latentibus. Itaque nemo iam serit ex samera, sed ex sobolibus*).

The difference between a tiny elm seedcase and a juicy bunch of grapes as "fruit" is of course not be be underestimated, and in the light of that contrast the elm could still very well have been called barren (*akarpos*) by Hermas. Another difficulty is the failure to distinguish in Latin or Greek between not bearing seed and not bearing fruit, a failure caused no doubt by lack of a similar distinction in biological knowledge. There is, however, perhaps more to it than that. The Atinian elm, which Hermas may have been contemplating was probably known to central Italians only under cultivation and might have been thought in popular lore to be totally sterile. On the other hand, consider the complaint of Horace (*Carm.* 2.15.4) that because of an increasing taste for luxury, cultivated fields are being replaced by lakes, flowers, etc., and the celibate plane tree prevails over the (married) elms (*platanusque caelebs / evincet ulmos*).[14] Here by inference the elm becomes fruitful in exactly the same way developed by Hermas, through the fruitfulness of the vine (*hotan oun epirriphḗ hḗ ampelos epi tḗn ptelean, kai par' heautḗs pherei karpon kai para tḗs pteleas, Sim.* 2.3).

The "marriage" of the vine and the elm, though itself a common agricultural term, did not escape the poetic imagination. Ovid also had his scene in an *arbustum* (*Metam.* 14.661-68), where Vertumnus comes disguised as an old woman to woo Pomona. He too sees a comely elm covered with grapes, which he admires. He too remarks that if the tree remained "unmarried" (*caelebs*) it would have nothing to offer except leaves, and that unless the vine clung to and rested upon the elm it would have to grovel on the ground.[15] But Pomona, he concludes, does not want to follow the vine's example:

[13] One wonders how he thought it reproduced without cultivation. Perhaps since it was not indigenous to central Italy he had never seen it growing except under cultivation. Joly refers to Daremberg-Saglio (*Dictionnaire des Antiquités grecques et romaines*, 1904, 3.1252), which cites only Columella to support the statement and seems unaware of Hermas (*Pasteur*, 215). Apparently the idea is not recorded elsewhere among ancient writers.

[14] See the similar complaint of Quintilian (8.3.8) given above.

[15] For a similar allusion, see Horace, *Carm.* 2.15.4, discussed above at n. 2 (*platanusque caelebs/evincet ulmos*).

ulmus erat contra speciosa nitentibus uvis:
quam socia postquam pariter cum vite probavit,
"ai si staret" ait "caelebs sine palmite truncus,
nil praeter frondes, quare petertur, haberet;
haec quoque, quare iuncta est, vitis requiescit in ulmo:
si non nupta foret, terrae acclinata iaceret;
tu tamen exemplo non tangeris arboris huius
concubitusque fugis nec te coniungere curas."

There was a shapely elm-tree opposite,
covered with gleaming bunches of grapes.
After he had looked approvingly at this awhile,
together with its vine companion, he said:
"But if that tree stood there unmated to the vine,
it would not be sought save for its leaves alone;
and this vine, which clings to and rests safely on the elm,
if it were not thus wedded, it would lie languishing,
flat upon the ground.
But you are not touched by the vine's example
and you shun wedlock and do not desire
to be joined to another."[16]

The context, the literary form, and the use of the parabolic figure are different in the cases of Ovid and Hermas, but the two passages have some significant elements in common. The speaker finds himself in a place where "he just happens to notice" a nearby elm covered with producing grapevines. It is not an image conjured at a distance, but rather he is for literary purposes physically present by an *arbustum*. The sight immediately reminds him of a human situation involving two complementary but opposite elements. In both cases the elm is seen as unfruitful in itself, and the vine is viewed as being in an inferior position if left to lie on the ground rather than to rest on (Ovid) or to cling to (Hermas) the elm. The similarities need not point to literary dependence but rather to common familiarity with symbolic use of a well-known sight.

An extension of the marital imagery of the *arbustum* is the reference to the tree whose vines have been removed as having been "widowed." It would follow that this too was a common agricultural term; however, it does not appear in the writings of the agriculturalists. Since it appears only in literary texts, it may be assumed to have arisen as a literary allusion. Horace (*Carm.* 4.5.30) depicts as an idyllic agrarian scene each farmer on his own hillside

---

[16] Ovid, *Metamorphoses*, trans. Frank J. Miller (LCL; Cambridge, MA: Harvard University, 1964) 2.346-47.

tying up vines on "widowed" trees (*condit quisque diem collibus in suis, | et vitem viduas ducit ad arbores*).

Catullus (62.48-57) combines the images of *vidua* and *virgo* by comparing the widowed elm growing alone and untended on the ground to an unmarried girl who becomes more valuable to both husband and father when wed. Demetz considers Catullus the first to raise "a technical term of Roman agriculture, if not a subliterary rustic idiom, to poetic brilliancy while unfolding its inherent pictorial possibilities."[17]

Juvenal (*Sat.* 8.78) speaking of his preference for honor and independent achievement, compares the alternative, seeking to live off the fame of another, to the desire of the vine lying on the ground for union with the widowed elm (*stratus humi palmes viduas desiderat ulmos*). Here for the first time the marriage of vine and elm is a negative image: in Juvenal's context it is better to remain lying on the ground!

Columella (*De re rust.* 5.6.18) warns against matching vines to elms with which they are not compatible in age: too young an elm will not support the weight of a well-grown vine, whereas too old an elm may choke and kill too young a vine; vine and elm should therefore be of similar age and strength (*at si teneram ulmum maritaveris, onus iam non sufferet: si vetustae vitem applicueris, coniugem necabit. Ita suppares esse aetate et viribus arbores vitesque convenit*). It is surprising that no literary author seems to have used this compatibilty theme metaphorically.[18] Seneca, however, reports (*Ep.* 86.20) that he has seen an old vine transplanted from its original tree (*vidi vitem ex arbusto suo annosam transferri*); if the transferral is done correctly, such vines take hold of and embrace new elms that are not their own (*tenet et conplexae sunt non suas ulmos*). The primary frame of reference is a serious discussion of transplanting old trees, and probably if the transplanting is meant at all metaphorically, it refers to the transfer of people of traditional old Roman sentiment into the more luxurious ways of "modern" life (see 86.5–14).[19]

Use of the image of the elm and the vine for various aspects of marital life was common, and occasional uses of the image for other social realities

---

[17] "The Elm and the Vine," 522.

[18] See only Hermas, *Sim.* 2.1-2 (*hoti euprepestatai eisin allēlais. Tauta ta duo dendra . . . eis typon keintai tois doulois tou theou*); cf. Mark 2:21.

[19] Even if an allusion to remarriage is intended by Seneca, which is unlikely, he does *not* use the expression "for a figure of human adultery" (against Grobel, "Parable II," 54). G. Snyder (*Shepherd*, 97) also misapplies Seneca's reference, saying he "describes the process very much like this parable" (i.e., *Sim.* 2). The only similarity is that both talk about the *arbustum* method of growing vines: Hermas gives a brief functional description, whereas Seneca tells how to dig up and transplant a mature vine.

are also known. But the use of the image of the elm and the vine to depict social groups interacting with one another is unique to Hermas.[20]

[20] This way of using the vine/vineyard image by Hermas is also confined to *Sim.* 2. He uses the image of a neglected vine in *Sim.* 9.26.4 as a simile for those who have neglected themselves by apostasy, and that of neglected vineyards in *Man.* 10.1.5 for those too much involved in worldly affairs. The parable of the vineyard (*Sim.* 5.2) turns out to be an elaborate allegory (5.5) along familiar lines (e.g., Isa 5:1-7; Mark 12:1-9 pars.; the vines are *ho laos houtos*, 5.5.2) but with a happy ending (*Sim.* 5.2.8-10). Three later Christian writers use the image of the elm and the vine in the same way. Clement of Alexandria may allude to *Sim.* 2 in *kai tēn ampelon hē ptelea eis hypsos anagousa eukarpein didaskei* (*Strom.* 6.15.19); Commodianus probably does with *estote comes numinis, dum tempus habetis/sicut ulmus amat vitem, sic ipsi pusillos* (*Inst.* 1.30.15-16); Ps.-Chrysostom surely does when he says: just as you excel in worldly affairs, so does the poor in holiness; just as you support him in this world, so his holiness sustains you in the next—as the unfruitful elm gives moisture to the vine, and the vine bears fruit for itself and for the elm (*Hom. on Matt* 13; *PG* 56.701). Origen (*Hom. on Josh* 10.1; GCS 7.358-59) cites vv. 3-4 to refer loosely to Josh 9:3-15. Funk's association (*Patres Apostolici* 1.523) of Caes. Arles *Hom.* 24 (*PL* 50.858; cf. 67.1090) is not convincing.

BIBLIOGRAPHY

Editions of and Commentaries on the *Shepherd of Hermas*

Bonner, Campbell. *A Papyrus Codex of the Shepherd of Hermas (Sim. 2-9) with a Fragment of the Mandates.* University of Michigan Studies, Humanistic Series 22. Ann Arbor: University of Michigan, 1934.

Dibelius, Martin. *Der Hirt des Hermas.* HNT Ergänzungsband; Apostolischen Väter 4. Tübingen: J. C. B. Mohr [Paul Siebeck], 1923.

Funk, Francis X. "Hermae Pastor," *Patres Apostolici.* 2 vols. Tübingen: H. Laupp, 1901.

Gebhardt, O., and A. von Harnack. *Hermae Pastor graece, addita versione latina recentiore e codice Palatino.* Leipzig: J. C. Hinrichs, 1877.

Hilgenfeld, A. *Hermae Pastor graece.* Leipzig: T. O. Weigl, 1866 and 1881.

Joly, Robert. *Hermas le Pasteur.* SC 53. Paris: Editions du Cerf, 1958.

Lake, Kirsopp. "The Shepherd of Hermas." *Apostolic Fathers* 2. LCL. Cambridge, MA: Harvard University, 1913.

Lightfoot, J. B., and J. R. Harmer. *The Apostolic Fathers.* London: Macmillan, 1891 and 1893.

Snyder, Graydon. *The Shepherd of Hermas.* Edited by Robert M. Grant. Apostolic Fathers 6. Camden, NJ: T. Nelson, 1968.

Weinel, H. "Der Hirt des Hermas." In *Neutestamentliche Apokryphen*, edited by Edgar Hennecke. 2d ed. Tübingen: J. C. B. Mohr, 1924.

Whittaker, Molly. *Der Hirt des Hermas.* GCS 48; Die Apostolischen Väter 1. Berlin: Akademie-Verlag, 1956.

Primary Sources

Aristides. *The Apologies of Aristides on Behalf of the Christians.* Edited and translated by J. Armitage Robinson. TextsS 1.1. 2d ed. Cambridge: Cambridge University, 1893.

Clement of Rome. *Epître aux Corinthiens.* Edited by Annie Jaubert. SC 167. Paris: Editions du Cerf, 1971.

———. *Der erste Clemensbrief.* Edited by Rudolph Knopf. TU 20.1. Leipzig: J. C. Hinrichs, 1901.

———. *The Apostolic Fathers.* Part 1, *S. Clement of Rome.* Edited by Joseph B. Lightfoot. 2 vols. 2d ed. London and New York: Macmillan, 1890.

Columella, Lucius Junius Moderatus. *De re rustica. De arboribus. (On Agriculture. On Trees.).* Edited and translated by E. S. Forster and Edward W. Heffner. 3 vols. LCL. Cambridge, MA: Harvard University, 1954-55.

Didascalia et Constitutiones Apostolorum. Edited by Francis X. Funk. 2 vols. Paderborn: Ferdinand Schoeningh, 1905.

Dio Cassius. *Dio's Roman History.* Translated and edited by Earnest Cary. 9 vols. LCL. Cambridge, MA: Harvard University; London: Wm. Heinemann, 1968.

Eusebius. *The Ecclesiastical History.* With an English translation by Kirsopp Lake and J. E. L. Outlon. 2 vols. LCL. Cambridge, MA: Harvard University; London: Wm. Heinemann, 1964-1965.

Hippolytus. *Refutatio Omnium Haeresium.* Edited by Paul Wendland. 3 vols. GCS 26. Leipzig: J. C. Hinrichs, 1916. Reprint. Hildesheim and New York: G. Olms, 1977.

Josephus, Flavius. *Jewish Antiquities.* Translated and edited by Louis Feldman. 6 vols. LCL. Cambridge, MA: Harvard University, 1969.

Justin. *Dialogue avec Tryphon.* Translated by George Archambault. 2 vols. Textes et Documents 8. Paris: Alphonse Picard, 1909.

————. *Opera quae feruntur omnia.* Edited by J. C. Otto. 1.1,2. 3d ed. Jena: Hermann Dufft, 1876.

Ignatius of Antioch. *The Apostolic Fathers.* Part 2, *S. Ignatius of Antioch.* Edited by Joseph B. Lightfoot. 2 vols. 2d ed. London and New York: Macmillan, 1890.

Irenaeus. *Opera quae supersunt omnia.* Edited by Adolf Stieren. 2 vols. Leipzig: T. O. Weigl, 1853.

Minucius Felix. *Octavius.* Translated by Gerald H. Rendall. LCL. Cambridge, MA: Harvard University, 1931.

Origen. *Contre Celse.* Translated and edited by Marcel Borret. 4 vols. SC 132. Paris: Editions du Cerf, 1967.

————. *Contra Celsum.* Translated and edited by Henry Chadwick. Cambridge: Cambridge University, 1953.

Ovid. *Metamorphoses.* Translated by Frank J. Miller. 2 vols. LCL. Cambridge, MA: Harvard University, 1964.

Suetonius Tranquillus, C. *Lives of the Caesars.* Translated by J. C. Rolfe. 2 vols. LCL. Cambridge, MA: Harvard University, 1951.

Tacitus, Cornelius. *The Histories.* Translated by Clifford H. Moore. *The Annals.* Translated by John Jackson. 3 vols. LCL. London: Wm. Heinemann; New York: G. P. Putnam's Sons, 1925-37.

Tatian, *Oratio ad Graecos.* Edited by J. C. Otto. Corpus Apologetarum Christianorum Saeculi Secundi 6. Jena: F. Mauke, 1851.

Tertulllian. *Quae supersunt omnia.* Edited by F. Oehler. 3 vols. Leipzig: T. O. Weigl, 1853-54.

Secondary Sources

Alfonsi, Luigi. "La vite e l'olmo." *VC* 21 (1967) 81-86.

Altaner, Berthold. *Patrology.* Translated by Hilda Graef. 2d ed. New York: Herder and Herder, 1961.

Audet, Jean-Paul. "Affinités Littéraires et Doctrinales du Manuel de Discipline." *RB* 60 (1953) 41-82.

————. *La Didachè: Instructions des apôtres.* Paris: Gabalda, 1958.

Aune, David E. "The Social Matrix of the Apocalypse of John." *BR* 26 (1981) 16-32.

Bammel, Ernst. "*Ptōchos.*" *TDNT* 6 (1968) 885-915.

Bang, M. "Die Herkunft der römischen Sklaven." *Römische Mitteilungen* 25 (1910) 223-51.

Bardy, G. "Les écoles romaines au second siècle." *RHE* 28 (1932) 501-32.

Barnard, L. W. "The Early Roman Church, Judaism, and Jewish Christianity." *ATR* 49 (1967) 371-84.

―――. "Hadrian and Christianity." *CQR* 165 (1964) 277-89.

―――. "Hermas and Judaism." *Studia Patristica 8.* TU 93. Berlin: Akademie-Verlag, 1966.

―――. *Justin Martyr, His Life and Thought.* Cambridge: Cambridge University, 1967.

―――. "Justin Martyr in Recent Study." *SJT* 22 (1969) 152-64.

―――. "The Shepherd of Hermas in Recent Study." *HeyJ* 9 (1968) 29-36.

Barnes, Timothy D. "Legislation against the Christians." *JRS* 58 (1968) 32-50.

―――. "Pre-Decian Acta Martyrum." *JTS* 19 (1968) 509-31.

―――. *Tertullian: A Historical and Literary Study.* Oxford: Clarendon, 1971.

Baron, Salo W. *A Social and Religious History of the Jews.* 8 vols. 2d ed. New York and London: Columbia University; Philadelphia: Jewish Publication Society, 1952.

Barré, Michael. "Paul as 'Eschatologic Person': A New Look at 2 Cor 11:29." *CBQ* 37 (1975) 500-526.

Barrett, C. K. *A Commentary on the Epistle to the Romans.* Black's New Testament Commentaries. London: Adam and Charles Black, 1957.

Barrois, G. A. "Debt, Debtor." *IDB* 1.809-10.

Bartchy, S. Scott. *MALLON CHRĒSAI: First-Century Slavery and the Interpretation of 1 Corinthians 7:21.* SBLDS 11. Missoula, MT: Society of Biblical Literature, 1973.

Bauckham. R. J. "The Great Tribulation of the Shepherd of Hermas." *JTS* 25 (1974) 27-40.

Bauer, Walter. *Orthodoxy and Heresy in Earliest Christianity.* Revised by Georg Strecker. Edited by Robert Kraft and Gerhard Krodel. Translated by Paul J. Achtemeier et al. Philadelphia: Fortress, 1971.

Beaujeu, Jean. "Les apologistes et le culte des souverains." In *Le culte des souverains dans l'Empire Romain.* Entretiens sur l'antiquité classique 19. Edited by Willem den Boer. Geneva: Fondation Hardt, 1973. 101-142.

―――. "La religion de la classe sénatoriale à l'époque des Antonins." In *Hommages à Jean Bayet.* Edited by Marcel Renard and Robert Schilling. Collection Latomus 70. Bruxelles-Berchem: Latomus Revue d'Etudes Latines, 1964. 54-75.

―――. *La religion romaine à l'apogée de l'Empire.* Vol. 1, *La politique religieuse des Antonins.* Collection d'études anciennes, Association Guillaume Budé. Paris: Belles Lettres, 1955.

Beauvery, Robert. "*Pleonektein* in 1 Thess 4, 6a." *VD* 33 (1955) 78-85.

Benoît, André. *Le Baptême Chrétien au second siècle: la Théologie des Pères.* Etudes d'Histoire et de Philosophie Religieuses. Paris/Strasbourg: Presses Universitaires de France, 1953.

Berger, A. "Nexum," *OCD* s.v.

Best, Ernest. *The First and Second Epistles to the Thessalonians.* HNTC. New York: Harper and Row, 1972.

Blenkinsopp, Joseph, "Deuteronomy." *JBC* 1.101-22.

Boer, Willem den. "Gynaeconitis, a Centre of Christian Propaganda." *VC* 4 (1950) 61-64.

Bonner, Campbell. "A Papyrus Codex of the Shepherd of Hermas." *HTR* 18 (1925) 115-27.

Boulvert, Gerard. *Domestique et fonctionnaire sous le Haut-Empire romain: la condition de l'affranchi et de l'esclave du prince.* Centre de Recherches d'Histoire Ancienne 9. Paris: Belles Lettres. 1974.

———. "Les esclaves et les affranchis impériaux sous le Haut-Empire romain." 2 vols. Dissertation, Université d'Aix-Marseille, Aix-en-Provence, 1964. A revised version of vol. 1 was published as *Esclaves et affranchis impériaux sous le Haut-Empire romain: role politique et administratif.* Naples: Jovene, 1970.

Bowersock, Glen W. *Greek Sophists in the Roman Empire.* Oxford: Clarendon, 1969.

Bruns, C. G. *Fontes Juris Romani Antiqui.* Tübingen: J. C. B. Mohr, 1909.

Bultmann, Rudolph. *History of the Synoptic Tradition.* Translated by John Marsh. 2d ed. New York: Harper and Row, 1968.

Cameron, A. "*THREPTOS* and Related Terms in the Inscriptions of Asia Minor." In *Anatolian Studies Presented to William H. Buckler.* Manchester: Manchester University, 1939.

Carcopino, Jerome. *Daily Life in Ancient Rome: The People and the City at the Height of the Empire.* Edited by Henry T. Rowell. Translated by E. O. Lorimer. New Haven: Yale University, 1945.

Cardascia, G. "L'apparition dans le droit des classes d'honestiores' et d'humiliores.'" *Revue historique de droit francais et étranger* 28 (1950) 305-37, 461-85.

Carrington, Philip. *The Early Christian Church.* 2 vols. Cambridge: Cambridge University, 1957.

Chadwick, Henry. "The New Edition of Hermas." *JTS* 8 (1957) 274-80.

Coleborne, W. "A Linguistic Approach to the Problem of Structure and Composition of the Shepherd of Hermas." *Colloquium* 3 (1969) 133-42.

———. "The *Shepherd* of Hermas: A Case for Multiple Authorship and Some Implications." *Studia Patristica* 10.1. TU 107. Berlin: Akademie-Verlag, 1970.

Collins, John J. *Apocalypse: The Morphology of a Genre. Semeia* 14. Missoula, MT: Scholars Press, 1979.

Coote, Robert B. *Amos Among the Prophets: Composition and Theology.* Philadelphia: Fortress, 1981.

Countryman, L. William. *The Rich Christian in the Church of the Early Empire: Contradictions and Accommodations.* Texts and Studies in Religion. New York and Toronto: Edwin Mellen, 1980.

Crawford, Michael H. "Money and Exchange in the Roman World." *JRS* 60 (1970) 40-48.

Daremberg, Charles V. *Dictionnaire des antiquités grecques et romaines.* Revised by Edmond Saglio. 5 vols. Paris: Hachette, 1877-1919.

Daube, David. "Participle and Imperative in 1 Peter." In *The First Epistle of St. Peter,* by Edward G. Selwyn. 2d ed. London: Macmillan, 1949.

Davies, O. *Roman Mines in Europe.* Oxford: Clarendon, 1935.

Degenhardt, Hans-Joachim. *Lukas: Evangelist der Armen: Besitz und Besitzverzicht in den Lukanischen Schriften.* Stuttgart: Katholisches Bibelwerk, 1965.

Demetz, Peter. "The Elm and the Vine: Notes Toward the History of a Marriage Topos." *Proceedings of the Modern Language Association* 73 (1958) 521-32.

DeVito, J. "The Leopards of Ignatius of Antioch." *Classical Bulletin* 50 (1974) 63.

Dibelius, Martin. *A Commentary on the Epistle of James.* Revised by Heinrich Greeven. Translated by Michael A. Williams. Edited by Helmut Koester. Hermeneia. Philadelphia: Fortress, 1976.

————, and Hans Conzelmann. *The Pastoral Epistles: A Commentary.* Translated by Philip Buttolph and Adela Yarbro. Edited by Helmut Koester. Hermeneia. Philadelphia: Fortress, 1972.

Dix, Dom Gregory. *The Shape of the Liturgy.* Westminster: Dacre, 1954.

Dodd, C. H. *The Epistle of Paul to the Romans.* MNTC. New York and London: Harper, 1932.

————. *The Parables of the Kingdom.* Rev. ed. New York: Scribner, 1961.

Donfried, Karl P. "False Presuppositions in the Study of Romans." *CBQ* 36 (1974) 332-58. Also in *The Romans Debate,* edited by Karl. P. Donfried. Minneapolis: Augsburg, 1977.

————. "A Short Note on Romans 16." *JBL* 89 (1970) 441-49. Also in *The Romans Debate,* edited by Karl P. Donfried. Minneapolis: Augsburg, 1977.

Driver, S. R. *A Critical and Exegetical Commentary on Deuteronomy.* ICC. 3d ed. Edinburgh: T. and T. Clark, 1951.

————. "Poor." In *Dictionary of the Bible,* edited by James Hastings. Edinburgh: T. and T. Clark, 1902. 4.19-20.

Duchesne, Louis. *Histoire Ancienne de l'Eglise.* 3 vols. 3d ed. Paris: Fontemoing, 1907-10.

————. *Liber Pontificalis: Texte, Introduction, et Commentaire.* 2 vols. Paris: Cyrille Vogel, 1886-92.

Duff, A. M. *Freedmen in the Early Roman Empire.* Oxford: Clarendon, 1928. Reprint. Cambridge: W. Heffer, 1958.

Duncan-Jones, Richard. *The Economy of the Roman Empire: Quantitative Studies.* Cambridge: Cambridge University, 1974.

Dupont, Jacques. *Les Béatitudes.* EBib. 3 vols. Rev. ed. Paris: Gabalda, 1969-73.

Dupont-Sommer, A. *The Essene Writings from Qumran.* Cleveland and New York: World, 1961.

Easton, Burton S. "The Epistle of James." *IB* 12.3-18.

Elliott, John H. *A Home for the Homeless: A Sociological Exegesis of 1 Peter, Its Situation and Strategy.* Philadelphia: Fortress, 1981.

Ellis, E. Earle. "Paul and His Co-Workers." *NTS* 17 (1970-71) 437-52.

Elze, Martin. *Tatian und seine Theologie.* Göttingen: Vandenhoeck and Ruprecht, 1960.

Fasola, Umberto. "Le due catacombe ebraiche di Villa Torlonia." *Riv. di Arch. Crist.* 52 (1976) 7-64.

Feine, Paul, and Johannes Behm. *Introduction to the New Testament.* Edited by Werner G. Kümmel. Translated by A. J. Mattill. 14th ed. Nashville: Abingdon, 1966.

Feldman, Louis H. "Jewish 'Sympathizers' in Classical Literature and Inscriptions." *TAPA* 81 (1950) 200-208.

Finley, M. I. *The Ancient Economy.* Berkeley and Los Angeles: University of California, 1973.

————, ed. *Slavery in Classical Antiquity: Views and Controversies.* Cambridge: Heffer, 1960.

Fitzmyer, Joseph A. "The Letter to the Romans." *JBC* 2.291-331.

Flusser, David. "Blessed Are the Poor in Spirit . . ." *IEJ* 10 (1960) 1-13.

Ford, Josephine M. "A Possible Liturgical Background to the Shepherd of Hermas." *RevQ* 6 (1969) 531-51.

Frank, Tenney. *Economic Survey of Ancient Rome.* 5 vols. Baltimore: Johns Hopkins, 1933-40. Reprint. New York: Octagon Books, 1975.

————. "Race Mixture in the Early Roman Empire." *American Historical Review* 21 (1916) 689-708. Also in *Problems of European Civilization,* edited by D. Kagan. Boston: Heath, 1968. 44-56.

Frederiksen, M. W. "Caesar, Cicero, and the Problem of Debt." *JRS* 56 (1966) 128-41.

Frey, Jean-Baptiste. "Les communautés juives à Rome aux premiers temps de l'Eglise," *RSR* 20 (1930) 267-97; 21 (1931) 129-68.

Fridrichsen, Anton. "Zum Thema 'Paulus und die Stoa.'" *ConNT* 9. Lund: Gleerup, 1944, 27-31.

Gagé, Jean. *Les classes sociales dans l'Empire romain.* Paris: Payot, 1964.

Gager, John G. *Kingdom and Community: The Social World of Early Christianity.* Englewood Cliffs, NJ: Prentice-Hall, 1975.

Garnsey, Peter. *Social Status and Legal Privilege in the Roman Empire.* Oxford: Clarendon, 1970.

Gesenius, Friedrich H. *Hebräische und Aramäische Handwörterbuch über das Alte Testament.* 17th ed. Leipzig: F. C. W. Vogel, 1921.

Giet, Stanislas. *Hermas et les pasteurs: les trois auteurs du Pasteur d'Hermas.* Paris: Presses Universitaires de France, 1963.

Girard, Paul F. *Textes de droit romain.* 5th ed. Paris: A. Rousseau, 1923.

Goodenough, Erwin. *The Theology of Justin Martyr.* Jena: Frommann, 1923.

Goodspeed, Edgar J. *Index Apologeticus sive Clavis Justini Martyris operum aliorumque apologetarum pristinorum.* Leipzig: J. C. Hinrichs, 1912.

Gordis, Robert. *Poets, Prophets, Sages: Essays in Biblical Interpretation.* Bloomington and London: Indiana University, 1971.

Gordon, Mary L. "The Freedman's Son in Municipal Life." *JRS* 25 (1931) 65-77.

_____. "Nationality of Slaves under the Early Roman Empire." *JRS* 14 (1924) 93-111. Also in *Slavery in Classical Antiquity*, edited by M. I. Finley. Cambridge: Cambridge University, 1970. 171-89.

Grant, Robert M. "The Chronology of the Greek Apologists." *VC* 9 (1955) 25-34.

_____. "The Date of Tatian's Oration." *HTR* 46 (1953) 99-101.

_____. *Early Christianity and Society: Seven Studies.* San Francisco: Harper and Row, 1977.

_____. "The Heresy of Tatian." *JTS* n.s. 5 (1954) 62-68.

Grobel, Kendrick. "Shepherd of Hermas, Parable II." In *Vanderbilt Studies in the Humanities*, edited by Richmond C. Beatty et al. Nashville: Vanderbilt University, 1951. 1.50-55.

Grundmann, Walter. *Das Evangelium nach Matthäus.* ThHKNT 1. Berlin: Evangelische Verlagsanstalt, 1968.

Guelich, Robert A. "The Matthean Beatitudes: 'Entrance-Requirements' or Eschatological Blessings?" *JBL* 95 (1976) 415-34.

Guinan, Michael D., ed. *Gospel Poverty: Essays in Biblical Theology.* Chicago: Franciscan Herald, 1977.

Gülzow, Henneke. *Christentum und Sklaverei in den ersten drei Jahrhunderten.* Bonn: Rudolf Habelt, 1969.

Haenchen, Ernst. *The Acts of the Apostles: A Commentary.* Translated by R. McL. Wilson et al. Philadelphia: Westminster, 1971.

Hanson, A. T. "Hodayoth vi and viii and Hermas *Sim.* VIII." *Studia Patristica 10.1.* TU 107. Berlin: Akademie-Verlag, 1970. 105-108.

Harnack, Adolf von. *The Mission and Expansion of Christianity in the First Three Centuries.* Translated and edited by James Moffatt. 2 vols. Theological Translation Library 19, 20. 2d ed. New York: G. P. Putnam, 1908.

Harrington, Daniel J. "Social Concepts in the Early Church: A Decade of Research." *TS* 41 (1980) 181-90.

Hatch, Edwin, and Henry A. Redpath. *Concordance to the Septuagint.* 2 vols. Oxford: Clarendon, 1897.

Hauck, F., and W. Kasch. "*Ploutos.*" *TDNT* 6 (1968) 318-32.

Heichelheim, Friedrich. "Interest, Rate of." *OCD* s.v.

Hellholm, David. *Das Visionenbuch des Hermas als Apokalypse: Formgeschichtliche und texttheoretische Studien zu einer literarischen Gattung.* ConBNT 13:1. Lund: C. W. K. Gleerup, 1980.

Hengel, Martin. *Property and Riches in the Early Church: Aspects of a Social History of Early Christianity.* Translated by John Bowden. Philadelphia: Fortress, 1974.

Hennecke, Edgar, and Wilhelm Schneemelcher, ed. *New Testament Apocrypha.* Translation edited by R. McL. Wilson. 2 vols. Philadelphia: Westminster, 1963-65.

Hilhorst. A. *Sémitismes et latinismes dans le Pasteur d'Hermas.* Graecitas Christianorum Primaeva 5. Nijmegen: Dekker and Van de Vegt, 1976.

Hock, Ronald F. *The Social Context of Paul's Ministry.* Philadelphia: Fortress, 1980.

Honigmann, E. "Nexum." *PW* 17.163-65.

Hoyt, Thomas. *The Poor in Luke-Acts*. Ph.D. diss., Duke University. Ann Arbor, MI: Xerox University Microfilms, 1975.

Jacobs, J. "Usury." *Jewish Encyclopedia*. New York: Ktav, n.d. 12.388-91.

Jalland, T. G. "Justin Martyr and the President of the Eucharist." *Studia Patristica 5*. TU 80. Berlin: Akademie-Verlag, 1962.

Janzen, Waldemar. "ʾAŠRÊ in the Old Testament." *HTR* 58 (1965) 215-26.

Jastrow, Marcus. *A Dictionary of the Targumim, the Talmud Babli and the Midrashic Literature*. 2 vols. New York: Pardes, 1950.

Jeremias, Joachim. *The Parables of Jesus*. Translated by S. H. Hooke. Rev. ed. New York: Scribner's, 1963.

Johnson, Luke. *The Literary Function of Possessions in Luke-Acts*. SBLDS 39. Missoula, MT: Scholars Press, 1977.

Joly, Robert. "Hermas et le Pasteur." *VC* 21 (1967) 201-18.

Jones. A. H. M. "Slavery in the Ancient World." *Economic History Review* 2nd series 9 (1956) 185-99. Also in *Slavery in Classical Antiquity*, edited by M. I. Finley. Cambridge: Heffer, 1960. 1-15.

————. "The Social Background of the Struggle between Paganism and Christianity." In *The Conflict between Paganism and Christianity in the Fourth Century*, edited by Arnaldo Momigliano. Oxford: Clarendon, 1963. 17-37.

Judge, E. A. *The Social Pattern of Christian Groups in the First Century*. London: Tyndale, 1958.

————, and G. S. R. Thomas. "The Origin of the Church at Rome: A New Solution?" *Reformed Theological Review* 25 (1966) 81-94.

Jungmann, Josef A. *The Early Liturgy: To the Time of Gregory the Great*. Notre Dame: University of Notre Dame, 1959.

Juster, Jean. *Les Juifs dans l'Empire Romain: leur condition juridique, économique et sociale*. 2 vols. Paris: Paul Geuthner, 1914.

Kajanto, Iiro. *The Latin Cognomina*. Commentationes Humanarum Litterarum 26.2. Helsinki: Societas Scientarum Fennica, 1965.

————. "The Significance of Non-Latin Cognomina." *Latomus* 27 (1968) 517-34.

Karris, Robert J. "The Occasion of Romans: A Response to Professor Donfried." *CBQ* 36 (1974) 356-58. Also in *The Romans Debate*, edited by Karl. P. Donfried. Minneapolis: Augsburg, 1977.

————. "Poor and Rich: The Lukan Sitz im Leben." In *Perspectives on Luke-Acts*, edited by C. Talbert. Special Studies Series 5. Danville, VA: Association of Baptist Professors of Religion, 1978.

————. "Rom 14:1-15:13 and the Occasion of Romans." *CBQ* 35 (1973) 155-78. Also in *The Romans Debate*, edited by Karl P. Donfried. Minneapolis: Augsburg, 1977.

Keck, Leander. "The Poor among the Saints in Jewish Christianity and Qumran." *ZNW* 57 (1966) 54-78.

Kee, Howard C. *Christian Origins in Sociological Perspective: Methods and Resources*. Philadelphia: Westminster, 1980.

Koester, Helmut. *Synoptische Überlieferung bei den Apostolischen Vätern*. TU 65; Berlin: Akademie-Verlag, 1957.

Kutsch, E. "Armenpflege." *RGG* 1.617-19.

———. "Armut." *RGG* 1.622-23.

Labriolle, Pierre de. *La Réaction païenne: Etude sur la polémique antichrétienne du Ier au VIe siècle.* Paris: L'Artisan du livre, 1934.

Lake, Kirsopp. "The Shepherd of Hermas and Christian Life in Rome in the Second Century." *HTR* 4 (1911) 25-47.

Langerbeck, Hermann. "Zur Auseinandersetzung von Theologie und Gemeindeglauben in der römischen Gemeinde in den Jahren 135-165." In *Aufsätze zur Gnosis,* edited by H. Dörries. Abhandlungen der Akademie der Wissenschaften in Göttingen; Philologisch-historische Klasse, 3e Folge, 69. Göttingen: Vandenhoeck and Ruprecht, 1967.

LaPiana, George. "Foreign Groups in Rome During the First Centuries of the Empire." *HTR* 20 (1927) 183-403.

———. "La primitiva communità di Roma e l'epistola ai Romani." *Ricerche Religiose* 3-4 (1925) 209-26, 306-26.

———. *Il Problema della Chiesa latina in Roma.* Rome: Libreria di Cultura, 1922.

———. "The Roman Church at the End of the Second Century." *HTR* 18 (1925) 201-77.

———. *Le Successione episcopale in Roma e gli albori del primato.* Rome: Libreria di Cultura, 1922.

Laws, Sophie. *The Epistle of James.* HNTC. San Francisco: Harper and Row, 1980.

Lazzati, Giuseppe. "Gli Atti di San Giustino Martire." *Aevum* 27 (1953) 473-97.

Leclerq, Henri. "Aristocratiques (Classes)," *DACL* 1.2, 2845-86.

Légasse, Simon. "Les pauvres en esprit et les 'volontaires' de Qumran." *NTS* 8 (1961-62) 336-45.

Leist. G. A. "Addictus." *PW* 1.352-53.

Leon, Harry J. *The Jews of Ancient Rome.* Philadelphia: Jewish Publication Society, 1960.

Lewis, Charlton T., and Charles Short. *A Latin Dictionary.* Revised edition of *Freund's Latin Dictionary.* Oxford: Clarendon, 1879. Reprint. 1969.

Loeb, Isidore. "La littérature des pauvres dans la Bible." *REJ* 20 (1890) 161-98; 21 (1890) 1-42, 161-206.

Lohse, Eduard. "Paränese und Kerygma im 1. Petrusbrief." *ZNW* 45 (1954) 68-89.

Lowe, A. D. "The Origin of *ouai*." *Hermathena* 105 (1967) 34-39.

McKenzie, John L. *Second Isaiah.* AB 20. Garden City, NY: Doubleday, 1968.

MacMullen, Ramsay. *Roman Social Relations, 50 B.C. to A.D. 284.* New Haven: Yale University, 1974.

Malherbe, Abraham J. *Social Aspects of Early Christianity.* Baton Rouge: Louisiana State University, 1977.

Malina, Bruce J. *The New Testament World: Insights from Cultural Anthropology.* Atlanta: John Knox, 1981.

———. "The Social World Implied in the Letters of the Christian Bishop-Martyr (Named Ignatius of Antioch)." SBLASP (1978) 2.71-119.

Maloney, Robert P. "The Teaching of the Fathers on Usury." *VC* 27 (1973) 241-65.

———. "Usury in Greek, Roman and Rabbinic Thought.," *Traditio* 27 (1971) 79-109.

Marucchi, Orazio. *Le Catacombe Romane.* Rome: Desclée, Lefebvre, 1903. 2d ed. Edited by Enrico Josi. Rome: Libreria dello Stato, 1933.

Marxsen, Willi. *Introduction to the New Testament.* Translated by G. Buswell. Philadelphia: Fortress, 1964.

Meeks, Wayne, "The Image of the Androgyne: Some Uses of a Symbol in Earliest Christianity." *HR* 13 (1974) 165-208.

————. "The Man from Heaven in Johannine Sectarianism." *JBL* 91 (1972) 44-72.

————. "'Since Then You Would Need to Go Out of the World': Group Boundaries in Pauline Christianity." In *Critical History and Biblical Faith*, edited by T. J. Ryan. Villanova, PA: College Theology Society/Horizons, 1979. 4-29.

Michel, Otto. *Der Brief an die Römer.* MeyerK 4. 10th ed. Göttingen: Vandenhoeck and Ruprecht, 1955.

Millar, Fergus. "The Imperial Cult and the Persecutions." In *Le culte des souverains dans l'Empire Romain.* Entretiens sur l'antiquité classique 19, edited by Willem den Boer. Geneva: Fondation Hardt, 1973. 143-75.

Milne, H. J. M. "A New Fragment of the *Apology* of Aristides." *JTS* 25 (1923-24) 73-77.

Moffatt, James. *A Critical and Exegetical Commentary on the Epistle to the Hebrews.* ICC. Edinburgh: T. and T. Clark, 1924.

Mohrmann, Christine. "Les origines de la latinité chrétienne." *VC* 3 (1949) 67-106.

————. "Statio." *VC* 7 (1953) 223-45.

Momigliano, Arnold. "Nero." *CAH* 10.702-42.

Mommsen, Theodore. "Observationes Epigraphicae: XLI. Senatus Consultum de Sumptibus Ludorum Gladiatoriorum Minuendis; factum A. P. C. 176/7." *Ephemeris Epigraphica* 7 (1888) 388-416.

Morgenstern, Julian. "Sabbatical Year." *IDB* 4.141-44.

Moulton, James H., and George Milligan. *The Vocabulary of the Greek New Testament.* London: Hodder and Stoughton, 1930.

Mowinckel, Sigmund. *The Psalms in Israel's Worship.* Oxford: Blackwell, 1962.

Musurillo, Herbert. *The Acts of the Christian Martyrs.* Oxford: Clarendon, 1972.

————. "The Need of a New Edition of Hermas." *TS* 12 (1951) 382-87.

Mylonas, George. *Eleusis and the Eleusinian Mysteries.* Princeton: Princeton University, 1961.

Nelson, B. *The Idea of Usury: From Tribal Brotherhood to Universal Otherhood.* 2d ed. Chicago and London: University of Chicago, 1969.

Nickelsburg, George W. E. "The Apocalyptic Message of 1 Enoch 92-105." *CBQ* 39 (1977) 309-28.

————. "Riches, the Rich, and God's Judgment in 1 Enoch 92-105 and the Gospel according to Luke." *NTS* 25 (1978-79) 324-44.

Nilson, Jon. "To Whom Is Justin's *Dialogue with Trypho* Addressed?" *TS* 38 (1977) 538-46.

Nock, Arthur D. "Religious Developments from the Close of the Republic to the Death of Nero." *CAH* 10.465-511.

North, Robert. *Sociology of the Biblical Jubilee.* AnBib 4. Rome: Pontifical Biblical Institute, 1954.

Olck, F. "Arbustum." *PW* 2.421-25.

Oliver, J. H., and R. E. A. Palmer. "Minutes of an Act of the Roman Senate." *Hesperia* 24 (1955) 320-49.

Pernveden, Lage. *The Concept of the Church in the Shepherd of Hermas.* Studia Theologica Lundensia 27. Lund: Gleerup, 1966.

Peterson, Erik. *Frühkirche, Judentum, und Gnosis.* Herder: Freiburg, 1959.

Pilgrim, Walter E. *Good News to the Poor: Wealth and Poverty in Luke-Acts.* Minneapolis: Augsburg, 1981.

Puech, Aimé. *Recherches sur le Discours aux Grecs de Tatian.* Bibliothèque de la faculté des Lettres 17. Paris: Félix Alcan, 1903.

Rahlfs, A. ⁽ânî und ⁽ânow in den Psalmen. Leipzig: Dietrich, 1892.

Rawson, Beryl. "Family Life among the Lower Classes at Rome in the First Two Centuries of the Empire." *CP* 61 (1966) 71-83.

Reicke, Bo. *The Epistles of James, Peter, and Jude.* AB 37. Garden City, NY: Doubleday, 1964.

Reiling, J. *Hermas and Christian Prophecy: A Study of the Eleventh Mandate.* NovTSup 37. Leiden: Brill, 1973.

Rengstorf, K. "*Doulos.*" *TDNT* 2 (1964) 261-79.

Riesenfeld, Harald. "Accouplements de termes contradictoires dans le N.T." *ConNT* 9. Lund: Gleerup, 1944, 1-21.

Rigaux, Béda. *Saint Paul: Les épîtres aux Thessaloniciens.* Paris: Gabalda, 1956.

Robinson, J. A. T. *Redating the New Testament.* London: SCM, 1976.

Roby, Henry J. *Roman Private Law in the Times of Cicero and of the Antonines.* 2 vols. Cambridge: Cambridge University, 1902. Reprint. Aalen: Scientia, 1975.

Rodewald, Cosmo, *Money in the Age of Tiberius.* Manchester: Manchester University, 1976.

Ropes, James H. *A Critical and Exegetical Commentary on the Epistle of St. James.* ICC. New York: Scribner's, 1916.

Rose, K. F. C. "Time and Place in the Satyricon." *TAPA* 93 (1962) 402-9.

Rossi, Giovanni B. de. "Gli Acilii sepolti nel cimitero di Priscilla." *Bull. di Arch. Crist.* 6 (1888-89) 37-49.

_____. "Aquila e Prisca e gli Acilii Glabriones." *Bull. di Arch. Crist.* 6 (1888-89) 128-33.

_____. "Esame archeologico e critico della storia di S. Callisto narrata nel libro nono dei Filosofumeni." *Bull. di Arch. Crist.* 4 (1866) 1-14, 17-33.

_____. *Roma Sotteranea Cristiana.* 3 vols. Rome: Pontificio Istituto di Archeologia Cristiana, 1864-77.

Roth, Cecil. "The European Age in Jewish History (to 1648)." in *The Jews: Their History, Culture, and Religion,* edited by Louis Finkelstein. Philadelphia: Jewish Publication Society, 1949. 1.216.49.

Rouffiac, Jean. *Recherches sur les caractères du grec dans le Nouveau Testament d'après les inscriptions de Priène.* Paris: Ernest Leroux, 1911.

Sabourin, Leopold. *The Psalms: Their Origin and Meaning.* Rev. ed. New York: Alba House, 1974.

Ste. Croix, G. E. M. de. "Aspects of the 'Great' Persecution." *HTR* 47 (1954) 75-113.

_____. "Why Were the Early Christians Persecuted?" *Past and Present* 26 (1963) 7-38. And "Rejoinder." *Past and Present* 27 (1964) 28-33.

Sanders, Boykin. "Studies in Luke's Editorial Methods and Their Situations." Ph.D. diss., Harvard University, 1975.

Schürer, Emil. *The History of the Jewish People in the Age of Jesus Christ.* New English version revised and edited by Geza Vermes and Fergus Millar. Vol. 1. Edinburgh: T. and T. Clark, 1973.

Schwartz, J. "Survivances littéraires païennes dans le 'Pasteur' d'Hermas." *RB* 72 (1965) 240-47.

Scroggs, Robin. "The Sociological Interpretation of the New Testament: The Present State of Research." *NTS* 26 (1980) 164-79.

Seitz, Oscar J. "Afterthoughts on the Term 'Dipsychos.'" *NTS* 4 (1957-58) 327-34.

_____. "Antecedents and Signification of the Term *DIPSYCHOS.*" *JBL* 66 (1947) 211-19.

_____. "Relationship of the Shepherd of Hermas to the Epistle of James." *JBL* 63 (1944) 131-40.

_____. "Selected Subjects in the Thought and Terminology of Hermas." Th.D. thesis, Harvard University, 1945.

_____. "Two Spirits in Man: An Essay on Biblical Exegesis." *NTS* 6 (1959-60) 82-95.

Sherwin-White, A. N. "The Early Persecutions and Roman Law Again." *JTS* n.s. 3 (1952) 199-213.

_____. *The Letters of Pliny: A Historical and Social Commentary.* Oxford: Clarendon, 1966.

_____. *Racial Prejudice in Imperial Rome.* Cambridge: Cambridge University, 1967.

_____. "Why Were the Early Christians Persecuted?—An Amendment." *Past and Present* 27 (1964) 23-27.

Smallwood, E. Mary. *The Jews under Roman Rule: From Pompey to Diocletian.* Leiden: Brill, 1976.

_____. "The Legislation of Hadrian and Antoninus Pius Against Circumcision." *Latomus* 18 (1959) 334-47.

_____. "Some Notes on the Jews under Tiberius." *Latomus* 15 (1956) 314-29.

Smith, Jonathan Z. "The Social Description of Early Christianity." *RelSRev* 1 (1975) 19-25.

Solin, Heikki. *Beiträge zur Kenntnis der griechischen Personennamen in Rom.* Commentationes Humanarum Litterarum 48. Helsinki: Societas Scientiarum Fennica, 1971.

Spicq, Ceslas. *L'Epître aux Hébreux.* 2 vols. EBib. 2d ed. Paris: Gabalda, 1952.

Stein, S. "The Laws of Interest in the Old Testament." *JTS* n.s. 4 (1953) 161-70.

Styger, Paul. "L'origine del Cimitero di Domitilla sull'Ardeatina." *Rend. Pont.* 5 (1926-27) 89-144.

Stylianopoulos, Theodore G. *Justin Martyr and the Mosaic Law.* SBLDS 20. Missoula, MT: Society of Biblical Literature and Scholars Press, 1975.

Sundberg, Albert C. "Canon Muratori: A Fourth-Century List." *HTR* 66 (1973) 1-41.

Taylor, Lily R. "Freedmen and Freeborn in the Epitaphs of Imperial Rome." *AJP* 82 (1961) 113-32.

Theissen, Gerd. *Sociology of Early Palestinian Christianity.* Translated by John Bowden. Philadelphia: Fortress, 1978.

―――. *The Social Setting of Pauline Christianity: Essays on Corinth.* Edited and translated by John H. Schütz. Philadelphia: Fortress, 1982.

Tkacik, Arnold J. "Ezekiel." *JBC* 1.344-65.

Townend, Gavin. "Some Flavian Connections." *JRS* 51 (1961) 54-62.

Treggiari, Susan. *Roman Freedmen during the Late Republic.* Oxford: Clarendon, 1969.

Urbach, E. E. "The Laws Regarding Slavery As a Source for Social History of the Period of the Second Temple, the Mishnah and Talmud." *Papers of the Institute of Jewish Studies, London,* edited by J. G. Weiss. Jerusalem: Hebrew University, 1964. 1.1-95.

Vaux, Roland de. *Ancient Israel, Its Life and Institutions.* Translated by John McHugh. London: Darton, Longman and Todd, 1961.

Veyne, Paul. "Vie de Trimalchio." *Annales. Economies. Sociétés. Civilisations* 16 (1961) 213-47.

Wacholder, Ben Zion. "Sabbatical Year." *IDBSup* 762-63.

Waltzing, Jean-P. "Collegia." *DACL* 3.2, 2107-2140.

Walzer, R. *Galen on Christians and Jews.* London: Oxford University, 1949.

Ward, Roy Bowen. "The Communal Concern of the Epistle of James." Th.D. diss., Harvard University, 1966.

―――. "James of Jerusalem." *Restoration Quarterly* 16 (1973) 174-90.

―――. "Partiality in the Assembly." *HTR* 62 (1969) 87-97.

Weaver, P. R. C. "Cognomina Ingenua." *CQ* 14 (1964) 311-15.

―――. *Familia Caesaris: A Social Study of the Emperor's Freedmen and Slaves.* Cambridge: Cambridge University, 1972.

―――. "Social Mobility in the Early Roman Empire: The Evidence of the Imperial Freedman and Slaves." *Past and Present* 37 (1967) 3-20.

Weinfeld, Moshe. *Deuteronomy and the Deuteronomistic School.* Oxford: Clarendon, 1972.

Westermann, William L. *The Slave Systems of Greek and Roman Antiquity.* Philadelphia: American Philosophical Society, 1955.

White, John C. *The Interaction of Language and World in the "Shepherd of Hermas."* Ph.D. diss., Temple University. Ann Arbor, MI: University Microfilms, 1973.

Wiefel, Wolfgang. "Die jüdische Gemeinschaft im antiken Rom und die Anfänge des römischen Christentums." *Judaica* 26 (1970) 65-88. Also in English in *The Romans Debate,* edited by Karl P. Donfried. Minneapolis: Augsburg, 1977.

Williams, George H. "Baptismal Theology and Practice in Rome as Reflected in Justin Martyr." In *The Ecumenical World of Orthodox Civilization: Russia and Orthodoxy. Essays in Honor of Georges Florovsky,* edited by Andrew Blane and Thomas E. Bird. 3 vols. The Hague: Mouton, 1974. 3.9-34.

_____. "Justin Glimpsed as Martyr Among His Roman Contemporaries." In *The Context of Contemporary Theology: Essays in Honor of Paul Lehmann*, edited by Alexander J. McKelway and E. David Willis. Atlanta: John Knox, 1974.

Wilson, William J. "The Career of the Prophet Hermas." *HTR* 20 (1927) 21-62.

Wright, George E. "Deuteronomy." *IB* 2.311-537.

INDEX OF PASSAGES CITED

PATRISTIC LITERATURE AND CHRISTIAN APOCRYPHA

INDEX OF PROPER NAMES